D0862185

What prepublication reviewers say about "Bank's Bandits."

"Army training readies new recruits for the rigors of battle, but nothing could have prepared these men for the innovative guerrilla warfare tactics they learned in Special Forces. An irritated military brass dubbed them "Bank's Bandits," but they became the original Green Berets. In recounting some of the most hilarious training events ever recorded, author Ed Fitzgerald has now made them an authentic part of the written history of Special Forces."

**B. Abell Jurus, Co-Author of *Men In Green Faces*
(A Novel of U.S. Navy SEALs)**

"There are two kinds of people who ought to read this book. Anybody who has never served in the military, and everybody who has. It is one of the half dozen best books I have ever read."

**Marshall N. "Mike" Heyman, Sedona, AZ,
Third Tank Battalion, 10th Armored Division (1943-1946), CIA (1953-1959)**

"Reluctantly quit reading at 0230, still laughing as I fell asleep. Looked forward to finishing it with the same anticipation as reading Ludlum. Began again as soon as I got home, just finished with the thought, 'Ed, you better have the second book in draft already, because all the military people I know will be in a lather for it.' I can't believe your memory for detail. You nailed those guys to a gnat's eyebrow. Your dead-on depiction of 'The Originals' is a classic and I only wish more of them were still around to enjoy this. I am proud you saw fit to share this novel with me, one that will delight all who respect the victories and professionalism of today's successors to the original Green Berets."

**Justin "Gene" McCarthy, LTC (Ret),
Special Forces (1962 to 1972).**

"When your husband comes running in from another room to find out why you are convulsing in laughter, when you desperately need sleep but still find yourself reading at three in the morning, then you know the book is a winner. Fascinating, genuinely exciting, surprisingly informative, and quite possibly the funniest book I've ever read."

Wendy S. Neal,
Esquire, Phoenix, AZ.

"I served in the 82nd in the 1980s, but I swear Ed Fitzgerald went through Jump School beside me with a tape-recorder in his fist. The best in-depth treatment of that experience I've ever seen in print. And I loved the way his "bandits" played hell with my 82nd mates in North Carolina and Georgia. This book is very funny--a great read."

William "Wild Bill" Yancey,
Chicago, Illinois.

"As an ex-infantryman who was not a jumper or involved in special ops, I was genuinely surprised to discover how much I enjoyed this book. This novel speaks to the universal experience of everyone who has ever served in the military, or who would like to know what that experience is like. Exciting, informative and full of humor, once I started I couldn't put it down."

Robert G. Younger,
Los Angeles, CA.

BANK'S BANDITS

THE UNTOLD STORY OF
THE ORIGINAL
GREEN BERETS

By

Edward F. Fitzgerald

Copyright © 2004 by Edward F. Fitzgerald

ISBN 0-7414-1830-4

Cover art and graphics provided by Clint McLaws, Mesa, Arizona

Published by:

PUBLISHING.COM

519 West Lancaster Avenue
Haverford, PA 19041-1413
Info@buybooksontheweb.com
www.buybooksontheweb.com
Toll-free (877) BUY BOOK
Local Phone (610) 520-2500
Fax (610) 519-0261

Printed in the United States of America

Printed on Recycled Paper

Published November 2003

DEDICATION

This book is dedicated to Colonel Aaron Bank (the "father of the Green Berets"), to Colonel Roger M. Pezzelle, to the original members of the 10th Special Forces with whom I had the great honor of serving, and to all of those later members of Special Forces who have gone on to bestow such pride and glory upon the Green Beret.

It is also dedicated to William C. Devereaux, Jr., who went absent without my leave in 1987, and who I can only hope is waiting patiently somewhere ahead, as he so often did in the past, for his "little brother" to catch up with him.

ACKNOWLEDGEMENTS

The author gratefully acknowledges the assistance of those, too many to name, who have encouraged him in rather belatedly undertaking and at long last completing this novel, including in particular the helpful suggestions received from the hard-working members of the Southern California Writers Conference. I would be unforgivably remiss, however, if I did not specifically thank B. Abell Jurus for the invaluable advice, assistance and editing unstintingly provided over many months, Justin "Gene" McCarthy for his helpful comments on the manuscript, and Cathlyn E. Stephen, M.D., for a great "catch" that has kept me at my desk and working, hopefully for years to come.

Lastly, I would like to thank Ginny, my wife and partner in the very best sense of that word. Without her loving and unwavering support and assistance from the first rough drafts through the final proofs, this book would certainly have never seen the light of day—for this work is in truth, in every way, "Ginny's book."

PROLOGUE

Special Forces? You mean the Green Berets? Guys sneaking out of the woods and shovin' cold steel up some poor bastard's tokus? Geez, Fitz. How'd you ever end up in an outfit like that?

When they find out, they always ask. First thing they need to understand is that I really hated the army.

Reporting for induction at the Boston Army Base in the fall of 1952, with the Korean War at full gallop, the heaviest piece of luggage I carried with me was a bitter hatred for all things military.

There I was, James Fitzpatrick, nineteen years old, right out of the Dorchester three-deckers and already a confirmed army hater. And there we were, a whole clutch of nervous and disgruntled inductees, crammed onto a bus for the trip to Fort Devens.

Even today, when I think of Devens, I think of a stockyard.

All of us in civvies when we arrived there. A kaleidoscope of clothing types and colors, with the disorganization of our attire accurately reflecting our variously disordered states of mind. Unloaded from the bus, herded into lines. New beef for the slaughter. *Hold your heads still, so's we kin hit ya square.*

Stripes. Double stripers. Triple stripers.

Yelling at us. Prodding us. Go this way! Go that way!

i

Running. Our arms full of brand-new army clothes, some of which fit.

Running from building to building, line to line. The stripes depositing us, finally, at a very late hour, into our stalls. Into our boxes. Into our barracks.

The next two weeks, total confusion. Written and physical tests. Marching. Running. Bullying and bear baiting. Only an army could call that orientation.

Then I was out of there. Out of Devens. On my way.

Luck of the draw. Most guys, Dix, Kilmer, Polk, for eight weeks basic training. *Me?* Sixteen weeks. Humping heavy-weapons around Fort Indiantown Gap, Pennsylvania.

A vacation spot. Selected by our masters because of its geographical similarity to the frigid, miserable, up and down, snow covered mountains of Korea. *Don't worry, guys! Under all this nice snow, we got your mud!*

Would the thrills never cease? Basic training. Like being forced to smell your own armpit. For a long time. After sixteen straight hours of arm-wrestling.

All of which makes what followed, well, confusing. How did I find myself, fresh out of Basic, a draftee heading for Jump School of all places--as a *volunteer?* Wait! Even worse. Heading for Jump School as a volunteer for Special Forces!

Well, I can explain. It will take me awhile, but I can explain.

It was a genuinely weird time. To apply an anachronistic term, the Korean War was never a prime-time event in this country. Hell, the bastards wouldn't even admit it *was* a war. A police action, that's what they called it. Yeah, right. Only one, you got cops running around, mortars and grenades, bawling into radios for air strikes. Only two, you got cops piled up in body bags beside those frigid fields where poppies never grow.

But, hey, look! Who could blame us? The nation had just got through fighting the war to end all wars--not once, *twice!* It was just flat out too much to ask. How would they put it today? *Here's my cell-phone. Call someone who gives a shit.*

In the fifties, civilians simply couldn't get excited about a pimple on their ass. Which is what it was. Korea. People just didn't give a damn.

Disturbing, though. The nation's youth at it again. Marching off to stem the yellow tide. The *pinkish* tide, as in Commie tide, to be more truthful. No bands this time, though. No crowds to wave them off. Packed into reconditioned liberty ships or, later, into huge transports, they left behind a country moving up, making it big.

When these poor bastards dove into the Korean War, they disappeared without a ripple. If they were *un*lucky, they left here sober and arrived there sick. If they were lucky, they left with a belly full of 3.2 beer and their blood pulsing to, "*I don't want no ricochet romance, I don't want no ricochet love!*" But they still arrived there sick.

Dumped in to a second-hand war, with second-hand equipment.

The insulated boots are on the way, men! Those fur-lined gloves are due any day now. Hey, don't call me no fuckin' liar. I've seen the requisitions!

Frozen feet. Lost toes and fingers. Ears coming off with the helmets.

Hey, Mr. Secretary! I got an idea! Let's use up all them crappy munitions we've had stockpiled since God knows when! They're costin' us a fortune.

Grenades that blew too soon. Mortar duds. Ammo sailing off into the sky or burying itself in the ground just feet in front of the troops. Swell. A real honey of a war.

And the GIs filtering home. Sometimes whole. Sometimes in pieces.

Did I tell you guys what happened the night the Chinese broke our lines?

Yeah, yeah, a hundred times. Shut up and drink your beer, willya!

Trying to find a place. Looking in vain for vacancies that didn't exist. The truth being that no one had even noticed they were gone.

It wasn't as though they didn't bring something back with them, of course. They did. It was a message carried back to the street corners of America. I remember it well.

How about it Charlie? You've been there. Is there something you can tell me? What it was all about? Something to remember when I get over there, things gets rough?

Sure, sure. You want a message? I got one for you, Kid. Gooks suck!

Oh, thanks a lot, Charlie. I'll have that stenciled on my shorts before I ship out.

A lot of people are simply too young to remember. What going into the service during the Korean War was really like. Being totally ignored by a country with too many things on its mind. New automobiles and television sets looming large. Houses with actual lawns. Still, a lot of people know what scrving in Vietnam was like.

Same shit, different day.

For those who don't know much about either, hey, this could be a worse place to start. With me, James Fitzpatrick. Come along for the ride. Kind of fascinated myself, to be honest, look back, figure out how things happened the way they did. Forget *why! How* will have to do. All I know, *how.*

We've all read those novels. Except for a single, seemingly insignificant misstep, a slight turn down a given road, all might have been peeled grapes and bubbling champagne for this hero, but one simple turn and the poor bastard's gone and done it. Stepped right into a sinkhole of hopelessness and despair.

Speaking of sinkholes of hopelessness and despair inevitably brings to my mind my local draft board. Which is probably as good a place as any to start. After all these years, that is still where my story begins.

CHAPTER ONE

The draft board. Easy to find. "Be there, six-thirty sharp," I was told. Even a moron would know this meant they'd start at seven-thirty, but I'm there a little after six.

Not what I expected. Thinking big, I guess. One of my problems. Looking for bricks and mortar. Guards in spiffy uniforms. Our federal government in action. What I found was a dilapidated wood-frame building on a Dorchester side street.

A couple of stores on the first floor, the Selective Service Board upstairs. A door at the top of the rickety stairs opened on to a narrow hallway, ugly yellow walls, dirt and grease ground into the divisions of the hardwood floor over years of use and abuse. A sign on the frosted window of a closed door at the far end said, "Hearing Room."

A clipboard hung on the wall. Sign in. Take a number. On a small table, a basket full of them on wooden slats, like some gyms use for locker keys. Big so you won't walk off with them by mistake.

Six guys ahead of me. By six-thirty, over thirty of us standing around in that chairless, airless corridor. The heat of that August day lingering, waiting with us, staining our underarms, exacerbating the ammonia smell of the nervous supplicants.

A lot of us smoking. Butt cans on pegs lining the walls. All of us clutching request forms and wooden numbers. Lining the walls, elbow to elbow. Two rather dull ceiling lights glowed above

1

us, above cracked and yellowed plastic saucers. The silence grim, the only movement, our hands going to our mouths with butts. We looked like a murder of crows settled on fences for the night.

Finally, the talk starting. A couple at a time. The conversation to the point.

Number Ten, chubby guy, glasses, nudging number Twelve.

"Whatta you using?"

"My back. I'm prackly a cripple."

"*Back*? Fug-get it. Every other guy here is back. You got no prayer, back."

Nineteen, further along the wall, piping up. "Shit, I gotta bad back, too. Can't lift a doughnut, the pain."

Number Ten stepping out and moving on, ignoring Nineteen. Asking the next guy further down. "Whatta you using, it might walk you out of here?"

Terrific. Here I am, a roomful of guys, all of them looking for a way out. Most with doctor's letters with their requests. Flat feet. Hernias. Incurable bed-wetters. One, a collarbone irreparably cracked in grade school. *It still hurts when I go like this. Honest.*

A few guys with typed letters on church stationery. Serious types with pallid faces. Looking like we might turn on them, pummel them, any moment. Like we cared.

Number Fourteen. Tall, thin guy, a pimply face and an intense look about the eyes. Pushes off the wall and heads right for me. Comes the length of the hall to shove his papers at me. "Is

2

this clear? Will they understand this, do you think?"

Jesus, why me?

It was a standing joke in my family. Drunks, crazies, simpletons, any place we went, they'd find me. Corner me. Sit down and tell their story to my open Irish kisser. *Send me your inebriated and muddled masses!*

The guys around us, nudging each other, smirking as I take the papers. Red-faced, I scan the single-spaced print. The imprint of The Immaculate Conception Church in Dorchester at the top. "I'm a daily communicant," Fourteen leans in to tell me as I read, his body odor so strong I have to avert my head. He keeps his voice low. "I work there six years, the church. *Everyone* comes to me. I'm practically a priest."

I read the theological dissertation. Rambling. Hard to follow. Densely laden with quotations. Plowing along, I get the drift. A well-crafted religious discussion as to why this church has to have this guy, and no other, as their janitor. Very strong on why it would be inappropriate for Fourteen, go over, get *his* ass blown, Inchon to the China Sea.

I hand him back the papers. "Good stuff," I tell him, watching him brighten. Seeing, oh, shit, the birth of hope. "I, uh, liked the priest's use of, uh, the Encyclicals."

Dropping my voice as soon as I said that. Shutting up. My Jesuit high school background pushing through. Stifle *that,* this group.

Almost ready to start the call. Huddles of whispered, heated conversation now. Anything to get that deferment. Slide out from under. Let this cup, oh, *please God*, pass.

And *me?* I'm trying to stand apart. Embarrassed to admit, this group, why I'm in their company. There to ask the Board to reshuffle their papers, move *up* my induction.

Could they possibly, oh, please, good sirs, take me in six months early? Could they move my induction date up to this September, next month, instead of February? That was *my* question, my request.

My thinking? If my two years are up in *September*, I'll be just in time. Just in time to start college on the G.I. Bill.

That's what I had reasoned out so stupidly.

It was exactly the kind of straight-line thinking the regular military prizes. They *love* that. And typical of guys my age. Skip over those minor details. Tiny quibbles. Like maybe the only way I'll actually come back is in a box. Like maybe September won't be such a big deal, I end up doing three years, the V.A., learning to tie my one shoe with my one hand.

They're calling the second guy now. The parade is starting.

To my left, number Six is the most confident-looking guy in the room.

"Poor bastards," he says, nodding at the heated discussions going on. "Wasting their breath. You know what you're looking at, them guys? At GIs, is what."

I nod silently, not wanting to get drawn into a discussion. Not wanting to tell him why I'm

4

there. "Me," Six continues, not lowering his voice, and pointing down at his brace-less legs but heavy-soled, mahogany colored shoes. "I got no sweat here. Polio when I was a kid. One leg's two inches shorter than the other. I got me a golden pass."

He demonstrates, walking away and coming back, a definite drop to his left.

Others nearby watching. Disgusted. *Polio? Can you beat that? Lucky sumbitch.*

Studying the floor. Wondering, not for the first time, if I am absolutely friggin' crazy. My sheep-stealing, sheriff-baiting forbears must be rolling over in their graves, seeing me here, *volunteering* to scratch my own name onto their two-year arrest warrant. *James Aloysius Fitzpatrick! Have you learned nothing at all from five hundred years of Irish history?* Apparently not a goddamn thing.

Oh, I had my reasons. Reasons you gave other people. The ones buttressed by logic and common sense. The reasons that offered some kind of future that wasn't limited to becoming a cop or going to jail.

College. That was the real crux of the thing. Two young brothers, my family eking it out. That G.I. Bill was the thing. My one-way ticket out of Dorchester.

I did have other options. My hole card, a starting job on the Boston Fish Pier. As a bait taster. See had it turned enough. For some reason, I leaned toward the army.

And, of course, there were those other reasons. The reasons you never told other people. Never. The truth is, you see, I was a secret hero.

Now, it's true I had never done anything heroic. Still haven't. Not to this day. But I knew, and that's what counted. Fact is, I'd been practicing the moves for years. The hero's moves. Mock smoking at ten with pencil stubs. The real thing at fifteen. Because they all smoked. Alan Ladd. Tyrone Power. Humphrey Bogart.

Got a light, sister? Thanks. I needed that.

The deep drag. Smoke drifting out of my nose for minutes after each long pull. The *way* you held them. The *way* you lit them. The *way* you ground them out. Oh, I knew all the cigarette moves. Looking around at that group in that smoke-filled hallway in Dorchester in 1952, hell, we *all* knew the moves.

And the walks. Man, how I practiced those walks.

There I was, five seven and two fingers, a hundred and twenty five pounds on a good day, trying to walk like John Wayne. See John Wayne walking up to his horse. See him keep walking under his horse without bending his knees. That was me, alright.

What's more, I could look around that waiting room, watch any of those guys cross the room, and name the actor. The hero. We all could.

The war was not going well that summer. We had the Red Chinese swarming down from the Yalu River. We had whole companies cut off and surrounded. We had retreats—wait, sorry, *strategic withdrawals to the rear*. And, right in the middle of all that, here I come, asking the Board to take me in early!

Going there that evening, I already had *my* interview pictured clearly. I was ready for the great wash of their approbation. Ready for their beautiful secretary, eyes watering, to slip me her phone number as the Chairman threw an arm across my shoulders. "By God, give 'em a couple of shots for us, Fitzie!"

"NUMBER SEVEN. FITZPATRICK!"

Heading down the corridor, I noted that all eyes swung to Six as he exited the hearing room. Our polio guy. Clearly rattled. Stopping right in front of me on his good leg, his arms spread wide. "Don't *worry* about it! They actually said that to *me! Where you're going, Kid, the ground will be uneven anyway!* Can you believe that shit?"

A collective moan from the listeners. A recognition of doom. It followed me in as the door shut behind me. The Board's secretary, two pencils haphazardly stuck in her gray hair. Miss Upham's Corner of 1918. Pointing to a single chair in front of the table. "Plunk it."

A reddish, heavy-looking wood table covered with files and papers, supplemented on one end by a rickety card table with spindly legs where the secretary sat, a thick steno pad in front of her. Five fat men in shirtsleeves. Four ignoring me, staring at the ceiling, as the chairman read his copy of my request. One painful word at a time, lips working.

Passing it down, finally, to the secretary, who read it aloud, scribbling on her pad as she did so. Five confused sets of pig-eyes staring at me. The Chairman, summing up.

"Alright, Fitzpatrick. What *is* this crap? Just what'n hell you trying to pull?"

Bureaucracy at work. The military mind in mufti.

I did the best I could. They finally *seemed* to get it. My request was granted.

Getting up to leave. Well, what do you know? The chairman *did* come out from behind the table. Gripping my arm, walking me to the door. Almost the way I had visualized the moment. The smell of fried onions and cheap ketchup making my eyes water as he shoved his face up close to give me his words of wisdom.

"Now you listen to me, Fitzpatrick. I got *your* number. If this is a scam and you don't show up on the 15th, I'll see your bony little ass in friggin' jail!"

Well, okay. Not *quite* the way I had pictured it, but it would have to do.

Heading for the exit door. Ten and Twelve still at it. Most of the hallway following their debate. "I'm in traction half the friggin' year," Twelve was protesting. "And you say, forget it? So whatta you, a doctor?"

"No, but my cousin is," Ten announced, waving his papers in his hand. "This here is his report."

"Oh, yeah? So whyn't you tell us, huh? What's *your* story? You're so sure it's gonna keep you home?"

Ten, looking around, grinning. Eyes alight. Everyone now listening.

"My cousin, the doctor," he told the group in a carrying whisper, waving the papers in his hand. "He used *this* condition to keep both my uncles out, the big one."

He said the words slowly, clearly having practiced the pronunciation, raising his voice just a bit and drawing out the syllables like a magician about to disappear a rabbit. "Stentorophonous sphincterismus!"

Jesus! We were all looking at each other. Completely lost.

Ten saying it again slowly. Translating it for us. "Sten-tor-o-phon-ous Sphinct-er-is-mus! Get it? Loud noises make me shit!"

CHAPTER TWO

Indiantown Gap, Pennsylvania. A notorious stockade and endless miles of temporary barracks. Snow starting in October. This is what I win? Terrific.

The first weeks punctuated by bombast and constant threats.

Fall in. Fall out. Strip. Bend over and spread those cheeks. Stand up straight. Suck in that fat gut. Piss in that bottle. Put on your clothes. Run. Walk. Jump.

Jesus, it was just one fun thing after another.

Tony Ventola from Bayonne, New Jersey, getting me in trouble. Making me laugh. Keeping a straight face himself as he cracks me up. Standing there with that innocent look as they make *me* run punishment laps, pump out extra push-ups. All of us bullied into submission by the stripes, never mind those gold and silver bars. But Tony, Mr. Charm, just coasting. Funny as hell but game, too. Tony Ventola getting the yellow helmet. Lemon head! Making squad leader. No KP for Tony. No guard duty. None of that shit for lemon heads. Tony still making us laugh.

I did, of course, become a soldier. Not the shoot back, give 'em hell soldier of my forties war movies. A basic training soldier. A last name. A number. A piece of crud.

"Hey, smart ass! Fitzpatrick! You think it's funny, this guy dropped his rifle?"

"No, sir, Sergeant. I...I..."

"I, I, my ass! We had one you wise mouths last cycle. Know where he is now? The goddamn stockade, that's where! Take off! Two laps."

After the first few weeks, though, it wasn't the stockade we feared any longer. It was standing out. Being noticed. Drawing the attention of the stripes.

Ventola tried to put me right. "Here's the trick, Fitz. Stay low. Under the horizon. If you know something, terrific. Just don't tell no one, see. Don't volunteer."

The sameness, the drudgery. It got to you. Days, weeks melded together. There were times, I couldn't even remember what being a civilian had been like.

Slog out to the ranges in the dark of morning. Slog back in the dark of dusk. Full field packs. Rifles. Mile after mile. Rain running in rivers. Then sleet. Then snow.

Ventola doing morning roll call. His announcements. "The sun was sighted in Pennsylvania yesterday, men. Too bad you guys were in the latrine. You missed it."

Nine at night and still at it. Corporal Krowse, known to us as Kroutsnout, pacing up and down and singing sweet songs. "Clean that shit! Make it shine. No one leaves this building until every one them fuckin' machines guns looks factory new. You call *that* clean? Do it again."

I was just starting to pick up another mud-caked gun barrel when I hear Ventola, outside the door, yelling in. Shocking me. "Fitzpatrick! Get your ass out here. I got a truckload of supplies to pick up, and you're gonna hump 'em for me if it takes all night."

The rest of the squad jeering as I grab my hat and jacket and head out. "We'll be done, an hour or so. Ol' Fitz will still be going, midnight!"

Climbing into the company two and a half beside Tony. Pissed to a fair thee well until I see his manic grin. Ventola chortling as we speed off. "I got beer, Fitz! Crackers. A canned ham. What cha think of that, Dogface? Got them, the post PX. Soon as I pick up Spivey, Moran and Hiller, we'll go behind the chapel, have us a party."

Good old Tony. God bless Tony. The Bayonne Bomber. What a pal.

Inspection tomorrow. All of us at attention by our bunks. Kroutsnout smoking one of his two-bit panatelas. Flicking the ashes on the wooden floor and grinding them in with the toe of his boot. Grinding *us*. "No one sleeps tonight, this barracks, until this floor is clean enough to eat off!" Dropping the butt of the stogie and taking time to mash it in good, all over the middle of the aisle.

"Whatcha been doing, Clarkson?" Kroutsnout pulling a two-tier bunk to one side. "Ya been saving turds under that bunk in case you get hungry later? *Scrub* that friggin' floor, I said! Make it shine!"

Climbing down off the ladder after cleaning the tall windows next to my bunk. Krowse, picking up a pail of the dirty water just used on the floors, splashing it all over the window. Gritty black water everywhere, running down the panes to the sill and dripping on to the floor. "If I can see glass in them windows when you get through, they ain't clean. Scrub them fuckers again, Fitzpatrick. Every inch."

Freezing October and November mornings. The snow on the mountains turning brown as we tramp upward. Mud finding its way through. Mud sucking at our boots.

December. On our bellies in the snow. Fingers stiff in wet gloves.

Krowse helping. Pointing. "Hurry up! Get that goddamn ammo up here!"

Slipping, sliding, trying not to drop the mortar shells as I run them forward. On those ice cubes in my boots that used to be toes.

Endless weeks of heavy weapons training. Jesus, has it ever been this goddamn cold, this miserable, anywhere else on this slimy earth?

Kroutsnout, no pack, no rifle, insulated boots that none of us have, with his battery-powered hand warmers in his gloves, trotting up and down the ranks as *we* slog along loaded with mortar barrels and base plates and heavy machine guns.

"Get your ass in gear, Hiller! That heavy .30 too much for you? Move! Up to that ridge. Let's go. There was chinks on our tails right now, you'd double time up there, alright, take my word. Pick up that gun and run! Move it, I said! It won't break."

Running across the uneven ground, slipping and sliding. Spivey ahead of me, a heavy .30 over one shoulder, the tripod under his arm. Stopping. Looking like he's going to go down. Bent over at the waist, gasping. I lumber up, shift my mortar barrel to my other shoulder and grab the tripod from him. Kroutsnout suddenly on top of us.

"What's the fuckin' holdup back here? Move it out, I said! Hey, YOU!"

"Who, me, Corporal?"

"What do you mean, WHO? What's this WHO, WHO shit, Fitzpatrick? You ain't no friggin' owl. Your foot don't fit no limb. Yes, YOU! Move it out!"

One thing, anyway. Moving, running, falling down even, you at least make some heat. After you get where you're going, that's the problem. Soaking wet when you stop. Then standing for an hour in the blowing snow waiting to get your turn at a mortar position. That's the fun part. *Jee-sus!* I am almost as numb as Kroutsnout's brain.

Kroutsnout and the driver in the cab of the truck, the one that brought out the extra ammo. We see them sitting in there, the heater making their hair flutter. Kroutsnout coming out from time to time to give us words of encouragement. "Don't tell *me* you're cold, you dog-asses! How do you think I lost these two fingers?"

Kroutsnout pulling off the left glove, showing us the stubs. Again. "Think I lost these here playing the pi-anna! Just wait until those chinks come pouring down on top of you greenhorns. Your ass will be warm then, alright. You just fucking *wait.*"

Kroutsnout moving away, down the line. Moran nudging me. "Know what I think, Fitz? I think old Snout *ate* them fucking fingers. One of

14

them days, he's always telling us about, the chow never showed up."

Clarkson, blowing on his hands. "Brighten up, guys. Tomorrow's Saturday, the end of week eleven. Five more and we're all out of this fucking dump. Forever."

Oh, sweet Jesus, there is a God!

CHAPTER THREE

Saturday morning inspection. Parading in our class A's. In the snow. The captain out there himself today. Our CO. Marching past him, despite myself, I stand taller. Chest out. Marching at a brace. "You're looking good, Men," he shouts over the stomp of our boots. "You're soldiers now, by God. Be proud to lead you anywhere, *anywhere.*"

Getting a charge out of that despite my cynical Irish soul. Feeling the warmth. Wondering if anyone else did. Wondering if anyone else felt the burn.

Back in the barracks, waiting for the lists to be posted. Guard duty. KP. And, please God, weekend passes. Something new for us, passes. None at all the first ten weeks. Then only about a third of the company on any given weekend. Wait your turn. Get a pass and you're gone, Saturday noon to Sunday night at ten. I was still waiting.

Ventola coming in the door, spotting me sitting on my bunk. "Hey, Fitz! The list is up. You and me, Buddy, we are both on it."

Jumping up. "Passes? No shit?"

"No, not passes. That won't be up for an hour yet."

I drop back on the bunk. Pisser. Tony continues. "I'm talking the OCS list, Buddy. Officer's Candidate School."

What *is* he talking about? Oh, shit, right. All those tests we took at Devens.

"You are qualified, my man. Me, too. On to phase two."

Yeah, yeah. I heard all about OCS guys. More written tests. Physical exams. And, if you pass them, you go to the officers' panel. Goody, goody.

Christ, I had forgotten we even took those tests. "Balls, Tony. Who wants that? All that extra time. For what? To become a second looey? There's a mule they keep in this camp for parades. He gets more respect than a second lieutenant. Eats better, too."

Tony laughing. Others coming over to listen.

"Four more years," I added. "You realize that? Count it up. The time in OCS, then three years *after* you get a commission. Hey, they can roll that list in a tube..."

"I know, I know," he said, dropping beside me. "The time bothers me, too. I got a year in college and I want to finish. Trouble is, what I hear, brass wants us to go there real bad. We say no, walk away, we're fucked. Won't even make PFC, this man's army."

Moran coming over. Mike a gung ho RA. Not a draftee like us. An *enlistee*. "Now, now, you got the wrong attitude, men. Someone's liable to think you boys don't like the army. And you a lemon head, Tony. Now, you listen to old Mikey. You're both bright guys. Play along. Go to OCS. Don't you go and make Uncle Sam cross."

I looked up at Moran. I liked Mike. He was a good shit. "You on the list, Mike? You going to OCS?"

17

"What, are you fucking crazy? I made it a point to flunk them tests. They shoot second looeys in Korea like they were deer in a pen. I'm going for stripes, Pal, stripes."

Well, shit. I know that made *me* feel a lot better.

Our little talk interrupted by Sergeant Drummond at the barracks door. "Ventola. Fitzpatrick. Clarkson." Reading five or six more names. "The CO wants to see all you guys the orderly room. Now!"

Standing at attention in front of the CO's desk. In basic, you don't see officers much. You see the CO every five, six weeks, whether you need to or not. Still, this guy actually looks like a soldier. Back from Korea where the word around camp was he did real good. And he has the chewed up ear and scarred jaw to make us believers. For us he is *the* big cheese. God in khakis.

"Now, I know most of you guys don't plan to make a career of the army. Good enough. But the army needs dedicated officers right now, and it needs them bad. And I take a personal interest in you men. You've passed the initial tests. You're all doing fine here at the Gap. I'm been watching your progress. I want every one of you to go on to O.C.S and give it two hundred percent and do us proud. Do you read me?"

Oh, yeah. I get that loud and clear. Let's see if I can rephrase it. We're losing our ninety-day wonders in Korea by the boxcar-full. You're getting all kinds of shit from the brass to send more guys to OCS. Either we accept our appointments with a smile or you, and the rest of

18

the brass, will make us the sorriest sonsabitches that ever lived. Did I leave out anything? Uh oh! He's right in front of me, holding out his mitt.

"Oh, yes, Sir, Captain. I certainly am considering it. Yes, very seriously, Sir."

Trooping back to the barracks. Balls! Become an officer, and it's three more mother-humping years eating with my fingers, shitting in a trench. Golly, how exciting.

Don't panic. Maybe they'll turn me down on that special PT test.

"Hey, McNamara. What PT score do you need for O.C.S?"

Balls! I already scored higher than that the last two times. That's what I get for showing off how many pushups I can do. Asshole.

Hey, maybe when I go in front of the officer's panel, they'll give me the old thumbs down. Too small. Too thin. My frame won't hold enough bullets to make it worthwhile, the chinks start shooting at the yellow bars. *Some* fucking reason.

"Hey, Clarkson. Don't they turn down about half? That's what I heard."

"Not the way *this* war's going. You shittin me, Fitzpatrick? Take a good look at the second looey they got running around Baker Company. Jesus Christ! If that mouth-breather can get through O.C.S., they'll give you a direct commission as a general."

Breezing through the written and physical tests. Getting the call. The officers' panel today. Dress in Class A's and look sharp.

"Private Fitzpatrick reporting, Sir. First Company."

Jeez, the guy in the middle looks OK. A lieutenant colonel. First colonel I've ever seen wasn't in some movie court-martialing someone. First time an officer has smiled at me since I came into this goddamn army. A lot of salad dressing on *that* chest.

Sit up straight. Jesus, look at that file! Is that all on me? Look at the croaker on the end. He keeps grinning at me like he was the tooth fairy or something.

"Yes, Sir. That's right. I did have Latin and Greek and French in high school."

Hey, maybe they'll send me to the Mediterranean, I get my bars. I could do that.

"Pardon, Sir? What branch would I like if I graduate? Uh, I think transportation, Sir. I've, uh, done, a lot of, uh, traveling."

Uh, huh. That went over like glue on a toilet seat.

"Sir? If I couldn't get that? Well, uh, I guess, uh, the Infantry, Sir."

Oh, sure, sure. Look at them now. Smiling and nodding. You birdbrain.

Back to the old routine. Slogging out to the ranges, running our asses off. Rub a dub dub, cleaning weapons. Two weeks creep by. Moran, yelling across the company square as we are milling around after falling out. "Hey, guys! The OCS lists are out!"

Heading toward the orderly room. "I can save you the trip, Fitzpatrick."

Moran's grin told the story. "You are on it, Baby. You, too, Ventola. Clarkson, Jameson, almost every one of you sorry bastards. Oh, Fitzie, what have you gone and done? But, hey, what's three, four years when you can spend it sleeping in mud and eating dogshit every other day? That's, of course, *if* those chinks miss you stepping ashore, which, face it, Fitz, *there ain't no chance!*"

Good God, almighty! How in hell did I get into this box?

I want more time in this friggin' army like I want seconds on that shit on a shingle breakfast they threw at us this morning. But, if I tell them now that I've changed my mind, I'll be a marked man. There'll be a permanent note in the front of my file. *Kick this man in the balls. Do it three times a day. He's been assigned to your outfit as a gong. Signed, the commanding general of the whole goddamn army.*

CHAPTER FOUR

A Monday morning. Early January. Ventola out in front of the platoon reading a sheaf of notices. The usual shit. Then a pause. "Special Forces," he said. "Today, after lunch, at the orderly room. Anyone who is OCS qualified, or who speaks a second language fluently—they are stressing *fluently*, guys—is excused from grenade practice this afternoon."

"*Excused?* To do what?" Carlson calling out what every one of us suspicious bastards was thinking. We didn't have thirteen weeks in the army for nothing.

"To fall out in front of the orderly room and march our asses over to the theater. Tell us about some new army outfit forming up at Fort Bragg." Tony gave his eyebrows a couple of Groucho Marx pops. "They're going to have *movies* and everything."

Carl Kowalski, who I happened to know spoke Polish fluently, yelling out from the back rank. "Fuck that. I'd druther throw grenades."

The whole platoon laughing. Ventola holding up a hand for quiet, the smile edging in. "Tough shit, Kowalski. Read this notice. Says, 'Dumb Polacks sit in front.'"

Only Tony Ventola could say that to Kowalski, make him laugh, not end up rolling around on the ground.

"Uh huh," Kowalski growled, "so's you eyeties can sit in back, get your beauty sleep. I ain't goin."

"As a matter of fact you are. I probably didn't read it right. All OCS guys, *and* everyone with a second language, are required to attend. Order of the Post Commander."

"Shit," Kowalski growled. "Can we bring some live grenades?"

Clarkson, next to me. "Why would we have to attend something like that? Special Forces, that's the entertainers, right? Singers, disc jockeys, musicians?"

Tony, shaking his head. "No, no. That's Special Services. This here is Special *Forces*. Don't ask me why. The first soldier said it's guerilla warfare, that kinda crap."

Kowalski again. "*Guerilla warfare?* You mean like behind the enemy lines, *that* shit? Hiding out in the hills, blowing up bridges, eating your shoes. They're looking for guys to do *that?* In *Korea!*"

Jameson piping up, pointing at his black skin. "Hey, I'm OCS qualified. Am I supposed to attend this stuff? They're gonna ask me do I want to go behind the lines in friggin' Korea? Like I'll fit in, right? No one will notice me. They must be soft."

The whole platoon howling. All of us picking up on it. Moran stepping out of the ranks and yelling down to me. "Hey, Fitzpatrick! Squint your eyes like this! I want to see if you'll pass for a goddamn chink. Oh, beautiful. Look at that, guys! Oh, Jesus, Fitz! Don't let them see you do that this afta. You'll be in Manchuria by Easter!"

****

23

Filing out, the lecture over. All of us talking at once. Like guys coming out of the fights. Or from a slam-bang John Wayne movie. Thrilled and scared by what we had seen, but definitely not wanting to show it. Playing it for laughs all the way. Typical.

Clarkson, talking to the group at large as we headed across the post for the two-mile hike to our company area. Just walking. No stripes on hand to fall us in, make us march "Oh, brother, can you *believe* that stuff? We kin volunteer, we want! Stop by the orderly room and sign up for an interview. These Special Forces guys will be here until *Sunday*, accommodate us! I almost had a orgasm, they said that."

Jameson. "Gotta sign up quick, though, or you won't get to take *their* tests."

Ventola, getting out in front and trotting backwards, pointing at us. His voice sounding like one of the old-fashioned newsreel announcers. "Alright, soldiers. We need a few, hand-picked men! If selected, you will join the most elite force of fighting men in the world. And, don't worry! It'll be weeks and weeks before we get you killed."

"As soon as we get close to our area," I chimed in, "I'm gonna run ahead so's I can get right at the top of that list. So they take me first."

"How about that movie, for chrissake!" Clarkson asked. "See our men jump out of planes! See them climb mountains! See them boiling in a rice pot when the friggin' chinks catch them behind the lines. Where was Tyrone Power, they made that turkey?"

"Oh, Jesus, they're going to teach us languages," Jameson chortled. "We'll speak it like natives. See how it works? Long as I speak good sing-song, those Koreans and Chinese will never notice I happen to be black. Blend right in if I learn the language."

Ventola pumping his arms like he was running the hundred. "Where is that list? I won't sleep nights until they tell me I'm one of them there elites. Hey, Kowalski! Bet you're glad they made you come along now, huh?"

"Yeah," Kowalski said. "What a break if you're picked, huh! First they send you straight to Benning so's you can learn to jump out of airyplanes. Ain't that grand! As long as you don't end up wit a oak tree up your ass."

Kowalski grabbing Tony by the back of the neck. "You know what I liked, Tone? That Ranger training at Fort Bragg they'll put ya through. Great stuff. Like swimming upstream wit a bag of cement on your shoulders. In case you ever come across a bag of cement drowning!"

Other guys chiming in. "Did you see them silly bastards chasing each other around that stage with friggin' knives? Watch closely, and we will see Sergeant Nelson take a Samurai sword away from his attacker."

"Yeah, yeah. If somebody as big as that guy Nelson wanted my sword, he could have it. I'd *give* him the friggin' sword! My underwear, too, he wanted that."

All of us getting in on the act. Throwing in my two cents. Clarkson then. "Hey, Ventola, you hear that? What Fitz just said?"

I repeated it for Tony. "My opinion, this whole thing is a gag. To weed out the real psychos. Brass doesn't want anyone around this army who's friggin' dangerous!"

****

Back in the barracks after chow. Sitting on my bunk. Slipping the materials out. Reading them all again. Keeping them inside an old *Life Magazine* so no one will notice. My palms sweating. *Medics, radio operators and language experts. That's what we need to get our teams operational. If you have the aptitude, and the intestinal fortitude, we will train you.* Christ!

Glossy pictures. A line of men in parachutes beside a plane. *Our men are trained jumpers!* Guys in fur jackets and mittens up to their knees in snow. *Our men are trained to survive under any conditions!* Two barefoot guys in martial arts outfits, facing off, while others kneel watching. *Our men are trained in hand-to-hand combat!*

And then, the critical words. The ones I kept going back to again and again.

Getting this unit organized and operational is one of the highest concerns of the Secretary of Defense. Orders of assignment to the 10th Special Forces Group will be given first priority over all other assignments, whether to Asia, Europe, O.C.S., A.S.A., or anywhere else.

First priority? Does this really mean, if I can do this, I can kiss off O.C.S.? I can say good-bye to those three extra years?

Lying back on my bunk, I could see that team of guys again. Marching on to that stage.

Their wings and jump boots glistening in the spotlights. Man! I got a quick flash of myself walking through Dorchester looking like that. *Kee-rist!* I broke out in a cold sweat. Then I started all over. Reading the materials. Looking at the pictures.

****

Everyone going about their business. Me, strolling casually downstairs and out the door. Into the dark. Across the square, toward the orderly room.

A few guys at the front of the next barracks. Bullshitting around. No one paying any attention to me. Slowing as I get to the front of the orderly room. A quick duck and I'm inside. The company clerk sitting at the back of the long room, his feet up on the night clerk's cot, reading. He glances up as I come in, then returns to his reading.

Sticking my fatigue cap under my arm, loosening my jacket. The room is hot after the cold outside. I move to the bulletin board, to the wall just inside the door. There it is. On a clipboard. "SPECIAL FORCES." The entire notice underlined in red.

All those wishing to apply, sign below for company duty passes. All candidates will report on Saturday to Headquarters Company, 0900 hours, for special written examinations. Each candidate must be O.C.S. qualified, or have fluency in a second language, and must pass one or more of the special aptitude tests for radio communications, field medicine or languages. Physical training exams and personal interviews on Saturday between 1300 and 1600 hours. Notification of acceptance or rejection will be received before the close of basic training. Good Luck!

Empty lines. Name, rank and serial number. The whole goddamn page empty. Almost 2100 hours, and not one name yet. What *am* I doing here?

I glance over at the duty clerk. He continues reading. His left hand gropes into a paper bag beside him on the floor and comes out holding an apple. He chomps into it noisily, his eyes never leaving the book.

I riffle through the papers on the bulletin board. As if I dropped in every night to make sure I was abreast of the latest SOP bulletins on cleaning latrines and banking the barracks furnaces. Slipping the clipboard off the nail. The clerk doesn't react. I turn slightly away from him. I grab the pencil dangling on its string.

Fitzpatrick, James A. U.S. 51183987. Private E2.

My hand so damp the stubby pencil keeps sliding in it. The letters look like they were written by an octogenarian. Oh, my good Jesus. Jump School, for chrissake! I was almost pleading with myself. *It's not too late! Don't do this! Haul your ass out of here.*

Slowly, carefully, the clipboard goes back into place. The pencil swinging carelessly beside it. I stare at my name. All by itself. Naked.

When the CO gets here in the morning, that single name will look like a billboard advertisement for asshole of the month. Screw it! I turn and head for the door.

"Durm Git." It came from the duty clerk, but I couldn't make it out.

I stop and look questioningly in his direction. He swallows two or three of the larger pieces of apple and repeats the words. This time they come out clearly.

"Dumb shit."

Then, in case I missed it, he looks right at me for the first time and inclines his head in the direction of the clipboard. "*Some* guys never learn!"

CHAPTER FIVE

The recollection of that train trip is still strong. From Boston, Massachusetts to Columbus, Georgia. An all night trip. Leaving that evening in the New England cold, greeting the dawn in the warm, Southern sun. For me, though, in that icy February of 1953, millions of miles separated the two.

Goodbye family and friends. So long fellow members of the human community. And hello *what?* Hello, Jump School? I already knew a lot about that. Hello dawn patrols, and heads shaved to the bone, and running until your feet are like hamburger. Maybe that explained the distance.

I moved down the aisle, then chose a double on the platform side. My parents were out there. Trying to see in through the steamy window. Trying to find me.

I shoved my duffle bag up on a rack and dropped the overnight bag on the aisle seat. It had the things I'd need. A copy of *For Whom The Bell Tolls* that I'd been wanting to read for years, but which I wouldn't be able to start that long night. The sandwiches my mother made and which would remain untouched throughout the trip, bringing a lump to my throat each time I saw the wax paper. Remembering her fingers folding each one so carefully. Handkerchiefs. Of course. Crisply ironed. My mother would put those in if I told her I was going to be fired out of a cannon in the morning.

I peeled off the heavy overcoat and unbuttoned the tight-fitting Ike jacket as I slid into the window seat. Sitting there in my straight-leg pants and low-cut shoes. *Wear low-cuts! Don't walk around Columbus, Georgia with your boots bloused if you haven't earned your wings. Not if you don't want to get your teeth kicked in.*

Screw them! What a lot of crap that is. I've half a mind to pull that duffle bag down later and put the goddamn boots on anyway. Half a mind! That's being generous, isn't it?

It was another miserable winter in Boston. I used my sleeve to clear a space on the frosted window. To see my mother and father standing there. This late night train was less than a quarter full, and the platform was almost deserted, but they were there. Trying to look cheerful. Like they were really enjoying themselves. Especially Dad. Like this was great fun and we were all lucky to be a part of it.

My mother cried all night the day I arrived home from Indiantown Gap and told them I had volunteered for Special Forces. That I was going to Jump School in two weeks. Oh, she put on a good show. In front of the relatives. In front of my two little brothers. But late that first night, I could hear her crying. Very softly. But I heard her.

My father was surprised too. At first, he was sure I was kidding. That it was another of my put-ons. Later, after he knew, he kept reminding everyone, himself really, that at least I wasn't going straight to Korea. From time to time, in the ten days I was home, I would catch him studying me. Trying to understand. Jump School! Guerilla warfare! What the hell?

How could he understand? I didn't understand myself. Not really.

Just before I left, we went out. Dad and I. Over to Uncle Fred's. Then with Fred and his brother, out to one of those Irish neighborhood bars in Jamaica Plain. I was in uniform that night. The only night I wore it on that leave. Uncle Fred had insisted. I knew how much he wanted to show me off to his pals so I made the concession.

Danny Boy on the jukebox. Pitchers of beer. The place full of ex-army men. Most of them served together. The Yankee Division. A few women there, too. Tough old gals with arms like stevedores. Out of the factories. The markets. "God, ain't he a picture of his Uncle Frank, though? Going to Jump School, is he? And him not half old enough to spit. Ain't he the brave lad, though? Jaysus, Mary and Joseph! But won't he make those Georgia girls swoon in that uniform of his! Give old Mary a kiss then. I used to bounce your Uncle Frank on me knee." Frank dead of tuberculosis at the height of the depression.

Uncle Fred had been in the Battle of the Bulge. In the big one. Doubleyou doubleyou two. We walked the war that night. Fred and all his pals. And Dad and I. The good times first. Then a few more pitchers of beer. Then the rough times. The names of the ones who didn't make it.

Oh, Christ! Little Donny McAvoy! Could ya ever forget him, Fred? Took one right in the forehead on D-Day. Sullivan buried him.

The names that finally made Fred lean forward, his head in his hands, choking over his beer. The times that brought silence to the long table.

The wet table, the dirty table. The table full of half-empty beer glasses. Full of ashtrays choked with cigarettes. Full of France. Full of Germany. Full of their war. Their memories.

In his own way, I think Dad understood some of my mixed emotions that night. *Ain't he brave though! Going to be a jumper, is he?* And me, a little sick to my stomach every time it was mentioned. I'll never forget what my father told me that night. Late that night. After we finally made it back to Dorchester in our dilapidated Chevy. Dad using both sides of the road. Weaving through the almost deserted streets. Three in the morning and doing about twenty miles an hour. With me helping. The blind leading the blind.

We lived in a three-decker at the time on Olney Street. I can still remember the two of us reeling up that stairwell, bouncing off the walls, and shushing each other with exaggerated hand signals. Then collapsing into laughter and shushing each other again.

Continuing, until we at last reached the top landing, where, to our absolute astonishment, my mother was waiting with the door open. She stood there waving us in, urging us to silence. Dad and I staring at each other, almost indignant. Of course we'd be quiet, woman. Hadn't we already proved that by the way we'd tiptoed in?

My mother, never one for reticence, was a model of restraint on that occasion, especially after I had taken pains to point out that "Fred bosh the beer."

Jesus! Was that *me?* My mother's expression remained unchanged.

33

"Really?" she said. "How much beer did he bosh?"

Stifling our laughter, trying not to wake my younger brothers.

Before I could try again, my mother turned me by the shoulders and pushed me toward the living room. "Go to bed, Jamie! Tell me about it in the morning. But go to bed."

I was sitting on the edge of the living room couch having a last cigarette when Dad came out. That's where I had been sleeping on this leave. My old room had been ceded to my brothers. Thomas Wolf was wrong. You can go home again. As long as you're willing to sleep on the couch.

I remember that Dad looked kind of funny, almost ridiculous, in his shorts and T-shirt, but he surprised me because now he was very serious. He came up, teetering slightly, put one hand on my shoulder to steady himself, then whispered hoarsely. "Hey, Jamie," he said. All that stuff we've been talking about tonight. Jumping out of planes. You want to know something? I don't give one good crap about all that."

He leaned further over me, making me look at him, making sure I understood. He had to do a little two-step in front of me to keep his balance. But I didn't laugh, not this time. I didn't even smile.

The truth is, it was a bit of a shock. In the first place, I had rarely seen my conservative, Knights of Columbus father when he'd had too much to drink. In the second, the words "one good crap" were the kind he never used at home. Never.

That was the first time I realized he had been bothered that night. By my uncle and all his pals. The Veterans. Lifting their glasses all night and urging me to raise the flag again at Iwo Jima. I nodded, to show I understood. He stepped back then, a little embarrassed. He waved his hand at me as though a lazy, erratic fly were circling between us.

He headed back for their bedroom, leaning forward and changing direction abruptly several times like a sailboat tacking into a stiff wind. He stopped once more, however, his hand on the bedroom doorknob. His whisper was like a vacuum cleaner going full blast.

"You remember what I said, Jamie. Forget Fred and all that Battle of the Bulge stuff. When you get to Benning, if you don't like it, if you don't want to jump, you tell them to stuff it. If you do, that'll be okay with me. You remember that."

He pushed against the door, and half fell into the bedroom.

It really was kind of comical, except that sitting there that night, I didn't feel like laughing.

From the train, I looked out at them, standing there on the station platform. My mother hanging onto Dad's arm. Their collars up against the bitter February cold. Most of the snow on the platform had been shoveled out of the way, but their legs from the knees down were lost in the clouds of steam coming out from under the train.

Dad was mouthing something at me, making gestures. A joke I couldn't follow. I had no idea what he was trying to say, but I laughed and nodded vigorously, and he grinned back.

The five or six minutes since I had sat down seemed like hours, and I kept having to clean the spot on the window to keep them in view, my throat constricted, the grin frozen on my face. Maybe if I went down to the platform between the cars, they could hear me. I started to signal to them that I was going to the back of the car, but just then the train gave a lurch, and a huge billow of steam poured out all around them. Another lurch, and the train started to move.

I waved. They waved. The train moved a little faster. They were dropping back then. I waved furiously, grinning. They waved back, growing smaller by the second, until finally they disappeared as the long, deserted platform rolled by my window.

Then the platform was gone.

I saw the rail yards. Boxcars on sidings. Miles of track. I sat back then, feeling slightly queasy. Next stop for me, Columbus, Georgia. Jump School.

You'll get to go to Fort Benning and jump out of airy-planes. Ain't that grand!

Oh, yeah. It's grand, alright. It sure is!

CHAPTER SIX

Almost eleven. The Southern sun bright outside the train windows. Everything hot and sticky.

From Washington, D.C. on down the train had been filling up steadily at each stop. I had dug the book out early that morning. Holding it in front of me for effect, but staring blankly at the pages. I didn't feel like company.

I didn't feel like anything, except maybe a letter from the Pentagon saying, whoops, sorry this was all a big mistake.

Damn. All over this country there are guys in the army just putting in time. Some guys always do things so easy. Why do I do everything the hard way?

Most of the passengers, young men with short haircuts. Some in sport clothes, regulars returning from pass.

A lot of guys in uniform. Some already wearing the round airborne patch on their hats, the shiny silver wings on their chests. Their uniforms, I noticed, were different. Shaped shirts, cut to fit tight to the body. Wrinkle free. Boots shining like glass.

A lot of guys like myself. Basic training stuck out all over us. Ill-fitting winter uniforms bereft of any insignia of rank. Jackets peeled off and ties loose, we sat there in khaki shirts, heavy OD pants and low-cuts. Jump School candidates. On our way. Sweating already.

The car was getting noisier. Bits and pieces of conversation drifted back to me.

So I told her, I'm not asking you to go all the way, baby. I just wanna put the tip in.

The sound of cards slapping down on the side of a suitcase. *Jeesus, Johnson! Three Jacks! You must be the luckiest sucker in the whole friggin' army!*

The sandwich man passing down the aisle. Paper-thin ham sandwiches. One buck. Christ! Can they spare it. Trees, houses, fields going by the windows. I continued to stare at the page in front of me.

"Are you actually going to eat that sandwich?"

I looked up. The guy speaking was a couple of seats away. A big guy, with one of those carrying voices. His left upper arm bore the red diamond of the Gap. He looked familiar, but he was not from my company. From Philly, by his accent. He was leaning forward, watching a guy in one of the seats across from him unwrapping his sandwich.

"You haven't traveled on trains much, have you, partner? Let me tell you, I've hung gypsum wallboard that was safer to eat than that ham. Be smart! Throw away the sandwich, eat the wax paper. That way we can tell the conductor exactly what you died from."

The guy took a big bite of the sandwich and just grinned. The guy from Philly leaned forward tapping him on the knee meaningfully. "I'm serious! Doesn't it have a slight green tint to it? Take a look. Not *that* side, Dummy. You can't tell through the mustard. The other side. Ah! Ah! You see!"

All of the guys leaning in to peer at the underside of the thin slice of ham. The guy from Philly peeled the bread back even further. "Oh, *Jesus!*" he said, staring down. "Oh, my God!"

The guy eating the sandwich had stopped chewing on his one mouthful, his jaws apart, and he looked greener than any ham could have. He glanced around, clearly looking for a place to spit, and the big guy jerked a thumb toward the far end of the car. "The Men's room," he said. "That way."

Our erstwhile sandwich-eater was on his feet and headed down the aisle, determined not to swallow. Looking like he might get sick before he got there. The guy from Philly, now holding the sandwich, watched his receding back for a moment, then he sat back and shrugged. "Oh, well," he said. "Waste not, want not!" He began devouring the sandwich, taking huge bites, chewing with obvious relish.

After a moment of shock, everyone watching began to laugh. The guy from Philly joined in as he tucked the last of the sandwich in his mouth. "It's just like they always told us at the Gap, men. We all gotta eat a pound of green before we go!"

Despite myself, I ended up joining in the general laughter. A moment later, the other guy made his way back down the aisle. His tie was loose, his shirt was open at the neck, and his face was still damp from splashing water on it. "Christ," he said bitterly. "Am I glad you spotted that! Green ham, for chrissakes! They oughta throw those bastards in jail!"

He was totally unprepared, of course, for the uproarious laughter that greeted this pronouncement. He looked around surprised, resentful. Everyone was laughing except the guy from Philly, who looked at the others, his face mirroring the resentment and disgust of the sandwich spitter. "Sure, sure," he said, waiting for the laughter to be replaced by respectful attention. "It's easy for them to laugh. Right? They didn't eat that shit!"

A little later, a young airborne trooper came swaggering down the aisle. He looked about twelve, especially with his head shaved to the bone, but he was giving everyone the flash from his wings. It was written all over him. *I've got mine, you poor suffering bastards, now it's your turn.*

The kid stopped next to the guy from Philly. Apparently satisfied with what he saw, he motioned for him to move in so he could drop into the seat beside him. It was half request, half order, the way he did it, but the guy from Philly made room. The trooper looking them over. Still swaggering even as he sat. A pipsqueak drawl.

"Y'all headin' for Benning? Jump School?"

The three guys all nodded and the kid actually licked his lips. It was like he'd just sat down to dinner.

Ten minutes later he was still going strong.

"And then, when y'all get to the planes, man, oh, man! That's when the fun really starts." He jerked his thumb up at his chest, tapping it

40

against the metal wings. "That's when y'all earn these, baby, lemme tell you. That's when y'all earn these, or you haul ass *out*!"

He leaned forward then, dropping his voice, but not enough. "Y'all just wait until it's your turn to stand in that door. WHOOOEEE! Man, y'all don't know what scared is! A thousand friggin' feet of nothin' out there. And theah you are! Like standin' on the top of the Empire State Building in New Yawk City."

Other guys in our part of the car had stopped talking and were listening.

"AAARRR you ready? AARR you friggin' ready to GO! WHOOOEEE! AAARRR you suckers a-go-in to jump! Oh, man! Y'all WILL PISS YO PANTS that day, baby, believe you me!"

That was when the big guy from Philly butted in. "No shit? Scared the piss right of you, huh? That's really fascinating. I have a brother who's a trooper. He's got three combat jumps in Korea, and he says jumping is a real ball. He loves it!"

He paused and let that sink in. "My brother did say it scares the crap out of some guys. You must be one of them, huh?"

The bluster went out of the kid like steam from a busted radiator. "Huh! *Me* scared? Aw, that's sheet, man! That's pu-wah sheet! Hell, ah love jumpin'."

"C'mon," the guy from Philly replied, grasping the kid's elbow. "Fess up. Did you really piss yourself when you went out that door the first time? You can tell us. We won't squeal."

41

The kid jerked his arm free and he was out of the seat and in the aisle, his face flushed. Finding himself submerged in a sea of laughter, though, his anger cooled. "Sheet," he said. "Ah tole you ah was just jokin' around. Sheet!"

Waving his hand, he added, but without heat, "You'll find out, alright. Y'all jess wait!"

He sauntered off down the aisle, not quite turning it into a swagger this time.

"Ten minutes!" This from the conductor. "Columbus! Ten minutes!"

Yeah, yeah. I heard you. I was staring out the window. What if I just stayed right on the goddamn train straight through to Florida. *Do you realize you're two years late reporting, Fitzpatrick? What's your excuse? Sorry, sir, I've been picking fruit.* Balls!

The train began slowing noticeably and there was suddenly a sea of men yanking down duffle bags, pulling on OD jackets and straightening ties.

You better button up there, boy, 'n you don't want some M.P. kicking your ass all the way out to Benning.

Christ. This friggin' army. Out in the packed aisle then, leaning forward on my duffle bag, a wave of heat moving in as the doors between the cars opened up. Watching the last of the grimy, smoke-stained houses next to the tracks slowly drift by the window.

A tap on my shoulder and I turned to find the guy from Philly standing behind me. The top of my head just about reached his shoulder. He

42

pointed to the red diamond on my upper arm. "Tell me, Stretch! What's a nice boy from the Gap doing in a pisshole like this? You didn't by any chance glom onto the same bait they dangled in front of my nose, did you?"

My mind seemed to be working in slow motion, but after a second or two I recovered enough to answer. "Well, I'm not really sure," I said cautiously. "I'm, uh, down here for Jump School, but I signed up for, uh. . . a new outfit."

I had dropped my voice to a whisper at the end, not sure what to say, and hoping he would let it pass. Not a chance.

"A new outfit!"

His voice rang like a gong, and I glanced around uncomfortably. I saw heads turning to look at us, from behind and ahead of us in the aisle. He cocked his head slightly to one side and his eyes focused on me like an eagle who has spotted a particularly juicy mouse. "A new outfit," he repeated loudly. "What *kind* of new outfit? What do you mean?"

I swallowed hard. The train was still chugging down the last hundred yards or so into the station, barely moving. There was nowhere to go. I leaned toward him, keeping my voice as low as possible, hoping to transfer a little of the confidentiality of my demeanor to him. He had to lean over to catch the words.

"It's a new airborne outfit," I whispered. "Sort of like . . .like, uh. . .the Pathfinders, I guess. . .or uh, like O.S.S., maybe. Up at Fort Bragg."

I was willing to let it go at that, but the Philadelphia eagle was listening intently.

"What's it called?" he stage-whispered back.

I swallowed hard again. I said it once, but he cupped a hand behind his ear, straining to hear, so I had to repeat it. A little louder. "Special Forces," I breathed hoarsely.

"SPECIAL FORCES!" The words from his mouth reverberated down the length of the railroad car. During basic I'd heard mortar rounds go off with less effect. I turned scarlet.

"Special Forces!" He brayed again, shaking his head as he looked at me, and I saw guys pushing themselves up on tiptoe, straining to look around their buddies, trying to get a look at the object of this excitement.

"Great suffering Jesus," he bellowed. "Guerilla warfare! Jumping behind enemy lines with a goddamn machete in your teeth. Eating cockroaches, sucking on stones for nourishment. *Special Forces!* Suckered you into that, did they?"

He shook his head again, in what I could only take as sincere commiseration. Then he added, in a tone that could easily be heard all over Columbus as the train chugged to a stop. "Special Forces, huh! Well, I have to take my hat off to you, my friend!"

And he did, lifting it to the ceiling, without completely straightening his arm. "I hope you don't have any special plans for the next ten years or so, Old Buddy. Once they drop your sweet ass into some Manchurian rice paddy, it's going to be a long walk out."

The line started moving then toward the doors. As I shifted my heavy duffle bag in front of me, a step at a time, I felt more like an idiot than I had at any time since I had first scrawled my name on that sheet at the Gap. Let's face it. The guy was absolutely right. In a few months, I'd be up the Yalu River somewhere, probably being served up as part of the Red Brigade's chow mein. The whole thing was sickening.

When we were almost to the door, I looked back and asked half-heartedly, "How about you? Where are you heading?" Truthfully, I didn't really want to know, but this time he leaned forward and I'm sure I was the only one who heard his words.

"Oh, they got me, too," he said softly.

I stopped, startled, looking up at him. He nodded, grinning broadly. His voice still low, he added. "That's right! We're all in this together, Partner, so stop looking so goddamned worried, willya."

We moved a few more steps and he laughed again. "The truth is, there's about as much chance of them dropping that Irish mug of yours into China as there is of them turning me into a ballerina! Brighten up, my friend. What the hell! Remember, we all gotta eat a pound of green before we go!"

CHAPTER SEVEN

On the platform, we shouldered the duffle bags, grabbed our hand luggage and became part of the endless line making the long trek down to the station. For some reason, following in the big guy's wake, I did feel better. A hell of a lot better. I tried to keep pace with his long strides. "What outfit is your brother in?" I asked. "Is he in Special Forces?"

The big guy looked down at me, obviously puzzled. "What brother?" he said. Then, remembering before I could answer, he broke out laughing. "Oh, *that* brother. Well, my friend, that brother was pure *sheet*. But it sure as hell put that little turd back in his commode, didn't it?"

And he laughed uproariously without breaking stride.

Inside the station little knots of men were forming as guys from different basic training camps spotted each other. We saw a small group from the Gap and kept going until we could drop our bags beside theirs. Only three of the guys were from my old company, but seeing them gave me an immediate lift.

Tony Ventola, Harry Fisher and Carl Kowalski. With me, they were the four from our company who made it out of the nine guys who had applied. All of them signing the list after me, that night or early the next morning. Until we fell in that Saturday morning at the Gap, I had not even known that anyone else had signed up. Seeing Tony, Fisher and some of the others lining up with me that morning had been like drinking

46

adrenalin out of the bottle. I got something of that same feeling now, seeing them there in the Columbus railroad station.

Backslapping, wisecracks all around.

"Jesus, Fitz!" Tony tapping my bag with a toe. "That duffle bag is bigger than you are. What you got in there? One of them Pottsville Pee-Ay ladies of the evening?"

Harry Fisher chiming in. Telling us he got so bored on his Ohio leave he hopped a truck to New Jersey and spent the last couple of days hanging out with Tony and a couple of the New Yorkers. "Ventola, you hot shit!" he said. "Show these guys what you were wearing the night we went up to Times Square, hit the dance clubs."

Ventola shushing him, and looking around, but then bringing them out of his pocket. A shiny set of railroad tracks. Captain's bars. He laughed. "I kept telling the honeys I just got back, got a battlefield commission. Christ, I couldn't buy the condoms fast enough to keep up."

Introductions all around. The big guy from Philly was Bill Denbeaux. William C. Denbeaux, Jr., to be exact. "Den-bow?" Kowalski asked. "You French, Bill?"

"Nah. Believe it or not, the name is Irish. Hell, they've been hanging Denbeaux's in Ireland for hundreds of years. I've got one cousin who pretends it's French, but he's a hairdresser, so what are ya gonna do?"

Denbeaux was not surprised that my name turned out to be Fitzpatrick. "Being Irish is bad enough," he admonished the group, "but a *Boston* Irishman!"

He went on to explain in a weepy brogue that would pass in any Dorchester gathering I'd ever attended, "Ah, the Boston Irish. A sad, mournful, disperate lot they are, by Jaysus. Not a good laugh among them since Parnell wint down. Just give them a few pitchers of beer, a drop of two of the 'cray-ture' and a dead body to wake through the night, and you'll really catch them at their best."

Everyone loving that, of course. Kowalski howling. Denbeaux doing a little jig in place as he began singing. *"Irishman, Irishman, bow down your head, go back to old Ireland, for Christ's sake drop dead."* All I know is, watching and listening to that silly bastard, I had the first belly laugh I'd had in days.

Picking up our gear, we followed the signs outside. There were busses marked "Fort Benning" already waiting. Lines of soldiers starting to board. Following some guys from the Gap into line, I looked back, surprised to see Denbeaux and Ventola standing off to one side watching us.

"Willya look at those dumb sonsabitches, Tony?" Denbeaux said, his voice carrying well past me.

Tony nodding. "They can't wait to get out there and get the carnage started."

"Lemmings," Bill added. "Throwing themselves into the sea!"

Fisher and me looking at each other, Denbeaux's brogue again. "Oh, Jaysus, driver, hurry it up, can't you? There's hours and hours of running me ass off in the blisterin sun I'll be missin' if you don't stop lollygaggin' around. Get me out of this sinful playce before someone drags me into win of them air conditioned ristrants and forces a cold pint down me throat."

Fisher and me laughing sheepishly and stepping out of line. "Hey, Carl," Fisher called to Kowalski. "What's the hurry? How about, you know, we grab a sandwich and a couple of frosties before we head out there?"

Like it was his idea.

Kowalski and some guy named Carver who was also from the Gap dropped out of the line to join us. We needed a place to leave our gear and the regular lockers wouldn't hold duffle bags, but Ventola dug into his bottomless reserve of charm. After a brief huddle with a singularly homely station clerk, he persuaded her to let us stack our gear in a corner behind her counter.

Outside in the bright Georgia sunlight, Denbeaux walked over to a cabbie at the curb and asked if the guy could suggest someplace to get lunch and a couple of beers.

The cabbie, who had to weigh close to three hundred pounds, heaved his enormous bulk out and leaned on the roof of his cab, producing a huge, plaid handkerchief as he did so. "Names L'il Clyde," he advised us. "Not to be confused with my cousin, Big Clyde. Can't miss him. He's a big, fat sumbee."

He kept a straight face with all of us laughing. Lifting his straw hat, he mopped the top of his baldhead. Then he dropped the sad-looking straw on to the roof in front of him.

"Son," he said to Bill, "don't never, I mean don't *never*, walk up in the noonday sun in Georgia and mention cold beer to a fat man."

He gave Bill a wink, and I noticed that his eyes moved over us, not missing much. His lips pursed as he looked at our heavy, olive drab uniforms. He looked thoughtful. "Lunch and that cold stuff we don't mention, huh?" he ruminated, looking off down the street. "Seems as how, 'n I were you, I might want to get away from this station and all these MPs. Find myself a place I could take off them horse blankets for a spell and enjoy my lunch. Any of you boys ever heard of Phenix City? Alabama?"

We all looked at each other blankly, but Carver cut in, impatiently. "Look, Pop," he said, and although I winced, the cabby's expression didn't change. "This ain't our day for no guided tour of the Southland. *Alabama*, for chrissakes! Alls we want is a sandwich and a beer, for cryeye. We gotta be out at Benning in a few hours."

Carver waved his hand indicating the quiet Columbus street. "There must be plenty of places within five minutes of the station here, we can grab a fast lunch."

Carver took a few steps away, Fisher and Kowalski moving with him. He gave us a disgusted, "C'mon let's go," motion with his head, but neither Denbeaux nor Ventola moved so I stood pat.

Bill folded his arms on top of the cab next to the driver. "Wait a minute. Alabama! That's right across the river, right? How far is this Phenix City, cabbie? What did you have in mind?"

The cabbie's head turned slowly back, pausing for just an instant as his eyes passed over Carver. He looked at Bill for a long second. "Man wants to grab a quick lunch, that's one thing." The words "quick lunch" came out sounding like a venereal disease. "They's hot dogs and sody pop in the station, you want you a quick lunch."

Denbeaux gave me a grin as the driver continued. "Now, me. Was I to find myself about to go off, spend five, six weeks with my Uncle Samuel, I wouldn't want no greasy dogs, hamburgers or sody pop. Me, I'd take me a ride down here to the 14th Street Bridge and go acrost the Chattahoochee River there to Phenix City."

The driver placed his battered straw in front of him like a plate, and he held his right hand just above it, thumb and forefinger about an inch apart. "Me, I'd want me a nice, thick, juicy steak, about like so. Charcoal broiled. With a big mess o' fries."

Oh, yeah! I liked the sound of that. The cabbie looked up from his "plate" to add, "And longside that steak, I'd want me a big ol' foamy jug of that stuff you don't never mention to no fat man in the noonday sun! Drawn from a tap. The good stuff."

He shut his eyes, drying his blotchy neck with the kerchief but continuing to speak. "Now, the goin' and comin' to this steak house is no more'n ten minutes each way. And the whole shootin' match will cost maybe a fiver apiece, you have three pitchers. Cab ride down there, fifty cents apiece. The tip I'll leave to you gentlemen."

Denbeaux had the passenger door open, and Ventola and I piled into the back. Fisher looked at the other two, but Carver shook his head. "Alabama! You guys must be soft. How do you know where that guy's gonna take you. You'll get a steak alright, and a Mickey Finn. Get rolled, beat to shit, end up on some friggin' chain gang. No thanks!"

Fisher hesitated. "Geez, I'd like to, guys. Sounds great. But maybe, I'll just grab something quick, you know? Get on out there, and well, you know, get settled."

His voice trailed off. He looked embarrassed. Kowalski shrugged, electing to stay with his buddy Fisher.

Denbeaux jumped in front. "Suit yourselves, guys," he yelled. As the cab moved away from the curb, Bill turned to look at Ventola and me. "They tell me that during the French Revolution, there were guys on their way to the guillotine who offered to hold the friggin' basket."

That drew a deep, appreciative chuckle from L'il Clyde, and we were off.

CHAPTER EIGHT

"Here he is. Hey, Clyde!"

L'il Clyde right on time, as promised.

Climbing in. Our bellies full. The three of us, awash in cold beer, glad to sit back and let the world roll by for a while. The cab taking us back, first, to the station.

I know I tried to walk with dignity and aplomb across the concourse to the counter where we had stored our gear, but if Denbeaux and Ventola were any indication of how I looked, the aplomb was all in my mind. The homely young lady had left for the day, but she had, I noted, pinned a note to Ventola's small bag.

Tony grinned and waved the note at us. Another conquest for the Jersey Jock. Denbeaux surprised me. Waving his finger under Tony's nose, he shook his head. "Throw that one away, Pal," he said, a loud burp in the middle adding unneeded punctuation. "She's a nice girl, that clerk. Marrying girl. Don't screw up her life, Tone, messing around with a nice girl like that."

Denbeaux, as I found out later, had six sisters at home. He didn't go for that shit with nice girls.

Ventola looked genuinely shocked, but then he nodded vigorously. "Right. She *was* a good kid," he repeated. "Took care of us, too."

With an elaborate gesture, Ventola kissed the paper and dropped it into a handy trashcan. "Not for the Bayonne Bomber. Not what old Tony needs, he gets a leave. I get to town," he added, confidentially, in a very loud whisper, "what I need is poontang."

At the moment, I had my own troubles. I was trying to throw my duffle bag onto my shoulder. Trying this several times and missing. Denbeaux shaking his head at my ineptitude, and effortlessly swinging his own up onto his shoulder. Grinning at me triumphantly. Until he fell backwards into the counter with a crash and dropped the bag again. Ventola, doubled over, watching this.

L'il Clyde shaking his head. Taking my duffle bag and Bill's under one arm and then grabbing Tony's with his free hand. "Gimme them duffles, boys. Least I kin see 'em! Bring your hand luggage along. I *believe* you kin handle them."

Back in the cab and heading for Fort Benning. Quiet and sleepy Columbus disappearing behind us. Fields, colorless now in the early dark of this winter day, going by the windows. Oh, Christ, oh, man. Jump School coming up.

Clyde slowing to a stop at the gates while the MP looked us over, then waving us in. Clyde wending his way knowledgeably through the brick buildings and manicured lawns of the permanent post. Then driving on through the regular company areas, past rows of white barracks and assorted support buildings. The latter of irregular size and shape, crowded in and looking over the shingled shoulders of the barracks.

Beyond all of that, the training areas, seemingly endless, surrounding us.

We were beginning to sober up, without question, but probably not enough. Ventola's beery giggle beside me. "Hey, Clyde, you probably know this place better than the cadre. How long have we got before they take us up in one of those World War Two crates, start kicking our asses out the door?"

All of us laughing. But not like earlier. Kind of a nervous, hollow ring to it, to be honest. And we all seemed to sense it.

Clyde looked at his watch. "It ain't eight o'clock yet, boys. Y'all want me to show you the towers?" He swiveled around to look at us. "You want a little look at them great big suckers they's agoin' to be dropping you boys off of in a couple, three weeks?"

Ventola leaning over, peering out at the white buildings going past, at the roads brightly lit by street and porch lights. "Sure, Clyde," he said. "Why the hell not? I'm gonna tell them I changed my mind in the morning anyway."

Personally, I wasn't exactly panting to see the goddamn towers. Not yet, anyway. But since neither Bill nor I said anything, Clyde took a left at the next intersection, leaving the rows of barracks behind. Trees going by, and fields. Then a bump as the cab left the road, and then the sound of gravel as we drove out toward an immense open space. Tall lights around the perimeter. Plenty of light.

"KEE-RIST!" That from Tony to my left, his head now out the window. The cab rolling to a stop. "Will you look at the size of those goddamn things. *Ma-rone!*"

Clyde out first. Denbeaux and Ventola out next. Me, last. Standing beside Ventola. Feeling the unsteadiness as I straightened up, but wishing I were a lot drunker at that moment. Drunk enough to laugh without choking.

There were four towers. Gigantic steel structures that seemed to go up forever into the darkened sky. We stood against the cab, leaning back, looking up. And up.

Four arms stuck out from the center of each main structure at the very top. We could see the hoops at each end to which the chutes would be attached. From where we were standing, those hoops each looked about the size of a dime. What was it that self-inflated little turd on the train had said? Two hundred and fifty feet from the end of each arm to the ground.

Denbeaux slapping L'il Clyde on the elbow. "I swear, Clyde, if my chute doesn't open when they drop me off that hummer, I'll raise holy hell with these bastards."

Ventola's laugh sounded like a cat coughing up a fur ball. I didn't even try.

Clyde motioned toward a tiered set of wooden stands off to one side. "They let people come out to watch, y'know. 'Cept on the windy days. When it gets windy, they's too many axe-see-dents!"

His next words were spoken softly. "Sometimes I drive out to drop someone off, and I come over here to watch. Man, it is somethin' to see when one of them chutes don't open. The way the body slams into that plowed dirt. Or when one of the boys gets his chute hung up on one of them there steel hooks. See them, 'long the side there?"

We saw them. Square angled metal bars sticking out from the structure.

"Man catches up on one of them, he hangs there while his chute tears itself in two, then jest drops like a stone. I swear, it wouldn't be half so bad if only they didn't kick so much and scream all the way down."

Clyde was still staring up at the towers, but all three of us were staring at him, absorbing the awful image. Then his head swung around slowly, and the big St. Bernard eyes crinkled at the corners, a broad grin splitting his face. "Shee-it," he chuckled. "Don't you city boys know when your leg's being pulled?"

He motioned to us to get back in. Slapping Denbeaux on the shoulder, he added, "You boys must be lots drunker than I thought. Why, they hasn't been a serious axe-see-dent on them towers since them eyesores was fust put up. When one of them ironworkers mashed a finger."

That didn't happen to be true, as we learned later, but those words sure made me feel better that night.

True to his word, Clyde drove us almost to the door. Just before we got there, a little incident occurred which shot us out of our temporary funk. Clyde rolling to a stop at a crossroads as road guards sprinted out in front of us to take up their posts. Standing at parade rest, panting. Two good-sized platoons double-timing toward us. White T-shirts. Fatigue pants. Boots crashing steadily against the asphalt.

These guys had been at it for a while. Rivers of sweat streaming down their faces and arms as they came abreast and hammered past. A Jump School instructor dancing along out to one side. Running backwards, needling them. His voice taunting. "What's the matter, girls? Getting tired? Pick 'em up, pick 'em up! Bring those knees up. What do you think you're in? The friggin' infantry?"

Boots crashing. Arms pumping. Legs pistoning. Knees coming up almost waist-high.

And there they were. In the second platoon. Almost unrecognizable. Every head shaved as bald as a billiard ball. Right in a goddamn row. Fisher, Carver and Kowalski!

I spotted them first. Pointing. "Look! That's Fisher! *Jee-sus!* And Kowalski!"

Denbeaux, then. "Oh, Man! Right in front of him. That's *Carver.*"

All of us exploding. L'il Clyde laughing harder than any of us.

"Well, now, ain't that jest about the purtiest thing you boys ever did see? Wanted to get right out here," he chortled. "Get theyselves *settled.* Well, they sure as sheet looks settled now, don't they? Ain't worrying about no god-damn Alabama chain-gang now, ah kin promise you!"

Clyde put the cab in gear as the road guards raced to fall back into line. We slid across the intersection and continued until we came to a large, grassy area in front of Headquarters Company. A stark white sign stood next to the pathway. "All Jump School Arrivals Report Here."

"Far as I kin take you, men. Use the walks now, and don't cross that grass, 'less you like doin' pushups for an hour or two. That'll be three bucks, boys," Clyde grinned. "No extry charge for the side tours."

CHAPTER NINE

We watched L'il Clyde roll away, a cloud of dust settling slowly behind his cab as it disappeared. I can't speak for the others, but I know that I felt like a kid left at the church in a basket.

Ventola moved first. He bent over to pick up his duffle bag, losing his balance momentarily. One leg shot out to the side at hip level as he tried to keep from falling. Watching, I saw his mouth open in surprise as he slowly tilted until he ended up sitting down heavily on the grass beside the bag.

"God damn!" he said, dropping each word like a precious pearl. "I have a late, late news flash for you, boys. *I am bombed!*"

Denbeaux and I each took an arm to pull him to his feet. When we let him go, however, all three of us looked like we were in a logrolling contest. Stopping, weaving in place, Denbeaux muttered, "My friends, there is just a chance that we may have sucked up one too many of those golden beauties."

A resounding belch punctuated those words, sending Ventola and me into another round of laughter.

"YOU MEN THERE!"

The voice slammed into the back of my head like a sledge. We all spun around, and the last of my laughter shattered into fragments at my feet. A tiny apparition over by the orderly room. Looking maybe, oh, god, like an officer. It bellowed again. "DID YOU HEAR ME! GET YOUR STRAIGHT-LEG ASSES OVER HERE! I MEAN NOW! DOUBLE TIME, YOU LEG BASTARDS! DOUBLE TIME!"

I was still trying to get the two hundred pounds of wet sand that used to be my duffle bag up to my shoulder when I saw Denbeaux's back shooting past me, straight across the square toward the officer. He had his duffle bag on one shoulder and his overnight bag in his other hand, knees pumping high.

"NOT ON THE GODDAMN GRASS, YOU LEG ASSHOLE! NOT ON THE GODDAMN GRASS!"

Denbeaux spun around like he'd been hit in the shoulder by a tight group of .45 caliber bullets. With their noses flattened first. Unfortunately, his duffle bag didn't make the same turn. It shot off his shoulder and scooted across the grass like a canoe going downstream. I could see Bill chasing it, booting it at every third step even as I got my bag up and double-timed down the walkway, around the square, toward our enraged superior.

Ventola, the dirty bastard, passing me at the last turn and skidding to a halt a good six paces ahead of me. I pounded up and stopped beside him, attempting to drop my duffle bag in front of me. As fate would have it, the bag hit one of my now jellied knees and jumped out of my hands and rolled forward. I saw it stop. Leaning against, almost *on*, the boots of the airborne officer.

Sweet Mother. Against his spit-shined, glass-like jump boots.

I started to make a grab for it just as Denbeaux thumped up to a stop panting at my side, but the officer's hand shot out like a traffic cop. Stopping me in my tracks. "Hit a brace!"

We didn't wait for an explanation. The three of us at rigid attention. Denbeaux's barely muffled breathing the only sound in the otherwise absolute stillness.

The lieutenant was wearing the most immaculate, wrinkle-free, skin-tight set of airborne Class A's I have ever seen, before or since. His left hand was still out in front of him, unmoving, and he was staring down at his feet with a look of absolute incredulity. When he spoke, his voice was almost a whisper, a good second's pause between each word.

"Your...filthy...cruddy...shitty...duffle...bag ...is...touching...my...*person*."

His hand dropped slowly to his side, and his eyes moved up to look at me. That was when I noticed that he was exactly my height. You could have laid a board across our heads without a slant. He looked about thirty. Narrow shoulders. A chin that could open cans. I stared back helplessly. Mesmerized. A puppy encountering a cobra.

His hand went to his back pocket and came out with a snowy handkerchief, which he shook out, holding it by one corner. Each boot was then lifted in turn onto my duffle bag, while he slapped at the spotless tips. An Italian waiter dusting a table.

Finished, he stepped over my bag and gave it a vicious kick with his heel, sending it rolling behind him to bounce off the building. Refolding and re-pocketing his handkerchief, he stepped in front of Denbeaux, nose crinkling. He sniffed loudly, looking around. He studied Denbeaux as if trying to identify an exact species of dead fish.

"Wait," he said thoughtfully. "I recognize that stink now. Indiantown Gap. The pisspot of the army."

He peered up at Denbeaux, his eyes narrowing, and his jaw set in what appeared to be barely controlled rage. In Bill's galloping charge after his fleeing duffle bag, his tie had worked down, leaving a gap. You could see that the top button of his shirt was undone. The lieutenant pointed at Denbeaux's throat, his words shredding the air between them.

"Do you realize that you've been running around MY Company square half-dressed? That you've been running all over MY grass half-friggin' naked!"

"Sir, yes, Sir! Sorry, Sir." Denbeaux's hand shot up to his collar.

"Who told you to MOVE, you insolent bastard? How DARE you move when an airborne officer is addressing you?"

The lieutenant pointed to the ground in a gesture that would become all too familiar over the next two months. "Drop! Drop DOWN, Straight-leg, and give me ten!"

Denbeaux dropped into the pushup position and began heaving himself up and down. His body, heavy enough to start with, was even further weighed down by a belly full of steak, fried chicken and French fries, and a parade of those golden beauties. I could hear him wheezing in agony as the lieutenant continued his walking tour, moving back past me to stop in front of Ventola.

The lieutenant's eyes bored into Tony. Two brown coals simmering. Then he smiled, but just with the bottom half of his face.

"Hi," he said, and his voice was honey dripping on toast. "Guess I gave you boys a turn, huh?" The smile opened a little wider. "Have a nice trip down here, Private?"

"Uh, Sir? Yes Sir!" Ventola's voice sounded like he was standing at the bottom of a well. A pause. The lieutenant appeared to be waiting for more. The slightest tilt of his head. Questioning.

Out of the corner of my eye, I could just see Ventola's expression. He was still at attention, but he was trying to return the smile. Trying to turn on the old charm. Under these circumstances, Tony looked like a condemned man sucking the last air out of the death chamber.

"Stop for a couple of cold ones, did we?" The lieutenant's eyes had come to life. They danced. His smile grew even wider. A lot of white teeth showing now. It was one of those comrades-in arms, "what-the hell, we're all in this together" smiles. "Have one or two with dinner maybe? Three possibly?"

"Sir? Beg pardon, Sir?"

The lieutenant's voice could have shriveled the leaves on trees across the compound. "Beg *pardon*, sir? Beg *pardon*? I *said,* did you have the friggin' nerve to come into my company area *drunk? That's* what I asked you, you stupid dung heap!"

Ventola wilted like a geranium in front of a blowtorch. "Uh, no Sir! Not me, Sir. I'm just, uh, not used to the heat, Sir."

"The *heat!* I'll give you heat, you beer-soaked bastard! See this square, Doggie? Our own homey little quadrangle? Let's see you pick up those cute little low-cut shoes of yours and trot your friggin' ass around this square! *Three* laps! Take off! Move! Move! HOOOOOOOOOOLD it!"

Ventola had broken into a trot to his right, but he braked to a stop, up on his toes, a basketball player trying to stay in bounds.

The lieutenant's arms were folded behind his back, but one arm came out to point at Tony's duffle bag and suitcase. His voice was soft. A smiling whisper. "Not going to leave *those* turds behind now, were you Leg? Some dog might come along and bury them."

As Tony hesitated just for an instant, the lieutenant's voice boomed, lifting the top of my now aching skull a good two inches. "PICK 'EM UP, DOGFACE! TAKE THEM WITH YOU! THREE LAPS. MOVE! MOVE!"

Tony bounded to his duffle bag, grappled with it for an unnerving second, got it up into the general area of his head and shoulders, and with a great athletic move, scooped his other bag up with one flailing sweep. Then he took off down the concrete walk, double-timing. The lieutenant's voice cracked again. At me, this time.

"What the hell are *you* looking at, you miserable dwarf! Feel left out, do you? Is your buddy having all the fun? Then join him, you short, disgusting little gnome! Three laps! Did you hear me! MOVE! MOVE! MOVE!"

The lieutenant was standing about two feet from the building with my duffle bag behind him. I raced around him, my smaller case already in my hand, and desperately struggled to pull the big, green bag out of the small space between him and the building. Without...holy mother of God forbid...touching his *person*!

He didn't move an inch. The duffle bag now weighed six hundred pounds, and it clung to the ground like a Galapagos tortoise, but at last I got it free and up to my shoulder. I was off after Ventola.

Behind me, I could hear the lieutenant addressing Denbeaux. "Well, now, *Stink*! What are *you* waiting for, you great pile of pig-shit? A postcard from Mumsie? That's *three* laps, Straight-leg! Take off! Move! Move! *Move!*"

I have no idea how far it was around that company square, around that grassy quadrangle. A hundred yards? Fifty yards? It seemed like a hundred miles. Any soldier in pretty good shape, fresh out of basic, ought to be able to run some distance with his goddamn duffle bag. That night it was like running uphill with a dead body. In thin-soled low cut shoes. Feet slamming on the concrete. Feeling like you were driving your tibias right up through your kneecaps. *Oh, my good Jesus, only half a lap!*

Passing Ventola. Being passed by Ventola. Denbeaux going by me. Second lap. Duffle bag on the right shoulder. Heave it around to the left. Back to the right. Juggling the smaller suitcase to do this. Passing Ventola again. He's carrying his duffle bag in front of him now, the top under his chin, like a huge canvas erection.

Over on the far side. Denbeaux just ahead. I cut the corner. Denbeaux's hoarse whisper.

"Stay...off...his...friggin'...grass...for...chriss akes...He'll...make...us...carry...*him*...like...a....go ddamn...papoose!"

Choking back laughter. Despite the awful pain. Despite the burning in my chest.

Crash! Ventola is down in a heap behind us. Tripped at the corner. Sprawled on *his* friggin' grass! Keep going. Lay them down. Whatever you do, don't stop. Last turn. Denbeaux thirty yards in front nearing the orderly room. Ventola still back on the far side. Jesus! Keep going.

No lieutenant. Where is that little shit? Staggering to a stop beside Denbeaux. Dropping the bags. Lean over. Breathing like a bellows full of marbles. If only I had the strength, I'd puke. Beautiful! Just beautiful. Welcome to the Airborne! All this and silver wings too!

Ventola finally beside me. Reeling. The lieutenant suddenly in front of us, clipboard in hand. Names. A few instructions.

"At all times in this area, from now until graduation, day or night. You *will* double-time. No exceptions. None.

"You are a straight-leg. You will stay one until the day they pin wings to your chest, *if* they ever pin wings to your chest. A Leg is a slimy, creepy, crawly thing. Legs don't jump. Legs stink. Do not forget it!

"Airborne men walk tall. They look you in the eye. Legs whine and crybaby. Legs want their Mumsies to hold their hands and make the nasty mens go away. The bad men ain't going nowhere, Legs. Remember that! *You* can go. Anytime. Anytime you want. Just let us know when you want to slide out of here on your belly, and you are gone! Good riddance!"

Uh, oh! What's he stopping in front of me for? What the Christ have I done now?

"During the first three weeks, I will be your peerless leader, you stinking cruds. Before you start a regular training cycle, it will be my job to find out what you are made of, what you've got inside. You will *love* this part of your training, Legs, because I am going to make it my life's work to drive you friggin' insane! I love to see you come apart. I love it when you quit, crying for your Mumsies!"

He was staring right at me. Nose to nose. His chin thrust out. Inches from my face. "You! Fitzpatrick!"

"Sir?"

"What in the Christ do you think you're doing here anyway? You might as well leave in the morning. Save us all a lot of trouble. You're too friggin' *short* to be an airborne trooper, and you know it!"

Jesus Christ! The colossal gall of it! This pigeon-chested, flyweight, bird-dropping calling *me* small! I could feel my face turning beet red as

I stared back at him, teeth clenched. Furious. He continued, shaking his head.

"Are you *sure* you're in the right place, you sawed-off runt? Where did they send the other half of you? To the friggin' boy scouts?"

He bent his knees as he finished, so he was actually staring *up* at me. His little pig eyes laughing at me!

Up yours, I vowed silently. I'll get through this friggin' Jump School, alright, you little turd. And the last thing I'm going to do before I leave here is come back to this company area and *accidentally* stomp on those precious, shiny boots of yours!

The lieutenant moving. More shit for Denbeaux. A few more digs for Ventola. Then, posted.

"Ventola! Barracks Three. Not *that* way, you dumb shit! Over *there*! Denbeaux, Fitzpatrick! Barracks Two. Move! Move it out!"

Pounding down the concrete walk again. *Oh, Jesus, yes*! Get me inside one of those barracks. Away from that venomous, strutting peacock. First Lieutenant Norbert L. Carpentier. "That's Car-PENT-ier," he told us twice. Lucky us. Must have flown him in straight from Auschwitz! Give him a couple of gas furnaces to work with and that sonofabitch would never leave the Post.

Inside the barracks at last. Leaning against the wall. Taking deep breaths. Neither of us at all drunk anymore. The barracks orderly, a young kid as bald as we'll be tomorrow, coming down the empty aisle, pointing upstairs. The second floor. Only two bunks left, an upper and lower.

We flipped a coin. Bill won the lower berth. Balls! I had four months in basic training in the lower bunk. Not a doubt, I'll roll out in the morning by habit, break both legs.

Falling on the bunks fully dressed. The empty barracks silent except for our breathing. Denbeaux from below. "Don't forget to leave a wake-up call, Fitz! Ten o'clock would be good! Tell them to go easy on the cream in my coffee."

CHAPTER TEN

I don't know which of us heard them first. The steady crashing of their boots as they came pounding up the road. The back and forth sing-song. The higher-pitched single voice of the instructor. The roaring response from the men.

"I can't *hear* you, turds, I can't *hear* you! What *are* you?"

"LEEEEEEGS!"

"What are you going to be?"

"AAAIIRRBOORNE!"

"What does the Airborne eat for breakfast?"

"LEEEGS!"

"Is everybody going to go?"

"YEEESS!"

"I can't *hear* you!"

"YEEEEEEEEESS!"

"That's better. Companeeeeeeeee-HOWT!"

"Look smart, Little Brother! Up and at 'em." It was Denbeaux standing up and slapping me on the leg. "Hop off there, you bog-trotting Irish bastard. I don't think you want to be caught in full uniform lying on that bunk. Not if one of those goddamn instructors pops up here to shake our hands."

I got the point. I was on the floor beside him unpacking as the guys began pouring through the doors down below and hammering up the stairs.

"Well, well, well. What have we here? A couple of late arrivals. Mutt and Jeff, I take it. Big shit, little fart."

It was one of the NCO instructors, looking us over. More instructions.

"Red diamonds? What do you think you are? Jewelers? Get that shit off your uniforms. All of them. What are you dumb bastards doing in OD's? You expecting snow, for chrissakes? Get your goddamn fatigues out.

"Low cut shoes! Jee-sus! Ain't they purty. Whatta ya gonna do? Go to a friggin' dance? Burn those bastards. Bury them. Get rid of them. Low cut shoes, for chrissakes! Don't never bring them out in a goddamn airborne barracks again. *Never!* We wear boots in this man's army, you assholes! Bloused boots!"

Watching his receding back. Yes, Sergeant. No, Sergeant. In a minute, Sergeant. Up your ass, Sergeant. Christ, I'm glad I wasn't lying on that bunk when *that* prick hit the top of those stairs!

Guys all around us in T-shirts and fatigues. Grabbing towels. Drenched. Falling onto their bunks. Dropping like flies.

Oh, my aching legs! How the Christ long did they run us? What time is it, for chrissakes? Only 9:30? You're full of shit! I don't believe it. It has to be midnight!

Down the other end, I spot Fisher. Working his wet T-shirt off over his head. Toweling off. Looking up and seeing us, he weaved his way down to us through the barracks full of sweating, griping GI's. Dropping onto the end of Denbeaux's

72

bunk, wiping his neck and bare chest with a towel.

"Shit, Denbeaux, I should have listened to you guys. While you've been drinking and screwing around, having a ball, they like to work our asses off. That was the third run since we got here."

He looked over his shoulder to make sure none of the NCO's were around. "Wait! Just wait until you meet friggin' Carpenter! Kee-rist!"

"You mean, 'Car-PENT-ier," Denbeaux corrected.

"Oh, you *did* meet that bastard, huh?" The name had brought attention from other guys around us.

Before I could speak, Denbeaux jumped in. "A lieutenant, real sharp dresser, right? Terrific guy. Hell, I hope they all turn out to be like him."

Fisher's jaw dropped and the whole end of the barracks fell silent, staring at Denbeaux as he put shirts and shorts neatly into his footlocker, continuing as though he hadn't noticed their surprise. "Fitz and I arrived, we were a little bagged to be honest, all that beer we put away, you know? The Lieutenant says to us 'Hey! It's after 9:00. I'm off the clock. You guys look like you could use a cup of coffee!' Ain't that right, Fitz?"

My startled attempt to respond was completely drowned out in the babble of voices that broke out at Bill's words, which was probably just as well. Everyone crowding in.

*Are you shitting me? CARPENTIER?
Lieutenant Carpentier? Offered you friggin' coffee!
He wouldn't give his mother coffee if it would save
her life!*

*You mean his "mumsie!" Yeah, right. Geez,
you guys HAVE to have the wrong guy.*

Denbeaux held up his hands, the babble
shutting down. "Hey! Easy. I think you guys must
be overreacting. Carpentier couldn't have been
nicer to us! Told us to drop over *any* evening, as
long as it was after hours. After nine, he said.
Told us it was his job to be a bastard during the
day, but the coffee pot was always on after nine if
anyone wanted to stop by. You know? Kick
around any problems. Or just bullshit a bit"

No one moved. They had even stopped
drying themselves.

"*Ho-lee Peter!*" This from one bug-eyed
listener with the name "Walters" on the fatigue
shirt he was holding. "I cain't hardly believe it!
That friggin' turd saying that! Drop by for friggin'
coffee! Shee-eet!"

From downstairs, an NCO bellowing. "All
right, you bird droppings. Lights out in ten
minutes. Ten minutes!"

The audience broke away, moving off in
small knots of astonished men, heading back to
their bunks.

*Carpentier? Our Lieutenant Carpentier?
Kin you believe that? He's gotta be one of them
Jekyll-Hyde guys. Whatta they call it? A split
popularity! Drop in for coffee! For chrissakes!*

74

Denbeaux and I laying out fatigues for the morning, using the windowsill and the chair between the double-bunks. Working fast to hack off the red diamonds on them with razor blades. The lights blinking off and on. Then, thirty seconds later, snapping out.

As I started to climb up onto my bunk, Denbeaux grabbed my arm and held me back for a second. Whispering. Trying to keep his laughter under control. "Oh, Jesus, Fitz! Can you see a couple of these guys getting up their nerve in a few days and trotting over there some evening? Expecting to be offered a cup of coffee! By that insufferable little bastard. By that little prick!"

Both of us having a fit of laughter as I climbed up and crawled under the covers.

"Goodnight, you friggin' dwarf," Denbeaux croaked.

"Goodnight, Stink," I answered. And I fell asleep almost at once. Dropping into a welcome oblivion.

CHAPTER ELEVEN

Falling out after another run. The third today and we haven't had noon chow yet. Getting easier, though, I have to admit. No one even winded. Just soaked to our insteps. Ventola out in the company street as we trot toward the barracks, waving at us.

"Hey, guys! The list is going up. Outside the Orderly Room! They're tacking it up right now."

Bill and I changing direction and moving out fast as others, hearing that, came piling back out of the barracks. Pushing in to the crowd near the Orderly Room door.

There it is. "Airborne Class 34. Company I."

Oh, Jesus, let me be on it. Almost three weeks of this physical training crap waiting for a new cycle. Shit, we haven't even started jump school yet. Get me out of this friggin' holding company, in the name of God.

Foran, pushing past us, looking sour. "Too bad, Foran. You ain't on it, buddy." Fielding giving him the needle. "Another week of Noballs Carp-PENT-ier for you, you poor bastard. Gimmie ten. Shine them boots! Fall out for another dawn patrol!"

Oh, Christ! Let me be on that friggin' list!

Looking over the shoulders in front of me. *Adams. Aldrich.* C'mon. Get your hand out of the way, willya? *Denton! Denbeaux!* Oh, the lucky bastard! *Felton! FITZPATRICK!* Oh, bless you. Bless everyone. Bless friggin' Carpentier. What a beautiful sight!

76

Hauling our gear to the new barracks. We start all over tomorrow. New NCO's. New schedule. The real thing now. Jump training. And about goddamn time, too.

Following Denbeaux into the barracks, walking along past empty bunks. Kowalski coming up behind to lift me off my feet, along with my duffle bag and overnight bag, swinging me around. "What are you looking so happy about, Fitz, you dumb Irish shit? The day after tomorrow you'll be standing in the door of one of them thirty-four foot towers. Three floors up, Baby. Until they kick your ass out into the wild blue yonder."

"Bullshit, Kielbasa Breath!" I told him as he set me down. "They won't *have* to kick me out, buddy. I always fall forward when I faint."

Other familiar faces. Jabs and handshakes as we pass. Felton, a new pal from the holding company, pointing at me. "Hey, you guys! Was I lying? I told you they had someone smaller than me in this outfit. Lookit Fitz here. He's so light he's gonna use a reserve as his backpack. Use a regular chute and he'd sail down to the Gulf of Mexico."

Bill stops, pointing at an empty double tier.

"What do you say, Fitz! Want to stick with the top, or you want to flip me for the lower this time?"

"Nah, Bill. I'll take the upper. Hell, I'm used to it now. Like to break my leg tumbling out that first morning, though. Hell, I've already made *my* first jump!"

I'm dumping stuff on to the bunk when I see him coming up the aisle.

"Hey, Bill! Look who's here! Anthony Ventola, Esquire. The Jersey Jock."

Kowalski chiming in. "Hey, grab this bunk, Tony. It's empty. Have you met the Frenchman? No, not Denbeaux. You know he's another thick Mick. I mean this guy, a real Frenchman. That's his name on that duffle bag."

Tony making a try at it.

"No, no, you dumb Dago," Kowalski laughing. "Not Fran-soyce Dew-boyce. It's French. That's Fran-swa Dew-bwa! See, Francois Dubois, got it?"

Francois also heading for Special Forces. Fairly tall and slender with a wiry, mountain-climber's build. Noballs Carpentier had made him shave his impressive moustache the day he arrived. "Just cheeken sheet," he'd growled at the time, giving us his heavy-lidded Gallic look.

"You continental types ought to hit if off real good, Tony," Bill told Ventola. "If I know this froggie, he's already got a nice, smelly cheese stashed under his pillow!"

'That's veree funee, Denbeaux," Francois retorted. "Veree funee. And we all zot that cheese smell was your zocks. Deeden we, Feetz?"

Kowalski looking around. "Hey, any of you guys seen Walters? How come he didn't get shipped over? He was here a whole week before we got here."

Donelson. "Poor bastard. He got kicked back a week by Carpentier."

"What for?"

Donelson looking mystified. "I dunno what he was thinking. It was crazy. Dumb fuck walked into the orderly room one night and asked Carpentier for a cup of coffee! Noballs gave him four laps on the spot, kicked him back a week."

Ventola staring at us. Bill and I going in to convulsions. "Hey, will you look at them! Denbeaux and Fitzpatrick. They think that's the funniest thing they ever heard. Loonies! This outfit is full of loonies!"

****

Starting in hot and heavy Monday morning. *Fall in. Line up. Straighten those ranks.* Who the hell is that turkey standing up there? All that salad dressing on his shirt.

The Airborne Department Director has a few words for us. Oh, swell.

The speakers echoing around the square. *Welcome to Jump School, Men. I am proud to have all of you with us. You all have something in here"*—tapping his chest—*"or you wouldn't be here at all. Your first week will be devoted to two things. First, you are going to learn four of the five basic jump techniques. You will drill on those until they are all second nature. The second objective of this week is physical training.*

Physical training? What the hell does he think we've been doing down here for the last two, three weeks. Modern dance?

Our boots thudding on the packed earth as we double-time out to our first training area. Fatigue shirts, T-shirts and bloused fatigue

79

pants. Helmets and helmet liners today. Our individual numbers stenciled on the fronts the night before. Each helmet with the distinctive chin-strap of the airborne trooper. Kowalski explaining that to us. "Keeps the helmet on your head, see, when your head is ripped off by a tree. That's so's they can read the number, tell whose head it is, cause you look different without your teeth."

It's early, but the sun is well up and already blistering. They let us file by a water bubbler at the corner of a field when we got there. My throat like a yard of sandpaper. Someone behind me. "I thought we got to wear khaki shorts when we train down here in Georgia. I read that somewhere."

Someone further back answering. "That's *summer*, Dimbulb. This here is winter. Ain't they got no calendars in Michigan where you were whelped?"

Lining us up again. *Drop those helmets and fatigue shirts right here, men, on the ground by your feet. We'll need those in awhile when we chute up.*

Chute up? Did I miss something? Jesus Christ, we're not jumping today, are we?

The instructor smiling. *First, we're gonna have a little run. Couple of miles is all. A warm-up. Platoon, ten steps forward, HAACH!*

Straighten those lines! Shoulders back. Riiight...HAACH! Keep those chests out! DOUBLE TIME...HAAARRRCH! Pick 'em up. Pick 'em up!

The instructor chanting, platoon answering.

80

I've got a girl in Ko-kee-mo.

EVER . . .BODYS. . .GOIN. . . TO. . GO!

Am I right or wrong?

YOU'RE RIGHT!

Am I right or wrong?

YOU'RE RIGHT!

What aaaare you?

AAIIRR-BORNE!

Can't heeear youuuuuu!

AAAAAIIRRR-BOOORNNE!

"That's better!"

Classes all morning, running from one to the next. For some we stand in groups to watch, for some we sit. For a while anyway. Most we end up rolling in the dirt.

Frequent breaks for push-ups and running in place.

Sit up straight. Pay attention. Wow, look at this. So *that's* what those goddamn chutes look like, huh?

You there! Muldoon. Out of those stands and give me ten. Whatta you think this is a kindergarten. Pay attention. Your life is going to depend on what you learn in these next two weeks. It's too late once you get to the planes. You got that, Soldier? It'll be too friggin' late, ask questions, you come out that door, your chute rips your balls off.

Rips your balls off? He's joking, right? *Right?*

81

You! Felton! You think that's funny, do you? Try laughing while you drop down and give me ten fast ones. MOVE! Knock 'em out!

Chutes on for the first time. Oh, man. John Wayne, eat your heart out.

Sergeant Baker in front of me. "Did you tighten those straps, Fitzpatrick?"

"Yes, Sergeant!"

His fingers going under one strap on my thigh, pulling it out four or five inches. "You call *that* tight? When I say tighten those straps, I mean *tighten* them!"

Sergeant Baker pulling on the strap end and holding my thigh down while his elbow almost hits me in the chin. *Holy Jesus! Bastard's trying to cut my legs off.*

All of us with backpacks and reserves on, the harness straps so tight it is painful just to stand. Never mind walk. Never mind run. Climbing two wooden stairs to a low platform with a mock door on it. To practice shuffling down, turning in, hopping out.

Baker barking at us. "Stay in line. Move. No, no, you asshole. Don't *walk*! Shuffle! Keep your left foot in front and *shuffle*. That's it. Straighten that line."

Near the mock door. "Alright, Trooper. The door is on your left. Shuffle up and stand in that door. Jesus Christ! Keep the left foot first, I said. Left door, left foot first. Right door, right foot first. That too much for you, Fitzpatrick? Too complex?"

Standing in the door. "Bend those knees. Back straight. When you land, bounce! On your toes. Then take off to the end of the line. GET READY! GO!"

Jumping! Feet together. In the harness, with the backpack and reserve on, I feel like a turtle in traction. One bounce and I go over sideways, right on my ass.

"Oh, swell, Fitzpatrick! Terrific! This here is a two-foot jump and you fall down! Didn't bust nothin', did you, Junior? Good, good. OK, Badass. End of the line. NEXT!"

A full hour of this. Out the door five or six times. Bouncing like I'm on a pogo stick. A waddling sprint to the end of the line after each one. Finally done. Oh, my God, does it feel good to get that chute off. What do they have in store for us next? The Iron Maiden? PLFs? What the hell is a PLF?

Now this, men is what's called a parachute landing fall. You're going to do these sideways, frontwards, backwards, until you roll and bounce like a rubber ball. Over and over. Every friggin' day that you are here you will do PLFs. Learn it right, and then don't think. Just do it! Do it until it's a reflex. Now, watch the instructors!

Three demonstrators in spotless white T-shirts. Looking like Rodin chipped them out of stone this morning. The platforms here about eight feet high, a sand pit below. *When you go down, men, I want to see that roll. Toes, calf, thigh, rump, and right up on to the top of the back, feet in the air. I want to see them legs up there at the end reaching for some sky.*

Fatigues and helmets for this drill, but no chutes and harnesses. Christ it looks high when you stand in this door. Eight feet looks like twenty. *Tuck in those goddamn chins when you go out the door, men, and keep 'em tucked. Stick them on your chests like glue. Hands on your chests like you were grabbing your reserve. OK, let's go. First man. Stand in the door. GO!*

A constant barrage of comments as we take our turns, run to the end of the line and do it again. *That one really sucked, Trooper! Call that a PLF? That stunk! Up, up. End of the line. NEXT! Stand in the door! GO! Hey, pretty good for a ten-year-old girl, Stretch. I said come out HIGH goddamn it. HIGH! End of the line. Next!*

Good news. No more classes for the next half hour. No waddling around in those goddamn chutes like friggin' penguins. No jumping out of mock doors. No, sir. Getting the word. *Going to have us a nice, relaxed half hour here, Men. Just a little PT is all.*

Balls! PT? Are they shitting me?

"Did I hear you groan, Trooper? Yes, YOU, Fitzpatrick! Drop! Get down and give me ten. Hurry up! Push 'em up! Think we've got all goddamn day! OK, up! Now, men, our first exercise will be pushups. Let's have twenty good ones. Ready? Drop! Down, up. Down, up. What's the matter, Fitzpatrick? We're only on five. Tired already?"

Run. Fall in line and run. The airborne shuffle. On to the next class. And the next! *Where the Christ are we going now?*

Lunch! Oh, my Good God, is it only *lunch*? Only half the day? We got all afternoon yet, more of the same.

****

At last, piling in to the barracks at five o'clock. "Let me in there, willya? Let me stand in that goddamn shower. Man! I'll never straighten these legs again. I'm a crip."

"Shit, my bunk is always upstairs! I think I'll catch a few winks on the stairs."

"Christ! How come, we're jumping in a sand pit and our feet look' like this?"

"That wasn't sand, Tony. It was teeny-weeny ball bearings painted yellow. I figured that out when I went over backwards. When my head hit. Or, could be concrete."

Denbeaux peeling off his T-shirt and examining the many bruises on his chest and arms. Laughing. "Hey, guys, if this is what they call getting us in shape, what would they do if they wanted to ruin us? Let's not get them mad."

We had only fifteen minutes left to get dressed before chow. I was lying, still wet from the shower, face down on my bunk, the urge to fall asleep almost overpowering. "Hey, Denbox, you oaf," I muttered. "When you're bringing my dinner back here tonight, try not to spill the gravy, okay?"

I was still face down when Denbeaux and Dubois dropped me on the floor. "Hey, Feetz," Francois said, everyone laughing as I scrambled up, "that PLF, eet zucked."

CHAPTER TWELVE

The morning run to the towers a scorcher. Doesn't the sun realize this is only mid-March, for cryeye? Full fatigues, steel pots and helmet liners, and I'm already soaked to my skivvies. And it won't even be eight hundred hours for fifteen minutes.

"Oh, my Jesus," Kowalski mutters, trotting behind me. "Are *those* the thirty-four foot towers? Who are they trying to kid? That's gotta be more than thirty-four feet up to them doors. From here, it looks like half a mile."

Marching up into the bleachers, sitting when we get the command. The backless wooden benches creaking from the uniform onslaught of so much human cargo.

Williams down to my left, doing his Orphan Annie voice, soft, but we can all hear him. "*Gloryosky, guys.* They're sending up a demonstration team to show us how easy this is. Look at the build on that sergeant. Where do they find these guys, anyways? Warner Brothers!"

The first guy rocketing out of the tower door in letter-perfect form. The guy yelling out the numbers as he falls. *One thow-sand, two thow-sand, threeee...* The cable squealing as he thumps at the end of the harness and sails off toward the high dirt bank where the catchers wait. Checking his non-existent canopy by arching his back and pulling the risers down and out until his hands are level with his shoulders. A perfect ride on the wire to his landing on the high dirt bank.

All of us grudgingly impressed, despite ourselves.

86

"Holy crap!" Benson saying just what we were all thinking. "That guy musta dropped twenty-five feet straight down before that harness stopped him. Four more feet he'd have been on the friggin' ground. Shit, I never heard they let you fall that far."

"It's okay, Benson," Kowalski reassured him. "You won't even notice the drop when you come out, being as how, one look out that door, you'll be unconscious."

More demo jumps. An officer at the mike verbalizing the finer points of form, the stuff we had spent all day yesterday practicing, then pointing at the scorer sitting below each tower door ready to grade our performances.

Alright, men. When you step into that door, call out your name and number good and loud so the scorer gets it. First time out the door we grade easy. Those who have heart attacks flunk, those who can still stand at the bank pass. After that we grade harder. Do this right, and you're on your way. If you can't handle this, you won't be jumping out of any airplanes. No learner's wings in this outfit, kiddies. Do it right or say goodbye, nice knowing ya.

He referred to his clipboard. *Alright, you all have numbers. They are on your helmets in case any of you can't remember two digits. One through forty-two will line up down here by the towers. One row for each door. The rest of you will take turns acting as catchers down where the cable meets the bank. You'll jump later. Move on down there now and report to Sergeant Wilson. C'mon, double time. Let's go.*

I didn't have to look at my number. Number 32. Swell! *We* get to go first. Isn't this fun? What are you doing in that line, Fitz? Me? Oh, I'm waiting my turn. My turn to go up and jump out a door on the third floor. For chrissakes, I have *got* to be soft.

Remembering just the scariest of the instructions.

If you don't keep your chin jammed onto your chest until that opening shock, your helmet is going to come flying forward and bust your nose wide open. Guess what? That will smart. That will happen because when you hit the end of the harness, the risers will snap up at about six million miles an hour right at the back of your neck. Got it? Dig those chins into your chests and keep them there!

Keep your feet together when you go out that door! If they are wide apart as you go down, chances are you will not like it when you slam to a stop and your ankles come together like castanets. If that does happen, just hope your boots fly off. Because after your ankles get through swelling, we'll have to cut your boots off!

I think I got that. Chin down, feet together, mess kit in my drawers to catch breakfast. I think I'm all set.

Ten guys at a time chuting up. All of us moving forward. Watching.

Guys already in harness, waddling in to the tower. Stomping up the staircase until they reach the top. Five at a time entering the metal room which is designed to look like an airplane fuselage, and which has one door, a black open hole, on each side.

Looking up and seeing the first guy stepping up to the door. Getting instructions from the jumpmaster. A slap on the back. A little encouragement.

We can see him stepping into the door. Calling out his name and number. Even from the ground we could hear the sharp slap on the rump, the barked, "GO!"

The first guy sailing out the door! All arms and legs. Popping up and down when he hit the end of the harness and bellowing in surprise. His helmet knocked down, covering his face. Not like those demonstrators. Not at all like those demonstrators.

I deliberately stopped looking after I watched the first few go out. Concentrating on the back of the man in front of me as we moved forward. Noticing that the guys around me all looked pretty pasty-faced. A few as green as their fatigues.

My turn to chute up. I had put the harness on at least ten times the day before, so it should have been old stuff. All of a sudden it wasn't. This one was for real. No mistakes. Not this time.

"Hey, Fitz, check my backpack, willya?" Felton, right in front of me, standing spraddle-legged while I check his harness. "Did I get them goddam straps straight?"

The left shoulder strap does have a twist in it. He has to unbuckle again so I can feed it straight across his shoulder. "Now, how the hell did I do that? Jeez, thanks, Fitz. Here, lemmee check yours. Christ, can't get them no tighter. Can you walk?"

I demonstrate, grinning. We'll start climbing as soon as the next stick goes out.

To my right, the scorer with his clipboard, waiting. From high above, I hear him.

"Den-bow, William. Twenty-three!"

The scorer looking at the name in front of him, then looking up. When he answers, he puts a little bite in it. Like, *I kin read!* "Den-BOX, William. Twenty-three."

I had to look up.

Out and down came Bill. Ass first! Legs apart in a "Y" and his eyes screwed shut. His arms wrapped around his reserve like a quarterback trying to run a sneak. A resounding "Whuuuumph!" as he hit the end of the harness, and then he was off, bouncing around on the cable like a puppet on a string, sailing away toward the dirt bank about thirty yards away.

Shit. He forgot to yell the numbers! All in all, though, not bad for a first one. Lucky sonofabitch! *His* first is over.

Yell the numbers! You go out of that plane and you yell three thousand and you don't get an opening shock, pull the goddamn reserve. If you don't, you are dead meat!

From up above. "Dew-bwa, Fran-swa! Twenty-four." This time the scorer, his finger on the typed name, spat in disgust before he bellowed back.

"Dew-boyse, Fran-soyce! Twenty Four."

We all knew what the scorer was thinking. It was all over his face. *I got my wings, you turds! I ain't talking like that for NO-body!*

Christ, look at that! Dubois! Coming out in perfect form! Legs together, hands in position, right hand on the reserve handle, chin tucked onto his chest. "*Won sow-zand, twoo sow-zand, threeeee. . .*" Whump! Man, that was perfect. Look at him sail along that cable. Look at him arch that back and check his canopy! His bellow ringing out.

"Vive L'Aaaaaiiirboooorne!"

His yell rolling out to us like a battle cry, as he flew away down the cable toward the bank. Everybody laughing. Everybody. Even the scorer. Even me. Crazy French bastard!

Oh, Jesus. Our turn. Here we go. Up the stairs. First landing. Steady. Don't run. Keep moving. Stay right behind Felton. Second landing. Moving up.

Third stairway. Moisture running in rivers down my back, down my legs. *Remember, oh most gracious Virgin Mary, that never was it known...that never was it known...*Oh, crap, I can't remember the words. Just get me out the door this one time, that's all I ask. Just don't let me freeze in that door.

At the top at last. Moving inside the tower building.

"*Check equipment!*" A bark from the jumpmaster and we all go into the routine, checking each other's straps, the last man turning around to get his checked.

"*Hook up!*"

Grabbing the cable, reaching up and slipping the eye on my snap-lock over it, pulling down hard to close it. Easy does it now. Put the safety pin through the hole. Damn. Hands shaking. The cable bouncing as others snap on. Can't get it through the hole. Try again. *C'mon you stupid, Irish twit!* Ah! That did it. Pin in and twist. I should yell at myself more often.

Christ, it must be a hundred degrees up here. Hard to breathe. Fitzpatrick, you bastard, you faint and I'll kill you! Concentrate!

Felton is second in line and now he's next.

The jumpmaster talking quietly to him and then stepping back.

"READY!"

I see Felton's head bob.

"STAND IN THE DOOR!"

Felton shuffling forward, turning right and moving into the open door. The jumpmaster now directly in front of me, just beyond Felton.

"Don't look down, Son. That's it. Stare straight ahead. Name and number. Okay, I heard that. Now yell it this time so the scorer can hear it. That's the stuff. Flex your knees now. Get ready. Nothing to it, now. Just relax."

The jumpmaster's right hand moving back. His left hand, which had been on Felton's shoulder to steady him, letting go. "When you feel the slap, go! Tuck in your chin. REEEADY! GOOOO!"

Felton! Still there!

The hand came back and slapped again! Hard! All of sudden, empty space! No one in the door.

The jumpmaster waving me forward. A hand on each of my shoulders. "OK, my lad! See how easy that was? Man went out the door like stepping off a curb. So will you! Now you just listen to me. Forget everything else, okay? You're gonna do fine."

He stepped back, a full arms-length away, one hand still on my shoulder, the other waving me forward. "Come toward me now. One more step. Perfect. Now when I tell you, turn into the door and stare straight ahead. READY! STAND IN THE DOOR!"

I swung into the door, my hands groping for position on the outside, feeling for the edges. I'm in the wide, open, empty door. An enormous void in front of me. *Oh, Shit!*

"DON'T LOOK DOWN, SON. Don't look down."

Staring straight ahead. Trying to focus on the horizon. Knees like jelly.

"Perfect. Lookin' good. Lookin' real good. Name and number now. Good and loud!"

I yell them out. From down below, from somewhere down there where I don't dare look, they come floating back up to me. "Fitzpatrick, James. Thirty-two."

"OK, Son. We got it made now. Flex your knees. When you feel the slap, out you go. Just like the mock doors. Just like you did all morning. All set?"

Nodding. "REEEADY. GOOOO!"

A hard slap at my thigh. A big dip. Uh oh, still *here!* A second big, *big* dip. Shit almighty. A hurricane all around me! Oh, my Christ, I'm OUT!

Tumbling! Head first! The whole world upside down! The harness jerking me to a slamming stop! OOOOOOOFF! Keeee-rist! That almost tore my shoulders off!

HEY! I DID IT! I DID IT! I DID IT!

Wild, bouncing slide down the cable toward the high dirt bank. A voice yelling at me. "Put your legs together, you Irish turkey! I don't want my balls kicked off."

Ventola! He and another guy grabbing me, stopping my slide. "Holy Jeez, Tony!" I was babbling. "Was that *great*? Oh, man was that ever *great*!"

"Yeah, yeah! I know. We saw you. Whatta ya call that dive you took, anyways? The dying swan? I thought we were supposed to come out *feet* first!"

"Feet first, head first, ass first, who cares?" I chortled. "I'm here, ain't I?"

Punching the release box on my stomach to let the leg straps drop down, putting my arms up so they could lift off the harness. In seconds I was skidding and sliding down the bank to the ground. Stopping. "Hey, Tone. Did I yell the numbers?"

The other guys on the bank all laughing at that. Ventola watching the tower for the next jumper. "Oh, yeah, Fitz. You yelled numbers alright. Fifteen and eighteen. I think you ordered the Won Ton Soup and the Pork Fried Rice."

CHAPTER THIRTEEN

Back at the foot of the towers again. Still on a high from that first jump. *This* time, oh, baby, I'm really going to snap one off for them. Now that I know what it's like. Ol' Dubois is not the only one who'll go back today walking proud. I'm gonna ace this.

In the harnesses again. Pull those suckers good and tight. Felton stopping just before we start up the stairs. Asking me to check his straps again. I notice he is white as a sheet, and I grin at him, slap him on the back, trying to pep him up before we start to climb. "Oh, sure," he says to me, totally inexplicably, "it's fine for you, Fitz. I've watched you. Nothin' ever bothers you, but this stuff scares the crap out of me."

Christ, I'm gonna have to learn poker. My fortune is made.

Staying right behind him on the stairs. Damn, the stairs are ridiculous. What are we? Jumpers or mountain goats. Felton looking grim as he rounds the turn in front of me, heading up to the next flight.

At the bottom of the third flight, Felton stops again. His hands out to the rails on both sides. Panting, trying to catch his breath. Balls. The guy is making me nervous now, and I'd been feeling great.

From below us on the stairs, voices yelling. *C'mon! What's the friggin' hold up?"*

Felton half-turns and looks back at me. He is dead white, something very close to panic in his eyes. More yells. *C'mon! C'mon up there! Move it out.*

"Hold your horses, willya!" I bellow down the stairs. Looking at Felton. I can hardly hear his words.

"I don't think I can do this, Fitz. Oh, God. I am just soooo scared."

Balls! Furry moths making wild swoops now, right down to my groin. And back. I force a smile. "Hey, Felton, old Pal. We're *all* friggin' scared. Me, too. But I can do this and so can you."

"Really, Fitz? You're scared, too?"

"Absolutely. You'll be fine. Just climb on up, okay, and we'll laugh about this later."

He nodded weakly. Then, his hands out and pulling on the rails, he began to climb again.

Perfect. This is just what I needed. I was just starting to feel good about this and now I *am* getting scared again. Screw that. Remember, you *liked* it, for chrissakes.

Finally, at the top again. Pushing into the tower behind Felton. The three other guys in the stick filing in behind me. Felton first in the stick this time. I could hear his breathing in front of me, the loudest sound in the tower room.

I reach up and hook on my snap-lock, noticing that Felton has left his open. I slip in the safety pin, easier this time I am surprised to find. The moths still dive-bombing my anus, and I feel a wave of anger. *Knock that shit off,* I tell them.

The jumpmaster barks and we do the equipment check on each other. I figure, fuck it, and I reach up and snap Felton's lock closed. I don't tackle the pin, though. I'm at a bad angle to reach it. Just then the jumpmaster waves him forward and I see him reach up for the pin as I shuffle to close the gap behind Felton.

The jumpmaster is talking quietly to him, and I hear Felton say, "No, no, I'm okay. Just a little...out...of breath."

I block them out. Talking to myself. Concentrate this time. Do it right. I am aware that Felton is in the door.

"GET REEEEADY."

Felton's knees dip as he crouches.

"GOOOOOOO!"

The simultaneous slap.

"NO...NO...NOOOOOO!"

Oh, Jesus! That was Felton! He had reversed his hands, shoving back, bracing them on the inside. He almost falls over backward.

The jumpmaster grabbing him, pulling him away from the door, then pushing him toward the tail of the tower room. Felton's arms and legs flailing wildly as he falls backwards against that wall. His face is terror-stricken.

Suddenly Felton crumples, his arms drop to his sides, and he slides down to a sitting position with his back to the wall. He is making a chugging noise and tears are streaming down his face, his head dropping on his knees as he rocks in place.

The jumpmaster's chest! Right in front of me. Blocking my view.

I look up. He is looking right at me. To my astonishment he is grinning broadly. He nods at me as though he and I share some special understanding of what has just happened here. I see his name. "MENENDEZ." He leans forward, slaps me on the side of the shoulder and speaks right to me.

"DAMN, trooper! I remember the first time a guy stopped like that right in front of *me!*" His voice is a throaty chuckle. "Ain't *that* a kick in the oysters?"

To this day, I still don't know why that struck me so funny, but at the time it was hilarious. The jumpmaster and I both laughing.

I saw his eyes flick once to my nametag, at the big inked letters on my shirt. His next words charged me up like my fingers were jammed in a light socket. "Fitzpatrick, huh? God damn good thing *you* were behind him, my lad. I can tell *you've* got the stuff! What are we going for this time, Fitz? A half-hearted plop out that door, or a leap and a brace and a score that will knock their eyes out? What's it going to be, Irishman?"

"SCORE, SERGEANT!" A bellow! The roar surprising me!

"I heard *that*, all right!" he laughed. Well, *alright*, then. Let's do it, Fitzie, my boy! Right up to me now. Oh, looking good, looking good. Stand in the door! OK, Irish. Give it to the scorer. By God, he got *that!* GET READY! GOOOOOO!"

Not a pause. Not a look around. Pumped to the gills! His slap barely touching me, almost chasing me as I went sailing out that door, hitting that brace, legs together, chin down. Yelling the numbers! "Wooonnnn thousand! Twooooo thousand! Threeeee..."

WHUUUUUMP!

Oh, *baby*! That was bee-u-tiful! Un-friggin'-believable! I *love* this! Sailing off toward the high dirt bank. Riding the wire! On top of the world.

Two different guys waiting to help me get loose. "Hey, Fitzpatrick. What was the goddamn holdup there? D'ja stop for coffee, or what?"

"Naw. It was...Felton."

"*Felton*? Christ! He was at Dix with me. What happened? Wouldn't he go? Huh? Hey, Fitz, don't run off. What happened to Felton?"

Shrugging, I scramble down the bank and fall into a trot, catching up with the others. Felton. God damn. The poor bastard. Man, I'd rather go out the door without a harness than be in his friggin' shoes. Oh, God. There he is now. *Walking* down. Lord! Walking down those flights of stairs. Past all those guys.

Standing in line and moving toward the towers, conversation drifting back.

How many have we lost so far today? Seven! Seven guys have quit? And the other half of the platoon hasn't even started yet.

Those poor bastards. They've been catching the whole time. Catching us and sweating it out. Hell, I'd rather go first anytime.

Yeah, who wants to wait around worrying.

Noticing several guys in line with puffy noses, blood crusted on their upper lips.

"Hey, Chas, did you bust that nose?"

"Naah, just gave it a wallop is all. Kept my chin on my chest the second time, though, didn't I?"

Balls! I hope we get one more jump in before they switch off. What the hell is that whistle? Damn and blast. Our turn to catch. Our turn to go to work.

Gathering at the other end to get our instructions. Sitting off to one side to watch and wait our turn up on the banks.

"Man, that was short shrift, wasn't it?" I griped to Kowalski and Benson. "How you supposed to get good when two lousy jumps is all we get?"

"Ah, don't sweat it, Fitz. They have to go real slow on these first ones. Wait until tomorrow. Sergeant Birch told me we'll get in five jumps each, some maybe six. Don't forget, some guys will quit tonight, won't come back tomorrow. On Wednesday, we start jumping out in sticks. Five at a time. Bing, bing, bing just like in the planes."

Anderson grabbing me from behind. "Yeah, and wait until *next* week, Fitz. Oh, baby! Them 250s! Them *biiig*, mother-humping 250s."

"Don't shake me," I said. "You mention those hummers, I may lose my dinner-- before I even get a chance to eat it!"

Sergeant Wilson up on the bank, yelling over to us. "All right, you guys. Knock off the chatter now and pay attention. When I call your number, get up here fast and relieve these catchers. The jumpers are coming out now!"

Watching the new crowd getting in their first jumps. My turn on the banks.

"Look at that guy, willya? Upside down and clawing the air like he was looking for hand holds. My good Jesus, we couldn't have looked *that* bad, could we?"

"Grab that bastard, Fitz, before he kicks us both off of here."

"Oh, yeah. You looked great, Stratton. We'll send you six glossies for your scrapbook! You'll be the one, your leg up in the risers."

"Get ready, Fitz! Here comes another one!"

****

Saturday evening. Our week on the thirty-four foot towers over. A four-hour pass and only a three-mile jog to the single beer hall on our end of the post. Piece of cake.

Stand in line, get the limit of two beers each and go right to the end of the line. Drink those two as we work our way back to the counter. Nicely oiled on the five beers each we have time for. Carrying the last one outside with us when we leave and draining it in five or six long pulls before we start back. Watching the time.

Ventola, Dubois, Green, Denbeaux and I. In required Class-A's. Ties and collars open as we trot back to our area afterwards. Falling automatically into an easy airborne shuffle. Plenty of wind. No strain. Laughing and joking as we run along. No worries. The 250s hours and hours away.

Starting to sing at the halfway mark, that last beer probably kicking in. We figured, the way

101

we sounded, any scouts around, we'd end up on Broadway. Punching out the new but already familiar words. Singing them to the tune of the Battle Hymn of the Republic.

> *There was blood upon the risers,*
>
> *There were brains upon the chute.*
>
> *Intestines were a'dangling from his Paratrooper's boots.*
>
> *They picked him up, still in his chute And poured him in his boots, oh...*
>
> *HE AIN'T GONNA JUMP NO MORE!*
>
> *NOOOOOOOOOoooooo...*
>
> *HE AIN'T GONNA JUMP NO MORE!*

CHAPTER FOURTEEN

Trotting down the asphalt road. The 250 towers growing larger at every step. Pushing up and into the clear blue sky ahead of us. Today was the day.

Turning off the road. The steady clop, clop, clop of our boots turning to a punk, punk, punk as we trotted across the plowed-up earth.

Heading across that rich brown circle, three or four hundred yards across. The drop zone for the towers. Heading toward one of the four tall structures standing there at the center. *Oh Jesus. Don't think about it. Just do it.*

They only use three of the towers, and three of the arms on each tower, at a time because the wind always blows in from one side.

What if it shifts around while you're up there?

Good luck!

Oh, thanks a lot. Thanks a whole heap.

Demonstrators going up.

Benson, behind me. "Wow! Are they ever up there! Look they're dropping loose."

"Man," I find myself saying, "look at them sail."

Kowalski, summing up. "Geez, look at them slipping into the wind! Boy, they're still hittin that ground hard, but look at those beautiful PLF's!"

I hate to think what mine are going to look like. Damn. Is it too late to join the Coast Guard? I swim like a friggin' fish.

An instructor with a clipboard. "Numbers twenty to forty line up over here."

Yipes, that's me. We're going up. Already? I mean, like right now? Oh, damn! Oh, God!

My turn. Running up to stand under the metal hoop, climbing into the harness.

"Hey don't look so nervous, my friend." The instructor in front of me, checking my harness. "You are about to have a ride you will never forget. By tomorrow you will be begging us for extra turns. I mean it. You just relax, son. Easy does it. I'm going to check out this chute and harness like you were my own son."

"NUMBER THREE READY!"

A tug at my shoulders, and all the straps pull tight. Then my feet leave the ground and I'm moving upward. About fifteen feet in the air, and all stop.

The loudspeaker barking. "Okay. Let's get a little movement there now. So, I know you guys are alive. All of you. Check your canopies. Arch those backs. Fine. Looking good! Now let's see everyone take a slip to your left. Climb up now, dammit. Get up there! Pull those risers down to your chest. Fine. Hold it. Okay, let up. Now, a slip to your right. OK! Fine. Let up. Okay, now. Everybody ready? TAKE 'EM UP!"

Ka-thunk, ka-thunk, ka-thunk. Somewhere behind me the cable cranking steadily. And up I go.

"JUST LOOK AT THE HORIZON. JUST RELAX, MEN, AND LOOK AT THE HORIZON."

The voice booming up at me from below. I stare at the horizon as the whole earth continues to shrink at my feet. *Oh, good Lord!* Steady. Relax now. Just stare ahead.

"HOW WE DOING, NUMBER ONE? HOW ABOUT YOU, NUMBER TWO? YOU'RE LOOKING GOOD UP THERE, NUMBER THREE. KEEP THOSE FEET TOGETHER, NOW. LET'S SEE YOU POINT THOSE TOES. THAT'S THE STUFF."

I can feel the wind coming from behind and to my left. The tower on my right. That means I have to slip left. I might have to take another, behind me, to keep from blowing all the way to Alabama. Jeez. It feels like a gale up here. I hope to Christ they know what they're doing.

Wow! That's Columbus! And, there's the river. And, goddamn! There's Phenix City over there! *Number three?* Are they calling number *three*? Hey, wait, that's me!

"DO YOU HEAR ME, NUMBER THREE? WAVE IF YOU DO! THAT'S FINE. HOPE WE DIDN'T WAKE YOU UP TOO SUDDENLY! HAVE A GOOD NAP? NOW! POINT TO THE WIND, NUMBER THREE. GOOOD! FINE. NOW WHICH WAY ARE YOU GOING TO SLIP? THAAT'S CORRECT. TO YOUR LEFT."

The voice moved off. To the others. I listened. My heart pounding now. My throat dry. A glance downward to the DZ below. Oh my God! Is that all I have to land on? That little, bitty circle? Jesus. Is *that* those huge stands? That tiny box?

"GET READY! TAKE UP YOUR SLIPS! PULL THOSE RISERS DOWN. GOOD. HOOOOOLD IT! HANG ON UNTIL YOU ARE WELL CLEAR OF THE

TOWER. COUNT A FULL FOUR SECONDS AFTER RELEASE, THEN LET UP. SLOWLY! SLOOOOWLY. DO YOU ALL UNDERSTAND? FOUR SECONDS, THEN LET UP! EVERYONE *REAAADY!* REEE-LEASE!"

The chute pulling me up, not smoothly, in hard, rattling jerks! One foot, two foot, three...*Christ!* A harsh, jarring clank of metal on metal and--*Oh, my Christ!*--I'm off! Ninety friggin' miles an hour! Wind rushing past me, everything happening at once.

A roar and rush of air past my left shoulder, past my face. The tower tipping away to the right, dropping away fast. Oh, Christ, I forgot to count!

"LET UP, NUMBER THREE!"

"LET UP, NUMBER THREE! SLOWWW-LY!"

Letting up on the risers, letting them out to full length, the world swinging in under me as I do so, the roar of the wind slowing, the horizon leveling in front of me, but rocking slowly back and forth.

"THAT'S IT! THAT'S IT, NUMBER THREE. FEET TOGETHER! POINT THOSE TOES. LOOK STRAIGHT AHEAD. REE-LAXXX! KEEP THOSE LEGS DOWN! THAT'S FINE!"

The ground! Slamming up at me in one great, bashing explosion.

WHUUMPH! Blaat! Christ! My mouth full of dirt. Dragging across the plowed ground, dirt hitting me in the face. Rolling over. A steady thudding against my back and bottom. Hey! Jesus! I'm dragging!

Bumping along on the ground, the chute still full of wind and pulling me. Bouncing me across the DZ.

Just to my left, an instructor trotting along, looking down at me. "Where you *going*, Trooper? You got an early date in Phenix City? *Pull* those risers down, right to your chest. Get those knees up on your gut! That's it! Now pull that left riser down to your shoulder and roll hard. *Roll*, goddammit! And come up running! That's it! That's it! Now run right into the middle of that chute. That's the stuff!"

The billowing chute collapsing in front of me as I run straight into it.

"Good, now run around it, turn it away from the wind and you've got it made! *Now* you got it, Trooper."

I could hardly contain myself as I raced around the deflating chute. I felt like leaping into the air, and in fact, once it was fully collapsed in front of me, I did leap into the air. An unplanned, exuberant leap of pure adrenalin.

Wanting to yell at the top of my lungs. Instead I slowed to a stop, grinning from ear to ear and unhooked one side of the reserve to let it drop. Punching the metal release box to let the leg straps of the main chute fall free, and then shrugging the harness off my shoulders. *Sonofabitch*. I did it! Off that humper of a 250! I've made a free fall jump!

Trotting back to my group to get in line again. All the guys ahead of me red-faced and grinning with the excitement. Whacking each other on the arm. "Man, was that a ride or what?"

"HOOOLD THAT SLIP, NUMBER TWO! DON'T LET GO! SLIP, SLIP!"

All of us looking up, the urgency of the barked commands turning our heads in unison. Two chutes sailing away from the tower, but one heading right for it!

Number Two had let up on his slip too soon. Sailing at the tower and crashing into it, bouncing off. His chute collapsing as we stood transfixed, helpless. The guy dropping beside the tower like a rock! Stopping suddenly about a third of the way down and swinging at the end of his risers like a yo-yo tossed in the air. His chute above him caught on one of those large, jutting hooks! Those life-saving hooks.

Holy Macaroni! Every eye watching the guy's pendulum swings, the other jumpers totally ignored as they sailed to earth.

"STAY CALM, NUMBER TWO! STAY CALM! WE'RE ON OUR WAY TO GET YOU. JUST HANG QUIET WHILE WE GET UP TO YOU."

All of us kneeling again, seeing the hoops cranking back down. Watching two instructors with ropes and belts over their shoulders scrambling straight up the grid construction of the tower leg toward the dangling trooper. Jesus, did they move fast. Monkeys in T-shirts. Racing up.

An instructor, standing at parade rest turns and nods at us. "Got it *now*, men? Take up the slip and *hold* it. A full count of four. Gets you well away from the tower, see? *Then* you let up, come down, land here in this kindergarten sand box. Got it?"

"Sure, sure," Muldoon whispers beside me, "but when do they change our nappies?"

****

Trotting back to the 250s in the afternoon. The airborne shuffle. The towers tall and erect in front of us, but not half so scary to me anymore. What a damn ride! Got two in this morning. Our turn now to rig the hoops for the others.

Everybody goin' to go?

YEAHH!

Everybody goin' to jump?

YEAHH!

What aarre yooouuu?

AAAIRBORNE!

Can't heeeeear yooouuuuu!

AAAIRRRBOOORNNE!

"That's better, troopers!"

Working the rings. Running out, forming a circle around the hoop, clipping the chute into place. Trotting back as they lift it up about fifteen feet, harness and risers on the ground below it. Passing Stratton waiting on one knee twenty yards away as we race back to clear the area. Stratton next up. Ready for his first.

"TAKE IT UP! HOOOLD IT! NEXT JUMPER, LET'S GO."

Stratton up and heading for the metal ring. His face strained. He didn't look at us as he passed, but all of us yelling encouragement. *You'll love it, Stratton. No shit, it's great! Piece of cake, Stratton.*

Quiet then, while he gets his instructions. The rest of us back at the apron. Sitting and kneeling. Feeling a good breeze over my right shoulder. It had picked up some, no question.

At least five or six guys from our platoon had refused to come over here this morning. They had stayed in the barracks until after we left for the towers. Most of us hadn't even known, hadn't even missed them until lunchtime.

Another six or seven balked at the rings and just wouldn't go up. Wouldn't put on the harness, or made them stop so they could get out. One guy half way up when he started bellowing. Made them bring him back down. Unnerving as hell to those of us still waiting our first turn. *Oh, Christ, don't let me do that! Not that!*

The guys who quit turning away hurriedly. Taking off, leaving the jump area. Some of them you could see were furious. Stamping around. Punching their hands. Like they were daring someone to say something. The others, most of them, just walking away. Trotting first, then walking. Dropping down. Sitting alone. *Christ.*

This morning a couple of guys had asked to wait until the afternoon. Moving out of the line of waiting jumpers, allowed to join the guys working at the rings.

Please, Sarge. I know I'll be OK, if I can just watch awhile first. I'll be fine this afternoon, I know it. Just let me watch for a little while, okay, Sarge? Please?

But neither of the two I had seen do that had come back with us this afternoon. When we fell out after chow they just stayed in the barracks. Starting to pack their things as soon as

110

the rest of us were outside. Wanting to be gone before we got back. Before the noisy, jubilant, back-slapping wave of men poured back into those empty barracks at the end of the day. Wanting to be gone before that, no matter what.

Oh, Christ! There's another one!

Where?

Number Three. Maybe he's just having trouble with the harness. Maybe there's something wrong with it. No! Shit, you're right. He's walking away, and they're calling up the next jumper.

Who was it?

Ventola.

What? Ventola? No, no! No way! I couldn't believe it. I just couldn't believe it.

Something must have happened. He must be sick or something. I could see him now. Tony. Walking quickly toward the stands, his head down, about fifty yards away from us. I jumped to my feet, starting to run toward him.

"HOLD IT, TROOPER!"

I skidded to a halt. The voice had come from my left. It was one of the instructors. Standing there in his immaculate white T-shirt, his legs apart, his hands clasped behind his back at parade rest. A friggin' statue of the Airborne Trooper. I glared back at him furiously, ready to break into a run again, but his words stopped me.

Not a command, though. Not this time.

"I know how you feel, Trooper. Believe me, I do. That guy's your buddy, right? Well, think a minute. What are you going to say to him if you do run over there right now, huh? What are you going to say to him?"

Damn! What am I going to say?

"You think he feels like bullshitting with you about what it's like to walk away? Forget it, Son. Leave him alone. There's not one friggin' thing that you or anyone else can say to him right now. Not one friggin' thing."

I stood there, and it seemed like all the joy had gone out of the day. I looked over at Ventola's receding back, watching as he broke into a run, as he left the plowed earth and headed on past the stands, then around behind them. Tony Ventola. The Bayonne Bomber. Trotting away. Out of sight.

I went back and knelt down with the others. A number of guys looked at me and shrugged, but none of us said anything.

Hey, guys! They're ready. They're gonna drop 'em!

The three guys at the top of our tower swinging lightly in the breeze, listening to the commands blasting up at them. Hard for me to see them, though. My eyes were watery and I was having trouble focusing. I stared at the ground for a minute, blinking hard.

There they go! Look at that! Oh, beautiful! Beautiful. Look at those guys sail!

CHAPTER FIFTEEN

Sunday night and the second week gone! Jesus did they go fast. Tomorrow will be our first jump from a plane.

The lights had been out for twenty minutes but I was having trouble falling asleep. Even as tired as I was. Even with five fast beers awash inside me.

Rolling over on my side, I could just make out Dubois, sound asleep already. Below him, in the gloom, Ventola's empty bunk. Terrible Tony. The Jersey Jock. We never saw him again. He was gone before we even got back that day. Reassigned. Where the hell do they all go, anyway?

Go to sleep. Relax. You worried about the 250s right? And they turned out to a ball. Damn, they *were* fun. But I don't know about these planes. Here I am, I've never even been up in a plane before, and tomorrow I'll be jumping out of one!

Stop thinking about it! Try to relax. Listen to the barracks. Everybody tossing and turning. C'mon. Go to sleep. Think of something peaceful. Something beautiful. Carolyn. Walking through the Boston Gardens with her last summer. Heading for the Arts Festival. The people. The flowers. Carolyn, beside me, her arm around my waist.

****

Kowalski climbing up in front of me. "We ride? In trucks? Jeez, and I thought they was going to double-time us all the way out to Pope

Field. Watch me break my leg falling out of the truck after all this training. Then they'll just have to go without me, huh? What a shame."

Rolling out of the company area. Crammed shoulder to shoulder into the back. Lighting up cigarettes.

Unable to eat any breakfast this morning. Some guys sitting there shoveling in the scrambled eggs, though! Sitting back, wiping their friggin' mouths. It was enough to make you sick!

Grover. Sitting right across from me. He was one of the goddamn eaters! Big old country boy. Tucking in like he was going out to milk the cows or something. He's staring across at me, smiling. Goddamn ox. I looked away.

"Hey, Fitz." It was Grover, leaning forward, across the space between us to tap me on the knee, motioning me toward him. "I seen y'all didn't eat no breakfast. You hungry? I got a chocolate bar." Tapping his pocket. "Think you could eat that?"

"Hey, no! Really. Thanks a lot though."

I smiled back sheepishly, really ashamed of myself. I tapped my stomach with my thumb, making myself heard above the roar of the truck motor shifting gears again. "Too nervous right now. I'll be plenty hungry later. Thanks, though."

"Shoot," he laughed, giving me a slap on the shoulder with a beefy hand, so hard it sent my helmet askew. "Shoot, we *all* nervous, raht! You change your mind, y'all let me know, y'heah!"

I sat back then, smiling across at him.

Grover. So while I had been watching him this morning, he'd been watching me. He hadn't missed much, had he? He saw me pushing the eggs around and leaving them.

Interesting. He was worried about me while I had been furious with him. Mad at him for taking it one step at a time. Time for breakfast? Eat the goddamn breakfast. Worry later. Grover's got the right idea. What a good shit he is. Salt of the earth.

Pile out, Men. Line up. As you go through the gate, give the man your name, rank and serial number.

Look at this! Mock doors.

The instructor waving us through. "Shuffle up, turn in, good jump out, and hit a good PLF when you land in that sand. *Great!* Next."

Heading then for the hanger. Into the long, half-moon structure. What's up now? Oh! Right. Piss call. Last chance!

The chutes. In Parachute Issue stacks. In kit bags. Grab one and take it along. Turn in the tag when your name goes on the manifest. Kelly laughing. "So they can find the sumbitch who killed you."

Okay, guys! Move along. Grab one. The chute inside is yours. Don't worry. They all work. We've got the best damn parachute riggers in the world right here.

Walking along with one of the kit bags bouncing against my right thigh. Finding my place. Setting my kit bag on the floor, very gently. Others already in front of me pulling on chutes. My hands soaking wet as I unzip the kit bag to take out the reserve and main chute packs. The yellow ticket wired to the handle staring up at me. Rigger's code and number. Every rigger has to jump one of his own chutes every month.

The straps stiff in my hands. Feeling new, unused. I stepped through the leg loops and started pulling the shoulder straps on one at a time. Fumbling. Having trouble. *C'mon!*

I looked up and down the line. To my right an instructor moving toward me. Checking each man thoroughly. Friendly smile at the man in front of him. Booming voice. "All set? Everything ready?"

The trooper nodding, white faced. I could hardly hear his, "Yes, Sergeant."

The instructor pointing to the floor, to the man's reserve, still lying there. "How about that? Want us to mail it to you, or would you rather wear it?"

Oh, my Jesus! I bent over to grab my own reserve. How could I forget the goddamn reserve? About every third or fourth man along the line doing the same thing. All of us laughing. Embarrassed. It was a weak, tinny laugh. No body to it.

"How about *these*, troopers?" The same instructor was holding up a kit bag, waving it above his head so we could all see it. "Gonna have a little trouble putting your chutes in these things at the other end if you leave them on the floor here, ain't ya?"

Oh, balls. They only told us fifty times. Fold the kit bag up and tuck it inside your harness, against your stomach, before you lock your straps in place. Goddamit. Now I have to start all over again.

I had just got my reserve back on when the instructor reaches me. He checked the leg straps first. Tugging on them to test the tension. The left one was too loose. He fixed it, pulling until it was like a vise, grinning at me. "Better being uncomfortable now, trooper, and have a nice, safe ride than to tear up your muscles when you get your opening shock. Remember that now. As tight as you can get it! Always!"

He went over the reserve, turning it very carefully, appearing to check every seam. Then the backpack. Quietly, behind me. "Beautiful. A-1!"

Like he was talking to himself. But I heard him. I didn't miss a word.

"You're all set, Trooper. Stand at ease. Smoke if you like. We got fifteen, twenty minutes yet."

Smoke? Oh, terrific. My cigarettes are in my pants pocket. I'd need a knife to get them out now. I looked around. None of the guys were smoking. Goode looked at me and laughed. "Doesn't anybody carry cigarettes in their shirt pockets in this goddamn outfit?"

"I say chaps, why so glum?"

It was the limey major. A British army paratrooper visiting Benning as an observer to compare our jump school training methods to theirs. Wearing his red beret at a jaunty angle as usual. Led by a cigarette in a long black holder, clenched between shiny white teeth, jutting out below his ginger, handlebar mustache. Can you believe this guy!

He extended a silver cigarette case open in front of us, and he came on down the line, insisting. "Go on now, Trooper. Help yourself there. Not as good as your American fags, but not all that bad, what? Go on now. Dig in there, lads."

Long, oval shaped English cigarettes. Almost flat. His lighter flashing. A deep drag. Damn that's good.

"Hey, thanks, Major. Sir, how did your tower pictures come out? Have they been developed yet?"

"Not yet, My Boy. Should be getting them back next week. They'd better be good or I'll have to bloody well do it all over again, won't I?" He laughed heartily at the prospect and we all joined in, remembering.

Last week, at the 250s, the crazy bastard had climbed up the outside of the tower to get pictures. On my fourth jump, as I hung suspended at the top, waiting, his voice floated up to me from just a few feet below. There he was! Leaning out into thin air, one leg hooked over a girder and both hands on his camera, looking up at me. His silly red beret tied onto his head with a shoelace. "Over here, Lad. Big smile now! You'll be jolly famous in England when these get developed, Old Chap!"

A click, a wave, a thumbs up, and "Give it a bloody good ride, Lad!"

I was almost laughing as I released and sailed away from him toward the ground below. Crazy bastard!

All of a sudden everybody began to turn around, looking back down behind us. A guy lying on the floor on top of his reserve, his head dangling down. A flurry of activity. Others leaning over him. *Hey, Sarge. Over here, quick. This guy's passed out!* Two instructors, moving fast, taking him out through the doors. Oh, sure. Out of sight. Out of mind.

Waddling forward. Our whole line advancing. One man, his face ashen, coming toward us. Between the rows. Walking fast, eyes down.

"Who the hell was that?"

"Alford. He's quit!"

Oh, shit! Damn, here comes another. Rafferty! I'll be damned. He's holding his mouth. Going to be sick! Oh Christ!

The line moving. My turn.

"Fitzpatrick, James A. Private. US 51183987."

Handing the guy at the typewriter the rigger's card. Moving on. Waddling toward the big hanger door.

Listen to those damn motors. Look at those goddamn planes! Like friggin' ugly beetles with holes in their tails. C-47's, they told us. Are they supposed to shake like that? The whole plane is vibrating like it's going to shake itself apart, for God's sake!

Kowalski pipes up. "Will you look at that friggin' pilot up in the window. He must be all of twelve! What is this, his first flight? Jesus!"

"Right, Sarge," I mumble. "Grab the rails and up the stairs. Gotcha."

Oh, God! *Hail Mary, full of grace.* Down the aisle. Geez, is this plane full! Bucket seats. Shoulder to shoulder, everyone facing the middle of the plane. Crammed in.

What the hell am I doing here with these gung-ho lunatics anyway? Take it easy. Take a breath.

More guys coming down the aisle. White-faced. Distracted. Grover! Damn, he looks terrified.

I lean forward, making myself do it, giving him a slap on the thigh as he reached me. Trying to grin up at him. God only knows how it came out.

He attempted a smile. His voice, barely loud enough to be heard above the engines. "Shoot, Fitz! Ain't this pure hell, though. Pure hell!"

Lumbering over to take his seat opposite me. Sitting there for a minute with his eyes closed. Taking deep breaths.

Two packed rows of sitting, sweating men. In the tail of the plane, men in white T-shirts, one with a headset on.

Who's getting on now? The English major! What the hell is he wearing, anyway? It was an Air Force pilot's chute. The kind you sit on. The kind that hangs down behind your ass when you walk. Must be going to fly along and watch us jump. His beret tied on with a jump boot shoelace, a big goddamn bow under his chin. Not caring a tinker's damn about how he looked.

Oh, Jesus. Here we go! The plane moving. Taxiing out toward the runway, making a dizzying half turn, the motors revving up to a screaming pitch.

Down the runway, faster and faster. Concrete flashing past the open doors. Suddenly disappearing. Green fields. White things. Houses? Shit, we're up! Already well off the ground. Climbing.

The plane banking slightly, my back jammed for a long half-minute or so against my chute, against the side of the plane. Across from me, all the legs shoving forward as the guys tried to keep their balance, to stay in their seats. Then leveling out, everyone sitting up.

Climbing steadily. The engines not as loud. A lot of sound swept away now, falling off behind us.

The jumpmasters dividing into teams. Two white T-shirts at each open door. One guy on each side kneeling, leaning out. Looking ahead. His face unrecognizable, blown into a strange, rubbery mass by the hundred and twenty mile per hour wind and prop blast flowing past him. Around his waist, a leather belt and thick wire leading off behind, attached somewhere in the tail of the plane. A monkey on a leash.

Christ. I was in the first stick on my side. Only six guys between the open door and me. Oh, Jesus!

"GET REAADY!"

My stick and the one across from us, leaning forward, preparing to stand up. Static line gripped in my left hand, a big bite taken up in the

121

line, which was trailing back over my left shoulder.

"STAAAAND UP!"

Pushing out of the seat. Knees like water. I grabbed for the static line cable with my right hand. Oh, God. *Just do it!*

"HOOOK UP!"

Holding the line with my free right hand, feeling it jumping around as others jammed their snap locks over it. Slipping the eye of my own static line over the cable and pulling down hard. I'm on. Now the safety pin. It's in! Through the goddamn hole!

I turned facing the tail of the plane, toward the open doors. Right foot forward, left foot back. Holding the bite in my static line. Right hand out, against the side of the plane. Steadying myself. Oh, God, I'll never get through this. Never!

"CHEEECK EQUIPMEENNNT!"

I looked at the chute in front of me. Running my eyes over it like I'd know if something were wrong. Are they kidding? I reached down, as taught, slapping the thigh of the man in front of me, telling him everything was okay, and feeling the whack against my own thigh from behind almost at the same instant.

"SOOOUUUND OFF!"

Down the line toward me. "TWO OKAY." A fraction of a second. "THREE OKAY." Each man calling out his check of the man in front of him. Down to me. "SIX OKAY." I used the opportunity to bellow. Trying to pump myself up. The calls continued behind me to the end of the stick. "TWELVE OKAY."

One of the instructors coming down the aisle. Checking us all out. Doing it right, Working swiftly. When his "TWELVE OKAY" thundered down the aisle, the stick was ready.

Suddenly, a shout from the English major. One we all heard despite the roar of the engines. "Cheerio, Chaps! See you below!" Two steps forward, into the door. The barest second there and he was out! Gone! Just popped out the door like he was going for a newspaper. No goddamn reserve. No helmet. A chute hanging off his ass that looked like a reject from an old John Garfield movie. But he was gone!

The jumpmaster, who had leaned out to follow his flight, pushing back and giving us all the thumbs up sign. Grinning.

A voice from the tail.

"Now, let's hear it. IS EVERYBODY GOING TO JUMP?"

"YEEEEEESSS!"

The intensity of the response that broke out automatically from all of us, including the jumpers still seated, took me by surprise.

"Let's go then! First man! STAND IN THE DOOR!"

Two white T-shirts closed around him. The same thing happening at the front of my stick, out of my view. Shuffle forward. Close the gap. Wait.

"GO!" I could hear the command, see the hand driving forward for the slap. He was gone. OUT!

The stick moving. "Alright! STAND IN THE DOOR! GO!"

Shuffle up. Wait. "GO!"

The man in front of me! It's his turn! I see the green fatigue pants, knees, in the door, just past the hip of the instructor in front of me. I hear the slap. A green mass filling the door. The tail of the plane dipping down and coming back up and he was gone! The whole goddamn door wide open. Just ahead of me!

"SHUFFLE UP!" I shuffle forward. I can't get a breath. I can't swallow. I see the two white T-shirts, one directly in front of me beyond the door, the other to my left. One is speaking slowly, clearly.

"When I tell you to stand in that door, shuffle up, throw that static line toward the tail. Throw it HARD! Then turn in just like you've been doing for weeks. Ready!

"STAND IN THE DOOR!"

Shuffling forward, trying to throw the static line with my left arm, but seeing it stop less than a foot from where I let go, grabbed immediately by the instructor who sent it flying down the cable. I turn into the door. Crouching, reaching for the sides, but sitting back at the same time. A white T-shirt one each side of me now.

"That's the stuff! Move up now. Move into that door. Let's go, Son. You have to get closer than that. Move up there."

124

A big breath. Shuffling up. At the door, the toe of my left boot sticking out over the edge. Hands at last in position on the outside of the doorframe on each side. The horizon directly ahead, moving straight up, then straight down, then up again. *Jesus!*

A face almost at my ear. "OKAY, Son! Just like the thirty-four foot towers. One spring and you're out! GET REEEEADY!"

He leaned back. Both of them did. I didn't hear the word, but I felt the sharp stinging whack on my thigh. Oh, balls! I pulled with both hands as hard as I could. Moving! Falling forward, my eyes squeezed shut.

OUTSIDE. A hurricane! The wind trying to rip me apart. Shocked by the sudden slamming force of it. Spinning me. Tipping me over. Deafening.

Upside down! WHOOMPH! A head snapping, shoulder jerking, legs flapping slam to a halt.

Silence! For a full two seconds, an eerie, absolute stillness. Hanging limp, legs and arms dangling. Listening to it. *Jee-sus.* I did it. I'm out.

Below me, like steps leading down to the ground, a string of toadstools. Open canopies. Four or five that I could see. A lot of space between them. Remembering, suddenly, with a rush, I reached up high to grab my risers, alert again as I did so. Pulling them down, arms straight out from the shoulders, arching my back to look up and check my canopy. Oh, beautiful! Beautiful! Look at that gorgeous, full, plump baby! Isn't that the most beautiful sight anyone ever saw?

The ride. Seeming not to move at all yourself. Rather, the earth moving gently back and forth below like a plate on a swing.

Pay attention now. Is there any wind? Am I going to hit the DZ? Where the hell is it?

Right there beneath me, growing larger. Coming up to meet me. Dark, rich earth. That's it. I'm okay. I'm on it. Damn, I'm coming down faster than I expected, though.

A tiny man in a white T-shirt. Getting bigger. He has a megaphone.

"THAT'S IT TROOPER! POINT THOSE TOES! C'MON! STRAIGHTEN THOSE LEGS AND GET REEEEEADY!"

A jarring thud, but I'm already rolling. Calf, thigh, ass, back and up! I'm on my feet and running right into the chute. Oh, baby! Was that a goddamn PLF or what? Damn! That was *fan-tas-tic!*

"Way to go trooper. We should have had a camera on that one!"

Heading for the trucks. An officer in fatigues is shaking hands with the jumpers as they leave the field. His uniform is covered with dirt, his own kitbag at his feet.

Well, I'll be a stuffed owl! It's No-Balls Norbert himself. The guy in front of me getting his handshake. Lieutenant Carpentier with his hand out to me. I take it. His grip vise-like as his eyes move to my stenciled name.

"Great jump, Fitzpatrick. Way to go! Welcome to the Airborne."

CHAPTER SIXTEEN

On our way to Fort Bragg, North Carolina. By bus. Twenty-five of us, our gear all over the empty seats. Special Forces bound. A sergeant and a couple of corporals transferring to the Group from other outfits and doing Jump School first to get in the door. The rest of us doing the triple bagger. Basic to Benning to Bragg.

I know what I was thinking. Whatever grief they gave us when we arrived in Jump School, they'll quadruple it when we get to Bragg. And I wasn't alone in expecting the worst. Most of us pretty subdued.

Some guy near the front of the bus. "Hey, Sarge. What do you think they'll do to us when we first get there? Run us a couple of miles with these duffle bags?"

"Hell, I don't know, Jimmy. Wish I did. I may end up sorry I ever transferred out of the goddamn infantry. I had it made at Fort Belvoir, these three stripes."

"What do you think, Denbox?" Stevens asked. "What are we in for?"

Denbeaux, on the back seat, holding court. At twenty-five, Bill was two to six years older than most of us who had come straight in from basic training. Bill had joined the navy at seventeen a few months before the war ended in 1945, then got riffed out just before he had a full year in when all the services had been ordered to cut personnel to the bone. Ironic for Denbeaux, though. One more month and his military obligation would have been completed. Instead, Bill had become draft bait just like the rest of us as soon as the Korean War broke out.

While the pure injustice of that would have driven me berserk, Denbeaux was clearly a master at rolling with the sneak punches life served up. He took it in stride.

"The way I get it," he told Stevens, "one of the hardest things to get used to in the Group will be those jump boots with the sharpened spikes on the bottom. I hear that learning to walk on those is a real bitch!"

Stevens, a very young eighteen, was clearly puzzled. Which was hard to tell in his case since he wore a look of constant surprise.

"*Spikes?* What spikes, Denbeaux? I hadn't heard anything about spikes."

Denbeaux, playing a live one toward the net. "You haven't *heard* about the spikes?"

"Well...well, I mean I've heard *something* about them, but, well, not what they were used for..." His voice trailed off.

Denbeaux leaning forward, his voice intense. "I'll tell you what they're used for, Buddy. They're for jumping behind the lines, that's what. Look! It's night. You're coming down in your chute and the Red Chinese farmers are rushing out of the woods to greet you with their pitchforks! So what the hell are you going to do, huh?"

Bill's feet in the air between the rows of seats, like he was riding a bike. "You come in kicking and slashing! That's what the goddamn spikes are for!"

Stevens's eyes, fixed on Denbeaux, were like headlamps. "No *shit*, Bill! *Really?*"

An explosion of laughter from the rest of us. From the whole rear quarter of the bus. Stevens flustered, turning away, beet red, disgusted. "Awww, Denbeaux, you are *so* full of shit."

Denbeaux winking at me. "Too bad they don't sell ham sandwiches on this bus, Fitz. You and me, we'd eat like kings!"

Chow break. Camp Gordon, Georgia. At the mess hall with tickets passed out by the sergeant as we got off the bus. Falling into line behind a couple of dozen guys in army fatigues. Heads turning to look at us. The room full of GIs looking us over. Our first time off an airborne post in uniform since we got our wings.

Standing a little taller all of a sudden in our skin-tight, cut-down shirts. In our Class A's with airborne patches on our hats and shoulders. Our metal wings flashing on our chests. Our spit-shined boots glistening below bloused pants.

Noticing being noticed. *We jump out of airy-planes. Ain't that grand?*

Mid-afternoon. Finally at the Fort Bragg gates. The bus sliding to a stop beside the guard hut. "HOME OF THE 82ND AIRBORNE DIVISION."

An MP stepping up to speak to the driver. Looking us over. The famous double A on his left shoulder. "Special *who*? Oh! *Those* guys! That'll be the Smoke Bomb Hill area, Pal." Then, for our benefit before he jumped down. "Just keep going. Past the main post. Past the hospital. Past the BOQ's. Past the goddamn woods and swamp. Keep going until you think you're at the end of the earth. When you figure this can't be it, you're there!"

Terrific!

The bus rolling on. Seemed like miles and miles.

Passing flat fields on both sides of the road. Sickly-looking scrub brush. Occasional trees, but new looking. Thin and bony with some evergreens thrown in. A few dirt roads running off between sun-baked fields. Beat-up signs with arrows.

"Rifle Range 32, Six Miles."

"Turn Off Car Radios. DANGER. EXPLOSIVES."

"COMBAT VILLAGE. CAUTION. LIVE AMMO IN USE."

Finally, another gate. A high chain link fence running off into the distance on both sides. "SMOKE BOMB HILL AREA -- AUTHORIZED PERSONNEL ONLY. DISPLAY PASSES."

And below that, "PSYCHOLOGICAL WARFARE CENTER."

And below that, just the two words. "SPECIAL FORCES."

130

Two MPs, one staying at the side of the bus with a grease gun, the other coming inside to check the large envelope with our names and transfer orders. Taking a head count as we sat silent, watching. Counting us twice before giving the driver the okay to proceed.

From Denbeaux, behind me, between his teeth. "Think *this* is bad? Wait until you try to get *out* of this friggin' place!"

Everyone busy all of a sudden. Wiping the scuffmarks off the toes and heels of our spit-shined boots. Shoving our shirts in, so they are neat and wrinkle-free. Checking the knots in our ties. Getting our hats on straight, cocked forward slightly with the twin peaks sticking up just right. No one talking now.

White barracks rolling by outside the windows.

Guys beginning to stand up in the aisle, duffle bags in front of them. The rest of us still sitting, but stiffly, peering out.

I looked at Dubois across the aisle. I get the Gallic shrug. The kind that says everything, but says nothing.

A sudden roar outside and above us. Two flat-topped brick buildings on our right, each two stories high. Then we saw him. A guy up on the roof riding a motorcycle! Racing toward the edge, skidding sideways, and disappearing out of sight. Coming back as we passed and this time flying into the air from a ramp. Two floors up, sailing across to the other roof and landing with a screeching, grinding squeal, black dust and stone flying up behind him.

"*Holy shit!*" From Kowalski, sitting halfway down the bus, as we left those buildings behind. "I got wings on my *chest*, not on my fucking back!"

Passing barracks and company areas, all appearing deserted at the moment. Denbeaux, very quietly, just for Dubois and me. "They're all inside, making bombs!"

The bus finally sliding to a halt. "This is it, men. Third Company."

All of us up now and moving out. The sergeant, his voice a bit shaky, pointing to the assembly area. "Fall in right here, men. Gimmie two columns, standing tall!"

The guys peeling off, running as soon as they hit the ground. Duffle bags on their shoulders. Double-timing into position. Every man hitting an airborne brace. Chin in, shoulders back, chest out. Backs like ramrods. Eyes straight ahead. Rigid.

Dubois, Denbeaux and me bringing up the rear. Racing to be in place before anyone came out of that orderly room. Before someone came out looking for a couple of asses to kick. *Shit almighty, why didn't I sit up front!*

The sergeant squaring his shoulders. A brisk about-face. Marching through the orderly room door. That's the stuff, Sarge! Let 'em know the quality merchandise is here. And, while you're in there, tell them whatever shit they're going to pull, how's about they start with the big guys first!

Silence. Time ticking by. Holding the brace. Then, the screen door swinging open.

Oh, my good Jesus! A master sergeant. Filling the goddamn door. One of the meanest looking sonsabitches I'd ever seen.

A flattened, broken nose that ran in three directions. Scar tissue over the eyes. A baseball catcher's hands. Fingers at some time broken, smashed and twisted. The kind of pot belly you could hit with a baseball bat, full swing, and all you'd get is splinters in your eyes. The nametape above his left breast pocket came into focus as he walked toward us. Beddaire. Master Sergeant Beddaire.

I wasn't worried about remembering it. I could always look him up in the yellow pages. Under *The Inquisition*.

He crossed the compound and began strolling along in front of us. Reviewing the goddamn troops. An easy gait. Surprising grace for a guy his size.

About three quarters of the way along our line he stopped, removing the stub of a cigar from the corner of his mouth. Everyone stiffened, straining to hear the orders we knew were coming, ready to spring into action.

Push-ups! I just knew it would be push-ups. Guaranteed!

"REEEEEE------LAXXXXX!"

The command exploded and I was in a deep crouch, halfway to the push-up position, still trying to figure out what the hell he had said.

All around me guys broke out in spastic movement. Some in a crouch like me, others starting left or right, others teetering in place, trying not to fall over. All of us struggling to understand the never-before-heard command. *Ree-what? Did he say repax?*

One hoarse whisper from the middle rank got it right. "I think...I think he said 'relax'!"

Beddaire watching us. Obviously amused. Removing the cigar again and shaking his head. "That's *right!* I said 'relax'! Just friggin' relax for a few minutes, willya? You guys fresh out of Jump School give me the heebie-jeebies!"

He waved his cigar in the air. "Light up, for chrissakes! Have a weed."

Pulling out cigarettes, I shook at least three on to the ground before I got one in my mouth.

Beddaire, still strolling, spotted a name stenciled on one of the duffle bags. Chewing meditatively, he mouthed the words with eyebrows raised. Slowly. "Fran-swah Dew-bwah." Then he looked up. "You-ain't gonna hurt my feelings none with *that* name, old buddy, let me tell ya. They call me 'Pete,' but my real name is Pierre."

His crooked grin showed stained, yellow molars. "No wonder I became a friggin' boxer," he told us, "name like Pierre Alphonse Beddaire. Father hadn't taken off somewheres in the Merchant Marine, I would have tracked him down, punched his lights out. What was he thinking, give an innocent kid from the

Bronx a name like that? Where are you from Fran-swah? Canada?"

"No, Sar-jant! From Montier-en-Der, Sar-jant. A small veel-age een. . ."

Beddaire's face lit up. "A real one!" he interrupted. "A *real* friggin' froggie. Man, I am *off* the hook, for *good*."

He gave Dubois a wink and swung around, continuing his stroll in the opposite direction. "It's about time this place got some class. We got Germans, Poles and Czechs coming out our ears. Lodge Bill boys. Do your time, get your citizenship. We also got Chinese, Phillipinos and even two Hy-wie-ans! But he's the first real Frenchman to hit this joint!"

Beddaire's voice rose then, like he needed to get our attention. "Welcome to Special Forces, gentlemen."

He walked as he talked. "The commanding officer of this here Group is Colonel Aaron Bank. Remember that name. Bank is a guy knows everything there is to know about guerilla warfare. Did his bit in O.S.S. when the last war was good and hot. Dropped into southern France near Marseilles long before the invasion. Place was crawling with Germans troops. Got that? *Your* CO, the guy running this outfit, was behind the lines in France in the days when, if the Gestapo grabbed your ass, they would burn your balls off with a blowtorch just to get the questioning started."

He was quiet, walking, letting that sink in. "Later on, after the invasion, when the

Krauts were bunkered in, hanging on by their toenails, he grabs himself a new mission. Called 'Iron Cross.' Jump into Bavaria, into the heart of the Nazi stronghold. Drop onto the Eagle's Nest, grab Hitler's bony ass, that was his mission. Grab the fucking Fuehrer himself, for crissakes!"

Beddaire threw his cigar butt down in disgust. "All ready to go, too, old Bank was. Had his troops all trained and ready. Would have pulled it off, too, guaranteed, if the brass hadn't chickened out, called it off at the last minute."

Beddaire paused again. "That's your CO, men. Quite a guy, Colonel Bank." Then he snorted. "But of course the man is an absolute looney. What kind of nut would jump into Nazi Germany, to go after the Fuehrer in nineteen and forty five?"

He stopped, looking us over. "Still, he's *my* kind of looney, I can tell you that. And yours, too, I hope, if you're gonna stick around this outfit."

Continuing down the line. "A word to the wise, men. There are plenty of guys like Bank in this outfit, as you'll damn soon find out. He's been rounding them up from every army post in the world. Ex-O.S.S. Rangers. Special Ops guys. Kind you can learn from. Guys who can blow the treads off a moving tank or steal a rosary off a nun's habit, she don't even break stride.

"On the other hand, there are some others paradin' about in this Group, officers, sergeants with stripes up the ying-yang, think

136

they know it all, but in fact they don't know enough to wipe their own asses, they're through! Guys who would get every friggin' one of you minnows killed in the first twenty minutes, you get dropped in with them on a real operation."

We stood frozen in place. Cigarettes burning unnoticed. "So what's the answer? *Learn*. And keep learning, that's the answer! And watch your step at all times. If you don't, it's going to be *au-revoir*, baby! *A-di-os*! See ya later!"

Crossing the company square with our gear, following another sergeant with the ubiquitous clipboard. This guy giving us our barracks assignments. Dropping out in threes and fours as our names are called, the rest moving on.

"Third platoon. Denbeaux! Dubois! Fitzpatrick! Green!

Going inside, the barracks empty. About eight of the top bunks at one end are unmade. Bare springs, mattresses rolled up. Bedding on top. All the rest have names on cards on each bunk and lettered on the footlockers.

Looking around.

Denbeaux going down the line, reading the name tags. "Sergeant First Class Gunnar Colte. Sergeant First Class Patrick Connelly. Corporal Coy Hadley. Sergeant First Class Casey Killian. Sergeant Juan Rivera." Every name a two or three striper. Denbeaux shook his head. "I have a feeling, gentlemen, that we have tiptoed into the wrong place. We must belong upstairs."

Up we went. Stopping at the top of the stairs in surprise. All the bunks up there empty! Bare springs and nothing else. No footlockers. *Christ.* Now what?

Anston Green, a Pennsylvania coal miner, expressing what we were all thinking. Speaking slowly but earnestly. "I ain't about to pitch my gear on top of no bunk which is atop no friggin' SFC. Not without being asked, I ain't. I ain't anxious to try learning to walk with a jump boot eight inches up my ass!"

We went back down to wait, leaving our gear on the floor upstairs.

After awhile, we heard them coming. Boots thudding on the asphalt. A loud babble of voices. Laughter. A lot of men double-timing down the company street, peeling off in small groups as they reached different barracks.

Some carrying weapons, others empty-handed. Some in grey sweat suits and sneakers, wearing baseball caps. Others in T-shirts. Most in regular green fatigues. White-stitched wings and name labels above the left pocket.

Stripes everywhere. A few corporals, but a lot more sergeants. A lot of sergeants first class, double-rockers. Shit! Master sergeants, three up and three rockers under. Four or five Masters that I could see. Trotting along with the others. All of them smiling and laughing, like guys running off the football field after a win.

One group broke off and headed for our barracks. We were standing at the far end against the wall. The four of us. Not knowing whether to stand at attention or not. Not knowing whether to shit or go blind.

The first guy in spotting us, coming down to greet us. Tall and blonde, he looked like one of the jump school demonstrators, except that his grey sweat suit was liberally stained with black grease marks, as were his hands, face and forehead.

He stuck out a huge hand, and then pulled it back just as Denbeaux reached for it. Catching sight of its grimy condition as though he hadn't particularly noticed until then. "Whoops! Here, grab an elbow."

He laughed, a big hearty sound as the others trooped in behind him. "Been unpacking Russian burp guns and Czech rifles all friggin' afternoon, and we had to dig down through six inches of grease just to get at the mothers. The name's Colte. Gunnar Colte. We've been expecting you guys for a week!"

Others crowding around then, sticking out hands. "Howdy. Calloway's the name. Any of you boys from Oklahoma? No? Shoot! Too bad."

Patrick Connelly shaking Bill's hand. "Where you from, Bill? Philly? No shit! I know Philly. What part? *Upper Darby?* Upper friggin' *Darby!* Hey, guys! This Denbeaux bum is a member of the ruling classes! *Jee-sus!* Lend me a few hundred, will ya, until my uncle straightens out? He's a hunchback!"

"Hey, where's your gear, guys?" This from Colte. "*Upstairs!* Shit, there's plenty of room down here yet." He jerked his thumb toward the empties right in front of us. "They won't use those bunks upstairs until the guys get back from Fort Sam and Fort Dix. That'll be a couple of months, anyway. Just pick yourself an empty and you might as well change into fatigues. It'll be chow time in less than an hour."

We started upstairs for our gear.

"HEY!"

Uh-oh. Colte again. Patting the bunk above his. Giving us a wide, evil grin. "On the other hand, I better tell you right now. If any of you bastards snore, you better not choose this one. I keep a Bowie knife under my pillow and we've buried three from this barracks already!"

CHAPTER SEVENTEEN

Special Forces. The first days.

"Holy Geez, Fitz," Kowalski said, dropping beside me after we got back from the rifle range, the whole morning on our stomachs, blasting away, "they got so many things going on around this joint I can't keep track of them."

"You're not kidding, Carl," I agreed. "They've got Russian language classes in the rec room right now, and when I went by Fielder's barracks there was a whole group of them in there practicing lock-picking, for chrissakes. All kinds of padlocks all over the floors and beds. I'm carrying my money in my mouth, here on out."

"Yeah. They even got me starting Polish classes in two weeks. That's sort of like carrying coals to Newcastle, ain't it?"

"Not if you speak Polish like you speak English, Carl," Green yelled going by, running outside laughing as Kowalski jumped up.

Grinning, Kowalski added, "Radio school starts Monday, I hear. I pity *them* poor bastards. Eight weeks frying their brains listening to code. You ain't in that, are ya?"

"Naah. That's not me, thank God. I'm gonna be a medic. They already told me at the Gap. I'll be going to Fort Sam Houston for sixteen weeks. Learn to be a field surgeon. So when we go behind the lines, no doctor available, I'll be right there on deck to take out your appendix with a rusty spoon."

"Geez, are you sure, Fitz? I heard that the guys going to Fort Sam left two weeks ago, just before we got here. Sixteen weeks. Next group won't go for four months. You sure they got you down for the medics group?"

"Absolutely, Carl. They promised me that at the Gap. None of that dah-di-dah-crap for me. I got their word."

****

Well, kiss my Irish ass! I can't believe this shit. *Radio* school. *Me?*

"Look, Sarge, this has got to be a mistake. They promised me Fort Sam at the Gap. And, see, I really *want* to be a medic, get that training, you know? Tough *what?* Oh, nice talk. Nice. And you an American soldier."

A lieutenant standing on a chair. A tough looking bird. Chest and shoulders on him like Charles Friggin' Atlas. "Alright, quiet down in here. Let's have your attention."

I am really pissed and I have plenty of company. The noise in the room receded grudgingly to an angry mutter. "I know a lot of you guys expected different assignments, as medics and language specialists. That was the plan. Problem is, availability on the one hand, necessity on the other. Some of you arrived here too late to make this last cycle at Fort Sam. We had to fill those slots or lose them entirely. We had no choice. And we gotta have those medics."

He let the wave of gripes subside again and went on. "And some of you were promised language school. Well, fine, but our problem right now is bigger than your preferred assignments."

A whisper near me in the back, just for our ears. "Is it bigger than this?"

I didn't have to look to see the guy's hand pumping the air in front of his groin.

"Our problem is that the regular army brass is already busting our balls and we aren't even set up here yet. The old-line regulars hate even the idea of an outfit like us. They're already trying to cut the measly budget the Colonel was able to squeeze out. So now we have to get our teams operational fast. We have to get teams into the field, both here and in Korea, to prove the value of special operations troops."

He looked down at us. "Men, you can't put teams in the field without radio operators. They're the lifeline. Re-supply, ammo drops, intelligence exchanges, all of that goes in and out over that radio."

Noticing the silence. All of us thinking that over. A hand going up in the front of the crowd. A sergeant, apparently getting reamed with the rest of us. The Lieutenant motioning for him to speak. "I hear you, Sir, and I can understand what you're saying. But why is it so important to get teams out there right away? I mean, as opposed to say, in six or eight months?"

The lieutenant's face lit up. His grin was satanic. "I'll tell you why, Sergeant. But all of you better keep this under wraps. I don't want to hear this being talked about at the post PX, or around Fayetteville. What I'm telling you now stays here, the Smoke Bomb Hill area, with Special Forces. Got it?"

He had our attention with that, alright. Little bastard knew his audience. "Why is it important to get our teams up and running right now? Because, gentlemen, in just a few months the 82nd has field maneuvers scheduled in both North Carolina and over in North Georgia. Colonel Bank has a job for us. For you new men along with the rest of us. Our job will be to go out there in the field and fuck up the 82nd six ways to Sunday! You all get that? We're gonna harass them, attack them, upset them, confuse them, and just fuck up everything they are trying to do beyond any possible redemption. Read that loud and clear!"

The same sergeant with his hand up. "So, summing up for the whole group here, Lieutenant, can I take it, then, that my assignment to language school is out the window, and that is final?"

"Yep. That's right. I guess you can say that everybody's orders are final, Sergeant."

Green, bringing an eruption of laughter from all of us, including the lieutenant. "Sir, could I ask you, is 'final' spelled with one or two 'fuck yous'?"

Denbeaux grabbing my arm on the way out. "Get ready to have your already besotted brain turned to mush, Fitz. We've both been dropped into the same hopper."

"There is no God, Bill. Eight weeks of radio school! Eight weeks of ditty dum dum ditty. Geez, Denbeaux, how I *hate* this friggin' army."

Denbeaux, for whom language school had just evaporated, started to chuckle. "On the other hand, Fitz, fucking up the 82nd, and getting paid to do it, now that sound's like something a couple of us Irishers ought to be able to get our backs into."

****

Damn! I've got to get someone to sew wings and new nametapes on all of my fatigues by Monday. Man, I *like* this Special Forces shoulder patch. That's class.

"Goddamn, Denbeaux. How did you get your uniforms all done so quickly?"

"There's a girl in the PX. She had an ad on the company bulletin board. Don't you ever read? I swear, Fitz, you could be on the list for Seoul tomorrow, I'd have to tell you in the chow line."

"Hey, she cut down your fatigue shirts, too. What did she do with the extra material, Denbeaux? Make pup tents? Put me down, you bastard."

Following Bill after he gives me a signal, a finger to his lips. "What are we going outside for? What is this, a military secret?"

Listening to Bill. Interrupting him. "Sure. Sure, I know who you mean. That real cute blonde who works behind the tobacco counter. Think I'd miss her? Okay, okay, I'm listening. Her husband's a transportation sergeant but she's crazy about paratroopers. *Come on,* Denbeaux! Are you shitting me? She did? *Really!* Honest to God! Just like that? Well, I'll be a sonafabitch!"

****

Fifteen minutes early for my appointment on Friday afternoon. A half hour walk from our company area. Leaving two hours after noon chow. Spotting the small house on the end of a long row. Five fatigue shirts and three Class A's over my arm. A pocketful of patches and blank nametapes. Listening to my jump boots clicking on the cement walk. My heart already jumping.

Oh, man. She loves paratroopers, huh? That friggin' Denbeaux. I just *know* he's screwing with me. Who does he think I am, Stevens?

Marching my virgin body along the sidewalk. Maybe not. Maybe he's giving me the straight goods this time. Will this be it, Fitz? Is this the day at last? Denbeaux's words the night before. "If you can't score with that little filly, Fitz, you better chuck it in now. Give up. Enter that monastery like half your relatives."

Pressing the doorbell. Christ, try to look relaxed, will you? For God's sake, you're just here to get some sewing done, that's all. Look casual. Be smooth.

Here she is now. Oh, man. That dazzling smile. Tossing her head to flip long blonde hair over her shoulder as she opens the screen door. Wearing a maroon silk Chinese dress of some kind that comes to just above the knee. According to Denbeaux, she wasn't wearing anything under it on his visit except stockings and a garter belt. He is so full of shit. Bastard is just busting my balls!

"Hi. You must be Fitzpatrick, right?" Her voice is like sugar on a spoon. "The Boston guy. I could tell from your voice on the phone. Come on in. The sewing room is all the way out back. Don't mind the mess, okay?"

Following her through the house and out to a screened-in back porch. A sewing machine. Two tables and several chairs covered with all kinds of clothes and material. Pin cushions and odd pieces of clothing on every surface. Baskets with more on the floor. A pleated skirt is lying on top of one pile facing me, rounded by the fabric underneath, and with the hem turned back in front. *Invitingly.* The sight is excruciatingly erotic to me. I swallow hard, staring at it.

"I told you not to mind the mess." She had misinterpreted my fascination with the pile of materials on the table, but she smiles again. "I keep on promising to clean up, but I always have fifteen projects going at once, so it's kind of hopeless. Well, now, let's see what you've brought me."

I pass her the shirts and begin pulling patches and nametapes out of my pockets. She is already sitting, her back to me, examining the shirts I have handed her.

"I...I can think of better things to do," I stammer, "on, uh, a day like this. Uh, rather than . . .uh, sew, I mean."

She glanced up at me, still smiling. "Oh, I don't know. I really like sewing. It's peaceful. And it gives me a real feeling of accomplishment."

Oh, Christ, Fitzpatrick. Come on. Give it one more try, you dimwit. "Uh, but there are things...that, uh,...that you could do...that, uh...you might like better."

Geez. Really brilliant. I'm stammering like a twelve year old.

She was clearing part of the table to make room for my shirts, and she glanced back at me over her shoulder. Eyes you could drown in. She was all business, though, counting the shirts and writing up the order. "Can you come back on Sunday afternoon? I'll definitely have the fatigue shirts ready, and one of the Class A's. I know you need the fatigues first, right?"

I was staring dumbly down at her, not answering, and I saw her brows knit as she looked up. Undoubtedly wondering what the hell was wrong with me. "Huh? Oh, Sunday? Sure, sure. That's fine. That'll be fine."

I took a step backward. Surely, she was convinced by then that I was a complete moron. Probably her only real question was whether I was dangerous. She was watching me, a slightly perplexed look on her face.

I took another awkward step backward. Her eyes followed me. She seemed as cool as ice. *That friggin' Denbeaux! I'm gonna kill that bastard.* "Uh...what, uh, what time Sunday? Should I come back? For the shirts?"

Smooth Fitzpatrick. Nice recovery. *"For the shirts."* She thought you meant for water polo over the "Y". My face reddened considerably as I turned to leave.

"What about that one?"

It took a full ten seconds for her question to register. Despite her pointing finger. She meant the fatigue shirt I was wearing. The one on my back.

"This one?" Oh, you are a real talker, Fitzpatrick. "This one?" I repeated, having to swallow to get it out at all.

I've always had a way with words. I was blushing like a goddamn fire hydrant. This was humiliating.

"Well?"

She was watching me. With what? Amusement? Irritation? Invitation? How the hell was I supposed to know? She *was* smiling. Does she want me to take it off, or what?

All of a sudden she was on her feet. Coming toward me. Damn! Months without even being close to a woman. *Months* without the touch of a woman. Just the smell of her perfume as she stopped in front of me made me giddy with excitement. The maroon dress was clinging to her hips and thighs, and all I could hear as she approached was the sound of her nylon stockings rubbing together as she walked.

She was only an inch or two shorter than I was. Without a word, her eyes on my chest, her hands moved up to the top button of my shirt. She began to unbutton it. One button at a time. Working downward. A tremor went over me as her fingers slipped inside, touching my T-shirt. Inadvertently, I was sure. I could hear myself sucking in my breath.

She glanced up at me then, her eyes dancing, making me return her gaze. She clucked her tongue softly. Then I felt her hand *inside* my open shirt, palm down, sliding slowly across my chest and abdomen. When it reached my belt, I could feel her tugging at it, loosening the buckle.

Her words were a bare whisper in the quiet room, and almost drowned out by the hammering in my chest. "I do *love* paratroopers. I don't know why, but I just *love* paratroopers."

Oh, Denbeaux, you are a gentleman and a scholar. Oh, lord what *is* she doing? My arms went up and around her shoulders, gently. Feeling her softness. Her hands between us, tugging at my T-shirt, before they slid around my waist and pulled me toward her as she moved backwards. Following her down, on to the thick rag rug next to her sewing machine. All of a sudden her hands were very busy. Deliciously busy. Oh, Fitzpatrick, you lucky sonofabitch. Get ready, for chrissakes! Get ready to stand in the goddamn door!

****

Denbeaux and Dubois already at a table eating when I made it to the mess hall just before they shut down the chow line. I dropped my tray beside them, catching Bill's eye. He shook his head slightly, his mouth full of chocolate cake so I ate in silence. I was ravenous. Dubois raised an eyebrow at the way I was shoveling it in. "I promise you, Feetz, we are not going to take zat tray away. You can zlow down, yes?"

After Dubois and the others had gone outside, Denbeaux, still drinking coffee, finally said it. "Ain't she a patch job and a half though, Partner?"

He tapped my wrist as I finally gave my fork a break. "Now listen to me, Old Buddy. You keep that one under your hat, understand? We got a long friggin' haul in front of us here, so just let's

150

be a little saving of the fruits that drop from the trees."

Outside, in the disappearing sun, Denbeaux stretched languidly and added, "As a matter of fact, at this very moment, I do believe I feel an emergency patch job coming on. But you just remember. Keep your lip buttoned, Buddy. I *hate* friggin' lines!"

CHAPTER EIGHTEEN

Reveille. 0600. Hit the deck. T-shirts, sweat pants and sneakers. *Let's go! Everyone outside.*

We loosened up in the company street, lined up in rows, but not in formation. It was more like a football team limbering up before practice.

Gunnar Colte was out in front. "Alright, men, shake it out. Do some knee bends. Stretch those muscles. Get loose. Everyone here? Let's go."

He led us out to the exercise field for our morning run. It was one mile around the perimeter, but we go around twice. Jogging, running, we set our own pace. The older guys who'd been at this for a while, shaming the younger guys. They flew past us doing sprints, tumbles and rolls and then coming up running. *Damn, these guys are in shape!*

We got into the spirit of it, working harder. Near the finish, Connelly dashed by me, challenging me to a sprint. He easily left me ten yards behind, sucking wind.

After showers, we fell out at 0700 for the AM report, with chow at 0730.

We fell in at 0830 in platoon formation. "Demolition teams! Over here! Rifle range fall in by the trucks. Radio School, follow Sergeant McInerney. TEN-SHUN. Left. FACE. DOUBLE-time...HAAAR!"

We trotted along past the other company areas for another friggin' morning with those hard rubber earphones feeling like growths on my head, reshaping my skull. Dah-di-dah-dit. I'm already hearing that shit in my sleep.

"Hey, Denbeaux. Look at those bastards climbing into that truck. Grease guns, carbines. Christ, those are Thompson sub-machine guns those two guys are lugging."

"Eat your heart out Al Capone," Bill laughed.

Fisher, ahead of me. "Some of the guys in our barracks ran that course with live ammo last week. Man, I'd *love* a chance to do some shooting at pop-up dummies."

Shit. Those guys get all the fun while we have to spend hours listening to code, developing my *fist,* as these commo birds put it. *Mother of Christ!*

"How about Dubois," I said. "That froggie prick is out in the open air blowing up buildings all day. Me, I got sixteen weeks heavy weapons training, the Gap, and they make *him* a damn demo man! There is no justice, Bill. No justice."

Two hours we spend pounding the key with a half an hour break. Which means twenty-five minutes of PT and five minutes learning to breathe again. Then we were back at it. We get a break for chow, then all afternoon, it was more of the same.

Sergeant McInerney gave us the word. "Okay, men, this hour is on theory. If you don't pass three hours of theory every week, you can kiss Special Forces goodbye."

Two evenings a week, seven to eleven, we got night combat tactics out in the boonies. Practicing silent approaches, walking and crawling. A growl from Colte. "What the fuck do you weigh, Fitzpatrick? Eight hunnard pounds? *Quiet*, for chrissakes! They can hear you in Canada!"

Two other evenings a week, classes in guerilla warfare, tactics and techniques. Lieutenant Bucky Walters. "Well, actually, men, we prefer to call it, 'Unconventional Warfare.' On account we ain't friggin' apes."

Saturday morning it was group lectures for all the new men. Lieutenant Walters again. I like Walters. We kind of think alike. "Now some of you college types want definitions. Okay. Unconventional warfare. What exactly does that mean? Write this down, men. First you sit in the friggin' hills starving and farting and slapping bugs until you stink. Then, you jump out and jam cold steel up the enemy's cooler until you hit his Adam's apple. Then you screw out of there. Fast! That's unconventional warfare."

He held up a hand. "And by the way, don't get caught. Definitely best not to get caught. You get grabbed out there in the deep woods by the 82nd, no officers or senior non-coms around, you'll learn exactly what a soccer ball feels like. *And* if you get caught out there on the real thing, do yourself a favor. Just bite your cyanide pill like a good boy and say, 'Goodnight, Gracie.' Because, when the toe-nail pluckers get through with you …well, let's not get into *that*. I have a weak stomach."

If we go *out there*? On *the real thing*? I gotta start reading a newspaper again. What the hell is happening in Korea right now, anyway?

Walters slapped a large printed chart with his pointer. "After you finish initial training in your specialty, you will be assigned to an A-team, the basic unit of a Special Forces Group. Every member will have a primary and secondary specialty, and all of you are expected to learn from the others."

"Now, listen up good. Colonel Bank has passed the word. We have only a few weeks to get ready. The deadwood goes. The fuck-ups are out. We have to prove ourselves, and fast, or we'll all be shipping out of here in a parade of busses!"

****

We broke into small groups and took our "angry nines" with us. The AN/GRC-9 radio was still in use from WW II. Seventy five backbreaking pounds of extra equipment for the radio team to pile on top of their rucksacks. Sergeant McInerney gave out the assignments.

"Okay, men, I'll be on the radio in the next barracks. Fitz, Denbeaux and Stack. Take turns. I want to hear your fist. And I want to see if you can take my code. Nice and slow, six words a minute. Accuracy first, speed later."

"You crank that friggin' generator first, Denbox, and I'll send. Let him see how this reads." My five-letter groups going out. My best work.

The message barely over when the return comes back. All three of us taking it. One signal repeated over and over.

"Hey, Denbeaux! What the hell is "QQQ"?"

Denbeaux and Stack howling. Stack translating. "It means, 'Get the bird shit off your antenna and send with your other foot!'"

"Oh, yeah? Smartass bastard. Here, Denbox, you give it a shot."

Two weeks later we were strung out over the countryside in groups of three. Hanging up yards of copper antenna. Finding the right frequency, which the instructor keeps changing. All three of us taking the incoming messages. Then one sitting on the generator stool cranking away while we take turns sending. Fisher, on the generator, his arm muscles screaming, summing it up. "This is what them jump school instructors did to get them builts. They're all friggin' ex-radio operators."

We trooped down what seemed like every road in the training area lugging all the radio gear. In addition to the main radio, generator and stool, you had your utility bag with codebooks, sending keys, earphones, yards of copper antenna on a spool, spare tubes and repair manuals. However, when we go *out there* on the real thing, they've promised us we'll get a radio the size of a shoebox.

Bill and I trotted back to the barracks from radio school after another endless day of radio practice.

"Hey, Denbeaux! Look at those guys over there. Hand to hand combat, for chrissakes. When do we get some of that?"

"Whoa! Did you see that guy go over? They're afraid to let you take those classes, Fitz.

Guy my size throws you like that, they'll never find the pieces."

"Oh, yeah, Denbox? When we get that stuff, I'm gonna bounce your dead ass so hard you'll look like the Hindenberg crashing!"

Back at the barracks. An uproar outside. The door flying open. Six sweaty, dirty guys piling in, all excited. Colte with his arm around Dubois's shoulders.

Colte giving Dubois a clap on the back. "Hey, you guys! You should have seen this froggie bastard in action this afternoon. You guys would have been proud of old Fransoyce here today, let me tell you. This was C-3. Plastic explosives. His first shot at the live stuff. Friggin' guy set his charges and rolled back those railroad tracks like they were goddamn rubber. It was beautiful. Bastard could give me lessons."

Casey Killian, grinning. "I have the feeling this wasn't your first time handling explosives, Frenchman. You were too goddamn cool. Am I right?"

All of us looking at Francois. He was taking off his shirt, using it to wipe the sweat from his face and neck. He looks up. Straightens. The ramrod bearing. The French knight in green fatigues.

"I 'ave blow up railroad tracks before, yes. Zee first time, ten years ago. I waz quite young, yes, but you do not forget zees things."

Colte asking. "How old were you that first time?"

"Quatorze. Ow you say? Fourteen. And after zat. A few more times I 'ave use ze exploseeves, yes." Adding very quietly, "Once on a beeg breedge full of Boche."

All of us silent. Dubois thoughtful, still wiping his face. Then, coming back from the memories. Grinning at Colte. "But, today, zat was fun, no! Today we blow ze sheet out of zoze tracks, deeden we, Partnair!"

Everyone laughing. Exchanging more stories.

I was flabbergasted. All through Jump School. Not even on the long weekend pass to Panama City after graduation. Not once in the weeks up here at Bragg. Living in the same barracks. Drinking up a storm on weekend nights in Fayetteville. Not once had he ever said a word.

Ten years ago. France in 1943. The goddamn Nazis everywhere. Jesus, the *Gestapo*. And Dubois was out there blowing up bridges, for chrissakes! Fitzpatrick, my boy, I'm afraid you've led a sheltered life.

****

"Holy Christ, Bill! Did you see those guys come in today from the radio team survival problem? Good God! Talk about the Bataan death-march."

"They were only out there ten days, Fitz. Isn't that right, Billy?"

"Yeah, but here's the thing, see. First they jump you out in the boonies in three-man teams. An old DZ out at Camp MacKall, which is where they run this problem. It's the asshole of the universe. You go in with one can of C-rations each. That's it. No more chow until you use your radio, find the next drop."

"What the hell does that mean?"

"Every night, between 1700 and 1800 hours, you get on the radio and get directions to where your next rations have been left for you. Two cans each, dinner and breakfast. No lunch. When you get your message, you have to decode it to get your map coordinates to find your chow. You get a different time and frequency each day."

"Oh, pisser. No wonder these guys come back looking like that. You don't find the chow, what then?"

"You get back on the radio the next night and try to do better."

"What's your chances," I ask, my criminal mind racing ahead, "of, you know, finding the rations without the message? How big is this friggin' place, MacKall?"

Fisher snorts. "I asked that, too. Smaller than New Mexico, bigger than Rhode Island, Sergeant McInerney tells me. It's huge. And they run you all day long to get to your rations before dark. Stop to take too long a piss, night is on you, you miss 'em."

Great, I thought. And perfect timing. It's been hotter than Africa here during the day these last few weeks, so now we get dumped in on this. Baking our brains out all day, freezing our asses off all night "What's the terrain out there," I ask.

"A lot of swamp. Mud and crap up to your chin. Grass up to your anal pore, and some places, bushes so thick you have to go around or cut your way through. During the war, when guys were trained to the breaking point, waiting to go overseas, they stuck them out there. So's all they'd kill would be snakes or each other. That's fact."

Snakes? Oh, thanks for mentioning that, Fisher.

"Fuck that," Wilson said. "I'll smuggle in enough rations to keep me fat for twice that time."

Fisher shaking his head. "Not on this problem. You go in empty. They make sure of that. They give two packs of butts to each man. One can of rations, a full canteen. That's it. Not even a lousy pack of gum. I asked."

Denbeaux and I working our asses off that last week. Playing tapes of code and checking the results. Laying out compass courses on maps. A man could friggin' die out there, MacKall, and never be heard from again.

Fitzpatrick? Sure, I remember him. He's the guy got lost at MacKall. He was found eating beetles and playing folksongs on his ribs.

"Balls! Send that shit to me one more time, Denbox. Send it *fast*."

"Hey, guys! It's all over the radio. No, not *your* radios, birdbrain. NBC. CBS. They expect a ceasefire in Korea any day now. The shooting is supposed to stop tomorrow, I think. Or maybe Saturday. This is no shit!"

Colte, coming through the door. "We're all going out tomorrow night and get blasted. The whole goddamn barracks. That piss-ass Korean war is over! Oh, that's right. Denbeaux and Fitzie can't make it. They're headed for MacKall. For ten glorious days to find out what they don't know about those friggin' radios. Too bad, Fitzie. I'll drink one for you."

Tomorrow. 0600 hours. Swamp bound. Everybody else will be out drinking and howling this whole goddamn weekend, and we'll be out at MacKall humping our asses just to stay alive. There is absolutely no goddamn justice. God, I *hate* this friggin' army!

CHAPTER NINETEEN

"Three-man teams. Let me through, will ya. Let me see the list."

"Who are you with, Fitz? Wilson and Miller. Hey, that's OK. They're good shits. Who's with Denbeaux? Garber and Stack. Not bad. You guys done okay."

"Just so long as I didn't win Stevens or Hillsop," I confided to Fisher, standing next to me, "I'm happy."

"Those two!" he groaned. "Yesterday, they were about to run their antenna off a public utility power line. So they'd come in loud and clear, Hillsop says! McInerney got there just in time."

Lining up at Pope Field a few days later for the jump in. Thirty-six new radio operators in twelve three-man teams. Our gear was spread out at our feet while Sergeant Santiago gave us the drill.

"Alright men. Lay your ponchos out on the ground and take everything out of your rucksacks. Empty your pockets, too. Everything goes on the poncho. Hurry up! We haven't got all day.

"You, Parker! Unblouse those boots. Do it! What's all this shit? Cans of Spam. Tuna fish. Nice try, Asshole. Okay, *everybody*. Unblouse those boots."

More sheepish faces as more contraband hit the deck and was collected. "What do you think we are, amateurs? We find anything else on anyone, you're off the problem and out of the Group."

Fisher reached down the front of his pants and came out with two small cans of crabmeat. Santiago scooped them up. "Too late for brain food, Fisher. You should have eaten that earlier."

Santiago passed out one map and one compass to each team. It was a piece of a map, really, part of a larger map of MacKall. It only showed the area where our teams would be operating, but that was plenty big enough. We also get a list of transmission times and frequencies, a different list for each team. Santiago summed up.

"Memorize the emergency frequency. It's monitored twenty-four hours a day. Use clear text. Don't frig around encoding the fact that one of you got snake-bit and is swelling up like a dirigible. If you miss three regular transmissions in a row, we'll be looking for you, sending Vs and trying to raise you. Try your antenna every which-a-way until you pick up our signal.

"If all else fails, don't panic. Get out in the open where the recon plane can spot you and stay put until a truck or ambulance picks you up. You all know how to use the snakebite kit. You want to eat the snake while you're waiting, that's okay, but cook it first. Don't want any upset stomachs.

"Last but not least. You'll have to hump your asses hard to get from one ration drop to the next. We plan it that way. Figure nine, ten hours on the move every day, not counting a stop for your radio transmission. So come morning, you'd better get your butts up. Unless you like looking for your C-rations in the dark.

"Use your heads. Study the terrain. Pick your routes. Supplement your diet, if you have time, with whatever you can find to eat. You've had some classes on that. Planted, running or crawling, food is food. You want to be part of a Special Forces team? Well, this is your first hurdle. You can climb over it, crawl under it, pole-vault over it, we don't give a shit. Just make your radio contacts every day, decode your goddamn messages, find your rations, and, oh, yeah--survive."

After repacking our gear we moved to the lines of waiting chutes to harness up. "Hey, Sarge." Stack asked him. "Are the riggers up here as good as the ones at Benning?"

"Hell, no, they ain't!" Santiago answered. "All these lazy bastards do is throw the chutes into a pack as fast as they can, then they sit around drinking and playing cards all day. Just make sure you got you a good reserve, that's the thing."

As we all gaped at him, Santiago broke up. "Shit, you guys *are* green, ain't ya? Hell, don't worry. The riggers here, they jump their chutes every month just like at Benning. Probably better at it. They'll work, alright. But, hey, if your chute does fail, don't come running to me. Okay, men. On the plane."

****

It was the tenth and final day and the six of us got to the rally point well before noon. It was an old abandoned airstrip. We set up our shelter halves for shade between trees. All of us had shaved, and we were in clean fatigues, washed yesterday in the lake for just this purpose. We knock every last bit of dirt off our boots. We took our time with all afternoon to kill. We ate the last of our extra rations, saving only a few candy bars for later. We buried the last of our garbage and made sure our spotless gear was neatly stacked. We had plenty of cigarettes. We spent the afternoon dozing, talking and smoking. Just the six of us.

Two trucks pulled in around 1800 hours. McInerney and Jacobs hopped down and stopped cold, astonished to see us sitting there. They strolled up to look us over, not missing a thing. McInerney spoke first. "Have a good problem, men?"

Denbeaux, who was lying on his stomach under the shelter half, lifted the tip of his fatigue cap and squinted up. "It was rough, Sarge. A real bitch! I'm so hungry I could eat my shoes. And *tired!* I could sleep for a week!"

"You don't *look* tired, Denbeaux. None of you do. And, if it comes to that, none of you look particularly hungry either."

"It's a front, Sarge. It's the Special Forces way, like you guys keep telling us. Ain't that right, guys?"

Nervous assents all around.

They wouldn't listen to me. I told them we should sit out in the woods, come in after dark with the rest of the teams. At least *look* tired and dirty, for cryeye. We're gonna end up court-martialed. I just know it!

McInerney and Jacobs nodded and walked back to the truck, straight faced. The six of us exchanged furtive looks.

Two more long hours passed, and it was after eight and getting darker by the minute when McInerney turned on a spotlight, letting it play out over the field in the direction the teams should be coming from. A homing beacon for the weary. *Don't quit now, guys, it's almost over.*

That's when we heard the next team coming in. Plodding up onto the broken concrete of the airstrip. Three guys in filthy fatigues, soaked to the skin and looking gaunt. "Shee-it! When did *you* guys get here? We wanted to be first. We really busted our humps." They dropped to the ground. Exhausted.

On they came. Team after team. Staggering into the light. A little after ten, the last three guys finally dragged in. Mud up to their waists, they struggled to smile anyway. "Man, what a fucking day. Where we started, had to come right through the middle of that friggin' swamp. We didn't, we'd a got here noon tomorrow."

The six of us climbed into the truck with the others. No one noticed our clean fatigues in the dark. Our shaved faces. Our barely controlled merriment. *OK, men. Pile in. Cookie's waiting with a late supper. Let's haul ass. This goddamn exercise is over!*

****

But it wasn't. Not quite. Back at Bragg, everyone dropped their gear in the barracks and went straight to the mess hall. Out in the light, a few of the guys began looking at us, puzzled. Most of them were so hungry that they wouldn't have cared if we'd been in tuxedos and wearing roller skates. They had eyes only for the food.

The mess sergeant spotted the six of us in line. "Hey, you men! This chow is just for the guys on the survival problem."

McInerney stepped up. "They were out there, Sarge. I *know!* I *know!* But they were out there. Take my word for it."

The word went down the line and through the hall. Now everyone was staring at us. Firing questions at us. *Hey, what's the scoop? What did you guys do? Stay at the "Y"? Hey, Miller, you prick, you put on weight out there? What's up with you guys, anyway?*

Five of us said nothing, letting Denbeaux explain. "We just used the water in our canteens to clean up, is all. Amazing what a little Ivory Snow can do if you pace it out."

Fuck off, Denbox! Ivory Snow, my ass! Clean this! Here, I'll hold it for you.

A crescendo of catcalls. Denbeaux just laughed and the rest of us managed a nervous snicker. Reaching the end of the line, with McInerney and Jacobs watching him silently, Bill held up a hand. "No dessert for me, thanks. I'm watching my weight!"

******

Actually, when you thought about it, it was obvious. But not to us. Not when you're out there waiting for the next Base message to tell you what direction you're going in the next day. Not when you're hard at it in the boonies, all you can

167

handle just to find your rations before dark. Not when, from dawn to dark, you are tired and hungry and soaking wet and every bone in your body is aching. Not obvious at all then, not to anyone. Well, not to anyone except Denbeaux.

Fifteen or twenty miles every day through woods, swamps, and streams, loaded down with gear, and always, right out there on the horizon, that beautiful friggin' lake. On your left one day, on your right another, but never close. Never *on* your ration route. A shimmering sliver of beauty, always just out of reach.

The third day. It had rained all night. Wilson, Miller and I plodding along in sodden fatigues, just beginning to dry in the morning sun. Seeing it again. The lake. Closer, but still a long way off. "Screw it!" I explode. "C'mon, guys! *One* quick swim. One good wash. We can do it. C'mon!"

Miller, objecting. "We'll never get there in daylight, Fitz, if we stop for a swim. We'll miss our rations."

Wilson, voting with me. "Screw it, Gerry. I vote for the swim. We'll find the friggin' rations. I can smell those lousy sausage patties right through the can."

The three of us trotting toward the lake, despite our aching bodies and the load we were carrying. My carbine, slung around my neck, bouncing off my chest all the way. Taking *forever* to get there. Scared witless now about the lost time. My stomach already growling at the thought of lost rations. The sun now blazing.

Oh, my God! The lake at last!

Holy *Kee-Rist!* Denbeaux's team already here! In the water, splashing around.

Look at this! Their pup tents are set up among the trees, ditched so the rain will run off. Their gear, all spread out. Can you believe these guys? Are they *crazy*? They'll never get that shit packed up in time to take off and get their rations tonight.

Denbeaux, from the water, "Gentlemen! Welcome to our happy home."

Stripping off and diving into the cold, delicious water, splashing around like porpoises. And then, sitting in the water along the shore, Denbeaux laid it out for us. "They got twelve teams out here on this problem, right? And we all have the same map. Big area, but first cut those corners off in your mind. Think of it like a giant circle. All the ration pick-up points have to be on this map someplace. And the guys running the problem, *they're* not being tested. They don't want to spend hours dropping off rations. They want to drop 'em fast and screw back to camp, sit around, tie into a few frosties."

The three of us listening, entranced. "So what they do, see, is drive *once* around the outskirts of this whole area in a big circle. They hit the twelve ration drops, see if last night's was picked up, drop the new. That's it for them. They're gone. The army way."

Bill made a big circle in the dirt at the water's edge. "Now picture a clock face. That's this whole area. They run a team one day from two to eight, all the way across. The next day, same team goes from eight to four, all the way across. Got it? They got *all* the teams doing this.

169

Passing each other like ships in the night. Through the swamp one day, up and down hill and through bushes the next. Busting our balls."

Miller treading water. "We keep seeing other teams in the distance, but they're always a long way off. No one close to our line of travel. We never cross the middle."

Denbeaux grinning. "That's the first thing I noticed. They keep us out of the middle. Away from this lake, this nice woodsy spot where you can camp out, get comfortable. One thing's guaranteed. They won't drop any rations out here. Got to keep the drops out at the edges of this map if you want to keep the guys hauling ass all day."

All of us absorbing that. Then Denbeaux put the capper on it. "Get it? This is the place to stay. Right here in the middle. Set up our radio, get Base in loud and clear, *leave* the radio right there! None of this running around every afternoon trying to find a spot to hang the antenna, hoping you can get a signal."

"Jesus," I said, "that's brilliant. But...but..."

"Look, we're here, we get our nightly call, decode it, get the new drop point. Fine. But, see, out here in the middle, wherever the drop is, we're already halfway there! We can send one guy with an empty rucksack. No shit to lug with him. Going empty out to the perimeter, any direction, it's a trot! He's there before noon, grabs the rations and he's back here before dinner. And this means, three guys, you work one day, rest two."

Wilson, unable to hide his awe. "This is *genius. Genius!*"

"If you guys want in," Denbeaux said, watching our faces light up, "we'll have *six* guys here to take and decode the Base messages. That can't hurt." We didn't need a lot of time to think it over. *Hell, yes, count us in! Count us in, Denbox, Old Buddy!*

The next day. Miller and Stack win ration pick-up duty, and Denbeaux and I headed off with empty rucksacks to see if we can find some real food. Rolling in wealth. Fifteen bucks that Denbeaux had tucked away in his sock. No one searching us for *money* at Pope. Who brings money to the boonies? Only the Philadelphia scrapple-eater.

"Of *course*, I brought money, Fitz," Denbeaux needles me. "A man without money, why, that's like a thirsty Boston Irishman the day before payday."

By ten we cross the perimeter of our map, heading out into "no man's land," walking and trotting all the way. We spot a dirt road, wagon wheel tracks. Then, a couple of miles further, a narrow but paved road that crosses it. We find the spore of civilized man. Crumpled cigarette packages. Candy wrappers. Empty Moxie and Dr. Pepper bottles. Well, the spore of civilized *Southern* man.

Hitching a lift from a farmer. *Hop on, Boys! A store? It's where I'm heading.*

A good old country general store. Bill put the whole fifteen on the counter in front of the proprietor, and we started stacking up the goods. Boxes of pasta. Onions, potatoes, cooking oil. Tomato sauce and beef stew. A gallon jug of cheap California red and six packs of Luckies. An iron fry pan and an aluminum pot. A two-pound bag of ground coffee and a one dollar coffee pot.

"How we doing on the money," Bill asked the owner, who had been running a tally with a stubby pencil.

"Appears you can keep on a wee bit, Major," the man said, studying his figures.

Inspiration. Bill grabs a couple of fishhooks and a ball of line. He picks up six candy bars and brings everything to the counterman. Pointing to the candy, he said, "And as many of these as your tally allows."

"How many of you fellers out there?" the storekeeper asked, putting two of the candy bars in the pile, as the farmer who brought us looked on amused.

"Six," Bill told him.

The guy looked at the ten and the five. "Slim pickins, I'd say, fifteen bucks for six growed men. Federals decide to quit feeding you army guys, or what?"

Bill's smile widened. "Well, the thing is, see, we're kind of sticking it to them, I guess. They dropped us out here on a survival problem. That's our mad money."

The guy shook his head. "That's your *insane* money, you doing your surviving at old MacKall." The farmer laughing with us.

The storekeeper pushed the other candy bars into the heap, reached behind him and dropped six more packs of Luckies on top. "We're square, boys," he said. A smile. "I throwed in the fishhooks."

172

Outside with the farmer, our rucksacks loaded, we jumped back on the wagon. The farmer drove us all the way back to the end of the first dirt road, to the edge of the woods. We had only about six miles to go to get to the lake. Handshakes all around. "Cain't take you no further, boys. Federal property starts here."

Back at camp. Denbeaux knee deep in the lake with a stick and his new line and hook. Tossing "sunnies" up on the shore as fast as we can pull them off and re-bait his hook. An occasional small lake bass. Wilson and Stack, already back from their ration run, started cleaning the fish. Fish in the pan, sizzling, four or five at a time. Mixed C-rations in the aluminum pot, spiced up with onions and fresh potato. An enormous and damn tasty stew. Fish still popping in the pan as it got dark. *Holy Mary, are these suckers good!*

The next night we had spaghetti and tomato sauce piled up in our mess gear. We passed the wine around, two inches in each cup, and around again. Hot coffee and fresh Luckies instead of those 1943 snap, crackle and pop Camels they gave us at Pope Field. The army sucks but, by God, this ain't half bad.

The last night, the last message. All of us cheered as we decoded it and found that the old airstrip was the rally area. *Why, Hell, we're more than halfway there right now! We kin stroll that far in three hours!*

A surprising explosion of anger from Stack. All of us turned to look. "*Shee-it, guys! We just run out of coffee!*"

****

Uh-oh!

The morning after we got back to Bragg.

Corporal Diaz, the company clerk, coming into our barracks. "Captain Beasley wants to see you."

"Who me?"

"Yeah, you Fitzpatrick. And where's Upper Darby? They want him, too. Better get over there fast. The man's waiting."

As Bill and I trotted across the company square, I was looking ahead for good places to throw up. "Shit, Denbeaux. What do we do *now*? Deny everything? Damn! We are dead pike, Brother. Dead pike!"

"Easy does it, Little Brother. Don't yell before you're gored. Probably wants to make us officers."

"Oh, riiight! Sure. We'll be back at the Gap tomorrow, you and me, Denbox. In striped fatigues. Doing *hard* friggin' time. Guaranteed."

Wilson, Garber and Miller were already there waiting. Stack came up right behind us. All of us were a little pasty-faced, even Denbeaux. We marched inside.

Captain Beasley was behind the desk. McInerney and Jacobs were off to one side. Goddamn finks. Dirty squealers.

Captain Beasley waved us toward chairs. "Sit down, men. Go on, sit down."

We all sat stiffly in front of the desk.

"I understand you guys really whacked the problem good. Beat the game as far as we can tell.

I've been over the reports. You made every single transmission on time and loud and clear. All of your rations were picked up except the last night. From what I understand, though, none of you had the hungry horrors, so we aren't worried about that."

He rocked back in his chair. "Came back in clean uniforms. Clean-shaven. Gear all in order. Fat and sassy as a bunch of Air Force supply sergeants, is the way I get it."

Beasley came around and sat on the edge of his desk. "Unconventional warfare. Do the job you're sent in for, but after that, beat the game any way you can. We couldn't care less. You guys beat the problem six ways up the middle. Most of the guys out there did fine. Showed they were first-rate airborne troopers. But you guys turned the game upside down, made it a real Special Forces operation. Congratulations."

Uh huh, I was thinking. Go on, finish up, Captain. Drop the other shoe. *But we're still gonna get court martialed because...?*

Beasley leaned forward. "It won't leave this room, men, you have my word, but I have to know. How the *hell* did you do it?"

All of us looked at Denbeaux. Denbeaux shrugged. "Well, you see, Captain, it was like this..."

Outside afterwards. Basking in the warm sun. Free men, all wearing shit-eating grins. High from the relief. "See, you dumb bastards," I said scornfully. "I *told* you guys we had nothing to worry about!"

175

CHAPTER TWENTY

Sitting in the back of the truck, I tried to keep my jacket between my bony bottom and the hard wooden seat. The truck bounced down the dirt road in and out of potholes, landing each time with a helmet-rattling crash. Eight of us were in the back. Wishing we were in front with the driver. So we could strangle him!

We were on our way back to the Smoke Bomb Hill area after another night problem, the fifth in the two weeks since the radio survival problem ended.

Out in the boondocks all goddamn night. In the pouring rain. A faint light was just showing in the rainy sky behind us. Soaking wet, I was mud caked all the way to my knees, and the stuff was drying in stiff, lumpy patches on my fatigue pants.

Colte gave us the word as we were dropped at the barracks. "Get all your gear and weapons cleaned up before chow, men. The morning is yours, all four hours to get some sleep. We got classes all afternoon. Be first in the chow line for dinner and you can get back and catch a couple more hours' sleep before we go back out tonight. We fall out at 2100 hours sharp."

Mother of Christ! To drive to another godforsaken corner of the boonies.

They had summed it up in the lectures. *Special Forces teams operate at night. We do our best work at night. We love the dark. We love rain and mud. These are our friends. That's when the regular army crawls inside to keep dry. To suck their thumbs. To write their mummies.*

"Yeah, right," I had said to Bill. "I'll bet the freezing cold is our buddy, too, in this outfit, but fortunately we don't get much of that here in North Carolina in June."

"Too bad!" Denbeaux had replied. "That crazy fuck Captain Badger is just back from the Aleutians, and he's dying to teach us to make igloos."

Map and compass problems. You'll work in two man teams. You better learn to read those maps, troopers. Get to point "X" by 0500 hours or the truck will be gone. Miss your ride, you'll spend all day walking back to camp. Twenty miles!

Connelly going past me. "Come on, Fitz. Let's double-time. Whatta ya say? We'll be the first ones to the truck."

The *very* first. Oh, goody gumdrops. "What's that, Sarge? Absolutely. I'm right behind you. Let's double-time."

Mock ambush problems. Find the crossroads in the dark. Set up a roadblock at 0400 hours on the dot. Rush out and shoot up the empty air. Bug out.

Connelly and I making a dead run into the woods. Connelly right behind me. Better not trip or fall. Fucker will run right over me.

"We do this to the 82nd, Fitz, you think those bastards are going to sit around after you hit them, discussing it? You got maybe four minutes head start. Like they give a fuck the umpire says they're dead. They'll be after us with anything they can lay their hands on. Bumper jacks, tire irons, probably. I know. I did a bit with the 82nd. Don't let them catch you in the woods."

Holy Shit! I'm running as fast as I can. This rucksack feels like a giant tumor.

"How far you think we've come, you short-legged little gnome?"

"A couple of miles, Sarge."

"Hah! Try half that distance, Junior. And one thing's for sure, it ain't far or fast enough. Don't look back, just run! Change directions! Zig-zag. Keep running!"

Another midnight outing. Paired with Colte this time. Moving fast through the woods toward our assigned checkpoint. Heading toward the "X" on our map. Still three or four hours to go.

"Getting hungry, Fitz?"

"Yeah, Gunnar. I could eat."

"Well, let's take fifteen. See what we got for din-din."

Colte's paw rummaging in his rucksack. Using a pen flashlight so he can read the labels, but keeping the light cupped.

"We got one can, 'Corned Beef Hash.' One can, 'Franks and Beans.' You like cold corned beef hash, Fitz? No, huh. Me either. But I just want you to know, out here on a problem like this, these five stripes of mine don't mean a damn thing. Out here we are equals, Fitz. We're gonna settle who gets stuck with the hash fair and square."

Good old Colte. A square shooter. I knew he wouldn't pull rank on me.

His grip numbing my shoulder. "Tell you what we're gonna do about this here can of franks and beans, Partner. We're gonna arm wrestle for it!"

****

Two days later, six of us were coming out of the woods when we heard the roar of water up ahead. Lieutenant Walters was out in front. Stopping us at the edge of the woods. "Tonight we cross the goddamn river, men. Now, I know it's pouring rain and that river is going by like Niagara, but that's the way we like it, right, guys? This is when the regular troops crawl in a hole somewhere. If there were any regular troops out here. Which there ain't."

Lunatics. Hey, I can swim, sure, but with a full rucksack! With a grease gun and wearing a poncho! I've seen this river. It's a hundred yards across if it's a foot.

"Now you new men, watch everything Connelly and Hadley do. They're going to use these trees and branches to make a raft for their rucksacks and weapons. One they can wade in and push in front of them, got it? And the rest of you are going to do the same. And the goddamn rafts had better float. If your raft sinks, and if this were a real problem, if you were really out there, you'd spend the next few months with no weapons, no underwear, and no friggin' cigarettes! Now, let's get to work."

****

179

Falling out in the company square the next morning. Lieutenant Ballbuster Walters is out front again. "Listen up, men. That is, those of you that didn't drown last night. Ah, I see they got most of the water out of you, Fitz. Fitz gave us a new idea last night, men. Drink the river dry first, then cross. Ingenious. Tonight, men, we go to the combat village."

"What's that, Fisher? I know you were there twice last week, but this time we'll be doing it in the dark. What? Of course with live ammo. No need to worry. When you guys are out there on the course, I'll be right behind you. Well, actually, I'll be up in the tower. I'm not a complete moron."

The combat village is a series of houses built close together on a simulated street. A touch of old Europe. Practicing team techniques for identifying and eliminating the enemy in close quarters. Practicing instinctive firing with pop-up dummies as we go through. Some are enemy soldiers, some are villagers. I held the team record for wiping out villagers. I even emptied a clip into a grandmother in a rocking chair. Well, dammit, it was dark!

Hey, c'mon. Leave off Fitz, you guys. At least he ain't hit the baby yet.

My opinion, that's because the baby is too small a target for old Fitz.

Yeah, yeah, pop up this, Green.

We went through those buildings that night like the Huns pillaging Rome. "Just don't trip jumping through those windows with that live ammo, men. Not unless you plan to go to Vienna, become one of them castrati."

180

"Hey, Anston, what's on this morning?"

"Hand-to-hand combat. On the PT field. Two full hours!"

"Fantastic! I've been looking forward to that. What? Not the radio operators! We have sending and receiving drill. Damn, damn, damn! We never get the good stuff."

Back to the endless practice. Ditty ditty dum fuckin' ditty.

"Hey, Fisher. How come the ones who really need this shit get to skip it? Well, look around you, for chrissakes! There must be at least fifteen guys missing. Stevens. That total fuck-up. And Hillsop. Where are they, huh? While we're getting knuckle cramps?"

"They ain't missing, Fitz. They're gone. The others, too. All of them."

"Gone? What do you mean gone? Oh! You mean, *gone!* Shit! Nobody told me. When did that happen?"

"Stevens, and a couple of the others, three weeks ago. Right after the survival problem. And the rest since then. Just didn't cut it on the night problems or the ranges."

"Balls. I kinda liked Stevens. Dumber than a bag of pork rinds, but a good shit."

Denbeaux plopped into the chair at the station next to me.

"Well, Partner. We better crank it up. The ranks are getting thin!"

****

181

More classes. Almost time to go into the field against the 82ⁿᵈ.

A headquarters major stepping up to the podium on the platform. He had more charts than Ike needed for D-Day.

Now I know some of you men were out on that supply drop last night, and you're pretty beat, but pay attention. Walk around if you need to. We have an Army Field Forces Test coming up, and we can't afford to flunk.

Tomorrow all of you will be assigned to an A-team. Your permanent team for the AFFT and afterwards. Get to know each other. The officer assigned to each team is going to be your leader for quite awhile. Get to know him. Learn the strengths and weaknesses of your team.

Sure! I can follow that. Good afternoon, Captain. You've met some of the strengths of your team. Those fellows over there playing tiddly-winks with those manhole covers. Now this is Fitzpatrick. He may look small, but he can throw up further than any of them.

Now, men, we have to do on this problem what you'd actually do in two years behind the lines. If your team were dropped in out there after a real war had broken out.

Out there? He's gonna start that shit again. Where is that anyway? Montana?

The first phase, intelligence-gathering. Two weeks to do six months work on a real operation. The job? Learn everything there is to know about your sector. Roads. Bridges. Traffic. Power stations. Armories. Troop encampments. You name it. You miss something like that in your sector, you can kiss this Group goodbye.

Well, I'll certainly keep *my* eyes peeled, Major. Now the fact that I wouldn't know a power station if my feet were plugs, that won't be a problem, will it?

Local law enforcement of all kinds. They are aggressor forces, too, working with the 82nd on these problems. How many, how well equipped? You better know. When it's time to wrap this up, we got to get close enough to stick the bombs right in their pockets.

Shit! Did you see the Major's eyes light up when he starts talking about bombs? He's a friggin' pyromaniac! There'll be a battalion of them, and at least *three* of us, right? *I'll carry the bomb, okay? You guys try to keep the singing down.* Christ!

Now, you've got a downed pilot. The aggressors will be looking for you and the pilot. Will you be ready to pass him quickly through to the next sector without getting him captured or the aggressors grabbing you?

Before the aggressors *grab* me! Grab me *where?* Jeez, what a terrific deal for us, huh! *We move the pilots out fast.* But we're still there' with those knee-cappers hot on our heels. Ain't that a pisser?

Are you the pilot? Hold this grease gun for me, will ya, Pal. Now gimmie that leather jacket, your papers and dog tags. Good. Now shut your eyes and count to five hundred. If you want me, I'll be in London, keeping your wife comfy till you get back.

In Phase Two of a Special Forces operation, it becomes your job to recruit and train a guerilla army from the local populace. Farmers. Students. Mechanics. Drivers. Anyone you can get to help you, to supply you, to fight beside you. Young and old, male and female...

Whoa up there, Cowboy! Slow that horse down. You are beginning to pique my interest. I guess you girls are all wondering why I've called you here.

However, gentlemen, on this upcoming problem, the AFFT, there will be no Phase Two.

No *shit!* What a surprise! Well, I don't need women. I've got that argyle sock. The pretty one.

On this AFFT we move right on to Phase Three. That's the part of guerilla warfare you have been training for so hard these last two months.

Sure, I'm with ya. Break your bones in the woods, then build a raft and drown. Smoke if you got them. No, not you, Fitzpatrick. You got your *matches* wet.

Phase Three means the invasion is on. The army of liberation is knocking on the door. The balloon has gone up. That's when your team will turn out in force to create havoc, destruction and chaos.

All ten of us? How about we compromise, leave off "chaos"?

First you hit all of your assigned objectives, the key targets in your sector. Then, with whatever you have left, that is, those of you not captured by the 82nd or ruled dead by the umpires, will hit everything that moves until the wrap-up. Night and day.

Night and day, we are the ones, if we haven't been ruled dead, or shot in the buns. *Didn't Cole Porter write that one?*

With whatever we have left? This major is definitely not a Dale Carnegie graduate. Hello London? Couldn't quite get your last message. Something about the balloon went where? Must be the clouds up here. The reception here is really a scandal. Be sure and try me again in August, okay? The second Tuesday is often sunny. Over and out.

We've got to work harder than ever, men. Forget sleep. Remember, the greenest member of a team may come up with an idea that will help you pull off a major coup. So stay loose. Exchange ideas. Consider your options. Have fun and good luck!

He's *right.* I have an idea. And this flashlight is perfect. But will he bend over?

CHAPTER TWENTY-ONE

The barracks was a bedlam of milling men, finding and shaking hands with their new team members. The lists just out. Nine-man teams for now, with more to be added later maybe. For Free Legion, the code-name for the AFFT problem.

"Hey, Denbox! Look at this! You and me paired up on the radio! Man, we'll bring in Tokyo, we have to, me cranking and you spinning the dials."

Denbeaux, as excited as I was. "We got ol' Francois, too. And Green. *Terrific!*"

The two of us going down the names. Gunnar Colte and Patrick Connelly, both! *And* Coy Hadley, the North Carolina snake charmer. Geez!

"We got the iron, alright," Bill chortled, "those three guys. Of course, they're all friggin' insane."

Now we understood why Gunnar and Pat had been taking turns running our asses off until our chests caved in. They knew this was coming.

"Who did we draw for a medic? Hector Gomez. Do you know him, Bill?"

"He was at Fort Sam until last week. Seems like a real good shit, too. Hey, who is this they have down for our team leader? Major Wendell Barnes? Ever hear of him?"

"No. Shit, I was hoping for Bucky Walters."

Gunnar Colte pushing through to join us. Shaking his head. "*Jee*-sus! I don't know about

186

this here team. What's Colonel Bank dumping on me anyways? A Philadelphia socialite and a Boston choirboy. What have I done to deserve this kind of punishment?"

"That's just what I was saying to Fitz, here, Sarge," Bill said. "We were hoping to get some real leadership, and look what we end up with. You and Pat. A couple of pathetic rejects the 82nd dumped on the Group."

"Yeah, yeah, right, Denbox! Too bad vaudeville's dead or you'd have a real career in front of you."

"The way I see it, Sarge," I said, "Denbox and I can *probably* carry you and Connelly, make you look good, if we can only get you in shape first."

Connelly coming up and grabbing me from behind, tipping me upside down and shaking me. "You're gonna make *who* look good, you friggin' pygmy? What do you say, Gunnar? Let's lock the little shit in a footlocker and leave him there until he stinks!"

Colte shook his head. "Naah, we do that, Pat, they might make one of us learn radio. Then our brains will be mush, too."

"Shit, that's right," Connelly agreed, dropping me unceremoniously in a heap.

"Tell me, Fitz," he asked. "Do you really send code with a Boston accent? Is that why no one can make out a friggin' thing you send?"

Green and Dubois arriving. Francois giving me a wink as I dusted myself off. "A Boston ax-zant. Zat's funee! I nevair noteece zat Feetz haz an ax-zant. Deed you, Anston?"

Green shaking his head. "Hell, no. I just figured all runts talked like that."

"Where the hell is Gomez, for chrissakes?" Connelly asked. "These greenies are ganging up on us. There he is now. Hey, Medic! Medic! Over here."

Gomez pushing his way toward us. Only about five-nine, but seeming almost that wide at the shoulders. A thick torso with no discernible waistline. With his spiky black hair and deep mahogany complexion, he looked more Native American than Latino, understandable since he had considerable helpings of both in his background. Later, the first time I saw him with his fatigue shirt off, I noticed the scar tissue running from his shoulders to his left wrist, one memento he had brought back from the Chosin reservoir.

When he reached Connelly, Gomez pushed Pat's eyelid back with a thumb almost the size of my wrist, studying the eyeball intently. "Uh huh. Just what I thought. The heartbreak of psoriasis, no question. Where's my enema bag?"

Coy Hadley coming through the door and finding us. "Sorry I'm late, guys. Heard ol' Fitz was gonna be on our radio team and I had to stop at the chapel first, do some serious praying. Then I heard Denbeaux was with us, too, and I almost stayed in the chapel. Hey, Gunnar, who's this here Major Barnes? Ain't crost his path before."

The barest change of expression on the faces of Gunnar and Pat. A split second's glance exchanged. Then Colte answering, but talking kind of fast for Gunnar.

"Major Barnes? Right, you haven't met him yet, have you? Well, let's see. He's career army. Was in Army Intelligence during the war. In England mostly, I understand. But his job was evaluating the reports from the French Maquis, and later from our own O.S.S. guys operating behind the lines. I'm told he knows a shitload about guerilla warfare. He's about thirty-eight, in uniform fifteen years. And, oh yeah, he just went through Jump School. So he could qualify to come here. That took some real guts at his age."

Holy shit, I don't like this at all. Colte going on the stump like that. Who's he trying to convince, anyway, himself or us? And Connelly silent. Looking off at the ceiling. What the hell is going on here?

Colte, stopping, our eyes on him. A *very* slight blush creeping up. "Okay, okay. Look, I just met the guy myself a few days ago, and I have to admit, he's, well, different. I don't know what to make of him yet, to be frank. But I'll tell you all this right now. *I'm* gonna give the guy a fair shake." His eyes moved from man to man as he let that sink in. "And so are you guys, or you'll fucking answer to me, and I mean that."

Oh, boy.

Green, never cowed, never shy. "You say he's different. *How's* he different?"

"Well, shit. I dunno. I'd say he's kind of, well, sort of British, I guess. That's the best way I can describe him. He did spend five years in England."

A pause while we all chewed on that one. Colte then adding, "He, uh, he carries a riding crop. And, uh, well, kid gloves!"

Even Colte couldn't keep the note of wonderment out of his voice as he made these last disclosures. A riding crop! Kid gloves! He might as well have told us that the major favored black lace undies. *Jee-sus.*

Colte was clearly concerned about our reaction, the thundering silence facing him. Gunnar making a good stab at putting humpty-dumpty together again.

"Hey, what do we give a good shit if Barnes is one of a kind, long as we all work together, get the job done. Let's face it. I ain't exactly your run of the mill SFC. I'm a guy's been up on charges three times for brawling on and off the post, years gone by."

The demented smile we were all familiar with was back. "Not to mention one shooting outside Seoul that no one was ever able to prove, and which they never will, unless .45s learn to climb out of boxes and swim to shore." All of us breaking up then.

"And I can tell you this," he finished, "I give every CO a fair shake, even though I've had more than one wanted to put me in friggin' chains. *Peacetime* COs, that is."

He spat that last part out like a bad clam.

****

At attention in the afternoon sun. Colte facing us. Thirty yards away, marching toward us across the company assembly area. Major Wendell Barnes.

Blocked fatigue cap on a small round head. A black, bushy mustache bristling on his upper lip. Riding crop and leather gloves in his right hand, slapping against his thigh with each step. Against an unarguably fat thigh.

His impressive stomach overlapping his highly polished belt. Head back. Left arm swinging high. *Christ Almighty. The fucking Black Watch passing in review. If the Black Watch has barrage balloons which carry riding crops.*

"Mother Mary!" From Denbeaux, on my right, the barest whisper. "Ain't he sumpin', Fitz?"

A warning glance from Colte shutting off my smirk before it started. A look that would blister paint.

Colte doing an about-face. His right hand snapping up in a salute.

"Sergeant Colte, Sir. Team present and accounted for."

The tip of the riding crop touching the cap. More of a flourish than a salute. The head still tipped well back, as if he wanted Colte to inspect his nostrils. A broad, toothy grin appearing below the fungus. "Good afternoon, Sergeant. Have the men stand at ease. I want to meet each one personally."

Well, kiss my instep! Personally. And me without my deodorant on.

The major coming down the line, shaking hands. A little chatter with each man.

To Gomez. "Ah, Spanish, eh!"

The guy was quick, alright. Perceptive.

Something I couldn't quite hear about tortillas. Patting his girth. Chuckling. He's a regular guy, no question.

Closer now. In front of Denbeaux. "*Philadelphia*, you say? You don't by any chance know the Vanderstadts, do you? The brokerage family. Big in copper, I believe."

Denbeaux, shaking hands vigorously. No change of expression. "Why yes, Sir, I do. They've been on my father's route for years."

What? Denbeaux's father, as I damn well knew, was a self-made millionaire at twenty-five who had lost his fortune in the depression, then died of a heart attack at fifty while Bill was still in grade school. Leaving a widow and eight kids. Bill was still pumping for water with the major's hand.

Barnes, clearly perplexed. "His, uh, *route?*"

"Yes, S*ir!* My father has one of the best garbage routes in Philly. He hits most of the main line families, so we know them all."

"*Really!* How *very*, uh, interesting." The major, finally retracting his hand, but not without a struggle. Bill holding on long enough to add, "It's really a great route, Sir. Around the holidays we eat like kings."

Denbeaux told me later that he just couldn't resist. The guy was so friggin' pompous. His father must have rolled over in his grave.

Barnes in front of me. A pudgy hand outstretched. Not quite so hearty this time, but still in there pitching. "From *Boston*, eh! Ah, yes.

192

The hub of the universe. The Athens of America. One of my very favorite cities."

But more cautious this time. "Uh, what part of Boston are you from, Fitzpatrick?"

"Dorchester, Sir. It's, uh, in the southern part of the city, Sir."

"Yes, yes. How very nice. We must have a long talk about Boston sometime. The Museum of Fine Arts. Louisburg Square. The Esplanade. Tea at the Ritz. Ah, what lovely memories I have of Boston!"

Oh yeah, I thought. Me, too. Watching the major marching stiffly back to Colte. We certainly must have a long talk about Boston, sometime, Major. Just you and me. About all the Boston memories we share.

Like being fifteen and hiding in a phone booth at Andrew Square while a bunch of the Southie Shamrocks roam by, swinging the sharpened buckles of their garrison belts, the leather wrapped around their fists. Looking for victims.

Like beating the Dorchester Heights Volunteers in a football game, six to zip on their home field, then running for our lives all the way to Fields Corner Station. Ducking a shower of rocks and hoping to find at least one cop with balls in the area.

Like the good old days as an usher in the Paramount Theater. Going home with black eyes and cut lips after we'd end up battling a pride of the Charlestown Townies or the Chelsea Tornados, who were trying to use the steel fire doors in the balcony as a free pass.

Sure, Major. We must have that chat real soon.

Well, we'd met the major. Our leader. No wonder Colte had problems trying to prepare us for that. Two weeks and we'll be in the field with him. The AFFT. That's when we'll know. That's when we'll find out where we stand.

CHAPTER TWENTY-TWO

Deep freeze. Two days of isolation and briefing in a tent city in the boondocks. Our last instructions before the jump in on the Free Legion, the AFFT. All very hush-hush. The teams actually involved the only ones out here.

Our team entering a large tent with a huge sand table in the middle. A three dimensional picture of the area where the problem is to take place. It was the first time I'd ever seen anything like that outside the movies. Impressive, I have to admit.

Finding our sector on the table. "Wow, you guys! This would be us, right here."

Green, beside me, looking down. "Where are the Nazis bunked in?"

We compared the table with our maps. Colte explaining. "The table is based on up to the minute aerial photography. Those maps you have are old. Make sure you note the differences."

Both Connelly and Colte pointing out hazards. The team discussing and selecting our own names for designated areas. "The Stockyards." "The Vineyards." "Mole Alley."

I started to write these down in a pocket notebook. Colte, coming over and grabbing it away, tearing off that sheet. "What are you, a fucking spy? You don't write this shit down, Dummy! *Memorize* it! Study this table, and your map, and put it all up here." His knuckles rapping my forehead.

It was Colte's job to select a DZ. Some of us trying to help.

"How about this spot right here, Gunnar?" Green offers. "A big open field. Plenty of room. In the dark that should be perfect."

Colte rolling his eyes at the tent roof. "Too big. Too perfect. That's the first place the 82nd will be watching. Screw that. I ain't getting my whole team captured on the jump in."

All of us crowding in now. Shit, this isn't as easy as it looked. Everyone chiming in. *How about over here? Oh, yeah. I see what you mean. Those power lines are too close. Hey, here's a...no, wait. Big paved road right over here. They'd be on us before we could get the chutes rolled up.*

Colte watching us until we quieted down. Then he pointed to a tiny football shaped green surrounded by woods.

We all stared. Is he shitting? That little birthmark? Damn, he's *serious*.

"*C'mon*, Sarge!" Green objected. "They make postage stamps bigger than that!"

"You turkeys have got to learn to fly one of these days. You ain't in jump school no more. Special Forces, we go out low, we get on the ground fast, we're gone. Get used to it. That spot is perfect."

"Geez, Gunnar," I said, "we know we're not in Jump School anymore, but..."

"No buts. You got woods all around, that spot. You got options, which direction to run, if them bastards show up while we're still there. It's big enough, take my word. I've done the math."

Denbeaux, wondering out loud. "Looks awfully small for nine men."

"We're gonna make two passes," Colte explained. "Five men go out the first one, four the second. It's perfect."

I kept looking at the scale given for the table, and then at Colte's DZ. On that table, I could cover the DZ with half my hand. With two of Colte's fingers.

We had the sand table tent to ourselves for the moment.

"Don't breathe a word of this to anyone, but Pat and I came out here two weeks ago, did a little surreptitious entry to get an look at this table," Colte told us, grinning. "Then Pat and I jumped this DZ a week ago. In and out, no one the wiser. It's perfect. Grass there is like a mattress. Am I right, Pat?"

Connelly nodding. "Good thing, too. Gunnar jumped us at eight hundred feet and I had to run along the DZ to get my opening shock."

Gunnar snorting. "Also, think about this. The DZs that the 82nd use are huge. They have to be, get whole companies on the ground with all their equipment. They won't even think of a DZ this size. Figure only lunatics would jump here."

Green, pressing it. "What height *we* jumping at, Gunnar?"

"Eight hundred." That toothy grin again. "You'll like jumping low, guys. It's like getting two opening shocks the same jump."

Coy Hadley, with over forty jumps, including one in Korea. "Hate to be the last man in the stick on this one. It's a night jump, right? No chance the last man will hit that purty little putting green. No chance."

Colte, both hands up. "Gentlemen, I promise you, I am not worried one whit about that. Of course," the manic grin again, "I'm jumping second in the stick."

****

Drawing equipment and packing it up. Carefully. First, the canvas-covered bundles to be pushed out in front of the first man in each stick. The stuff we divide up and carry off once we're on the ground. Two light thirty machine guns. A bazooka. Medical supplies. Mock sticks of C-3 explosives. Boxes of blank ammo and grenades. Flares and flare guns. Cameras. Can't have that stuff coming out after us, landing on top of us after we're on the DZ.

Next, packing up our personal gear. Sleeping bag. Rucksack. Extra clothes. Forty-five automatic. Grease gun, M-1 or carbine. Cartridge belt. Canteen. Compass. Flashlight. Map. Rations. Cigarettes. Candy bars. Books.

Ah, *books*. A necessity for six weeks in the field, but only two each. Two real lasters for me. James Jones' *From Here To Eternity* and Edmund Wilson's *To The Finland Station*. I remember Green, weeks later, hunting for something to read and looking at Wilson's tome in utter dismay. "Look at this shit! Karl Marx, for chrissake! Engles. I always knew you was a commie pre-vert, Fitzpatrick!"

Colte parceling out the rest of the gear that has to go in with us. Bill and I divide up the radio equipment first. Then the whole team in a circle as Colte deals out stuff he couldn't jam into our bundle. More blank ammunition. A few more grenades. Binoculars. Two machetes! *What the hell are those for? Where is our sector, anyway? Borneo.*

Sergeant Beddaire, sticking his head into the tent. "Major Barnes! Captain Beasley! If you'll bring your teams into the main tent, gentlemen, Major Caldwell has the most recent aerial photos of your sectors. Taken this morning."

Viewing close-ups taken that morning of the DZ Colte had picked out. A close look at some of the nearby roads. Pictures of some of the nearest aggressor encampments and vehicles.

Major Caldwell up in front. "Sergeant Beddaire, will you drop that canvas over the window and close the door flap. Thank you. It's not as dark in here as we'd like, but I think you men will be able to see this movie quite well. Study the terrain around your DZ. We'll run this twice. If you miss your DZ on the jump and end up in the trees, you want to know which direction to go in when you climb down."

Climb *down?* Fuck that. I can handle six weeks in a tree. I got books.

"Alright men. Now go back, try to get some rest. Trucks will be here at 2100 hours to take us to the planes. We should be in the air by 2130. ETA at your DZ should be about 2140, and it will be nice and dark by then. Stick close and don't wander off."

"Hey, Sarge. Here comes Major Barnes now. What in hell's he carrying, anyway? He's lugging more goddamn gear than we packed, our bundle!"

"Keep it down, Green. Hey, Fitzpatrick, Denbeaux. Get over there, will ya, and give the Major a hand."

Connelly, as Bill and I go by him. "What the Christ we're going to do with it after you get it over here, damned if I know."

The major's car pulling away. Barnes already huffing and puffing as we reach him. Gear hanging off every moveable joint in his body. Struggling. Not on parade at the moment.

Barnes giving me a toothy smile as I grab an armful, the bush lifting to bare his front teeth. "You know what they say, Fitzgibbon. Be prepared." He actually laid a finger next to his nose and gave me a wink. Santa Claus in fatigues. "We old soldiers," he confided, "we know the drill when we go in the field. Watch us and learn."

Back at the team tent. Laying everything down. Colte listening to the major and trying to keep a bland expression. "What's that, Major? Could we pass out some of this stuff among the men? Just for the jump in? Well, sure, I guess."

Colte looking at the mound of stuff. "Sir, may I ask what this is? A sleep hammock! Ah, I see. You find them better than a sleeping bag. Uh, huh."

Connelly, quietly. "It is a little bulky though, isn't it, Sir? Let's see. I think I can sit it in on top of your rucksack, lash it down, but we'll have to lighten your rucksack a bit first."

Items coming out of the top of the major's rucksack. Items that had stretched it to the bursting point. Connelly trying to keep his voice light. "Hey, guys. Can we give the major some help with this small stuff. The major needs a hand."

Can I roll it in a fist first? Lose it in that caterpillar under his nose?

"Yeah, sure, Sarge," I mumble, going forward with the others. "I got *some* room. I guess."

"Coy, can you take this?" Colte not looking at Hadley. Afraid to. "This, uh, map case. Great. It can go under the flap of your rucksack."

Coy taking it and responding to a comment by the major. "Yeah, that sure *is* a fancy map case, Sir. A real dandy."

All of us receiving some of his shit. Blank faces. Connelly, like he'd just opened a Christmas package. "Paté, Sir? And smoked oysters. Yes, Sir. A little civilization to go with us."

Dubois coming over to me in the corner of the tent, turning a fat can of pipe tobacco over in his hands as I opened my rucksack to try and shove in three cans of shrimp. Dubois trying to figure out how he was going to get his prize in his already bulging, but carefully packed rucksack. Looking at me. Nostrils flaring in anger.

Denbeaux holding a clay bottle of aftershave. Murmuring, "Gee, thanks, Santa. Just what I always wanted!"

Barnes had taken up a parade rest stance in the doorway. Surveying the bustling encampment. Hannibal waiting for the men to round up his elephants. Looking very satisfied indeed.

Colte beside him, lean and straight, also staring out silently. Jaw clenching and releasing. A hard, white knob just below his ear coming and going. A blinking light. Caution.

The major's voice rolled across to us. "Excellent night for a jump, Sergeant. Not a cloud in sight. We couldn't ask for a better start."

The force of Dubois's snort making me choke to keep from laughing. Denbeaux starting to whistle softly. We all knew the tune. *"Ha-pee-days-are-here-a-gain..."*

Stuffing the last can of the major's shrimp into my rucksack. Tightening the straps again when I heard the snap. An unmistakable sound. Balls! My toothbrush. Oh, right you are, Major Blimp, you asshole, Sir. We couldn't be off to a better start.

CHAPTER TWENTY-THREE

Hanging in the harness! Silence all around me except for the creaking of my shoulder straps. Straining my eyes to see through the darkness yawning below me. Shit, I'm already low. Very low! Not much time at eight hundred feet. Is that it? The DZ?

A light colored, sandy looking patch moving away to my right. Already too far away to slip toward. A deeper darkness coming up under me.

Right below me! Coming up fast. Spreading out. Are those cabbages? No, they're not in rows. Getting larger fast. Bushes?

Bushes, my ass! Those are goddamn trees!

WATCH IT! WATCH IT! CROSS YOUR ARMS AND COVER YOUR FACE! CROSS YOUR ANKLES! QUICK! FRIGGIN' TREES! FLYING UP AT ME!

Damn! Smashing in! Branches lashing me, whipping me. Cracking under my boots. Loud, popping noises as I crash into them.

Out into open space again. I'm through! The ground! WHOOMPH! Damn! I'm down! And I'm OK.

Rolling onto my knees. Up onto my feet. The risers still hung up in the trees above me. Pulling on them. Looking around nervously in the gloom as I haul and tug. Pretty dark in here. Tall, straight trees on all sides. Seeing that there is plenty of space between the trees now that I am on the ground, but a lot of branches touching each other about twenty or thirty feet above me.

One more good tug and my chute pulls free and comes floating down to land at my feet. Thin, broken branches all around me. One big branch a few feet away. Jesus! Did I hit *that?* Damn, was I lucky! Not a goddamn scratch!

Dropping off the harness. Shoving the chute into the kitbag. My heart pounding! Where the hell *is* everybody? What the hell happened to the goddamn DZ anyway? I don't think I even saw the bastard. Which way to go to find the others?

Behind me. Running footsteps. I spin around, trying to see. I'm in a small clearing.

Coming through the trees. There is he is! A black silhouette. A big guy, dropping behind a tree just as I spot him. *Holy Christ!* He's pointing his friggin' rifle at me! Not loaded. It couldn't be friggin' loaded. This is just a problem!

"AND THE RAINS CAME!"

The hoarse, harsh whisper reaching me. The rifle unwavering. Pointed right at my chest. The password! That's the goddamn password!

"AND NO WATER FELL!" I practically shouted back the response.

"Shee-it, Fitz! Stop yelling, willya! You trying to get us all captured, or what!"

Hadley. It was Coy, lowering his rifle and coming to his feet in a bound, trotting over to me in a half crouch. He gestured at the trees around us with his rifle.

"Damn, Fitz. Four men in our stick and they drop three of us out here in the woods. I didn't have a fat pig's chance at a bar-bee-que of hitting that DZ."

Do you know where it is, Coy?" I asked. "The DZ?"

He peered back at me. "Don't *you* know? Didn't you see it? Sheet, it's right over thisaway. Don't know how they 'spect a man to hit it though, when they drop his ass two counties away! Come on, and keep your ears peeled for them aggressor fellas. These here woods might be full of 'em."

We took off then, Hadley in front, with me trotting five yards behind him.

"HOOOOLLDD IT! FREEZE!"

Hadley dove to the ground in front of me, his kitbag bouncing off to one side as he did so. His weapon came up to his shoulder again, pointing ahead in the direction from which the icy command had come.

I hit the ground a split second behind him, staring at the canvas weapons-carrier in my hand. Pisser! I hadn't even gotten my greasegun out yet. It was real handy, all zipped up in the case like that.

Shit! I began quietly unzipping the bag, hoping Hadley wouldn't notice.

From out in front. *"And the rains came."*

From both of us, in unison. "And no water fell!"

On our feet coming together. Connelly! Looking us over. Grinning.

"Okay, hotshots! Follow me and keep the noise down."

Moments later, I could see it. Open space. The missed DZ. Hearing other footsteps. Brush rustling. The three of us taking cover. A figure approaching out of the dark. Again the crack of Connelly's voice. The figure skidding to a halt. A stunned silence. The password repeated by Connelly. We could hear heavy breathing.

"Sacré Bleu! I 'ave forgot zee password!"

Connelly suppressing a chuckle. "Get out here, you crazy froggie! Some goddamn part-ee-zan you are. *'And no water fell!'* That's the tickler. And you better friggin' remember it. We ain't home yet."

All of us running then, along the edge of the DZ, heading for the assembly point. Other figures emerging in the gloom. Colte waiting at the corner, carbine at the ready. Denbeaux trotting up and stopping beside him. The unmistakable silhouette of Barnes coming toward us from somewhere out on the DZ where *he* landed!

First man out of the plane, Barnes had hit the DZ alright, but in the middle instead of at the closest edge, so half of us ended up in the trees. A few seconds delay in the door is all it takes with a small DZ. Fat-ass bastard! I could learn to dislike that man if I put my mind to it.

"Green! Where the hell is he?" Colte, asking all of us. "Where was he in the stick? Who was he behind?"

"Me, Sarge," I answered. "He was right behind me."

Even as I spoke, I tried to remember whether I had seen him at all on the way down. I didn't think so. I was too damn busy trying to find the DZ.

Colte to Connelly. "Pat. Take Fitz and go back to where he landed. See if you can find Green. Leave your kitbags and rucksacks here. Make it as fast as you can. We'll unpack the bundles and be ready to move as soon as you get back. I just hope he hasn't broken a goddamn leg, or worse. These friggin' trees can do you in!"

Connelly and I, carrying only our weapons, running back along the tree line. He cut in abruptly. It was where we had come out, although how he knew, I had no idea. Getting nervous again. If there were any aggressors around, it would be just our luck to get caught in here now.

Connelly stopping, pointing to the ground. Broken branches. Shit, yes. This is where I had landed, alright.

We trotted on for another couple of minutes, and I think Connelly and I both heard it at the same time. We crouched, listening. Yeah! Someone muttering not too far away.

We crept forward cautiously. There he was at the edge of a tiny clearing. Still hanging in his harness. Swinging back and forth, his toes about a foot off the ground. His arms were crossed in front of him, a fistful of branches clutched in each hand. Hanging on for all he was worth. Bouncing gently up and down, but never quite touching the ground. Heavy foliage was jammed all around his chest, shoulders and face.

Connelly clapped a hand over my mouth just as I was about to speak, and motioned me to silence. His teeth flashed in the dark like a

Steinway grand. He lowered his weapon to the ground and went forward, moving like a cat. At Green's feet he melted to the ground, rolled over on his back, and cupped both hands over his mouth.

His voice, barely audible to me, drifted up to Green from as though from somewhere far below. "Haaaaa...loooooooo. Greeeeeeen!...Where aaaaarrreee...yooooooo!"

Green thrashed furiously against the smothering branches, desperately trying to free his face enough to answer, without for one second easing his iron grip on the life-saving branches. "HEEEERE!...UP...HEEEERE!"

Connelly was on his feet beside Green long before the last "here" had been swallowed by the surrounding foliage. Pat's voice, full force, was right at Green's ear. "Well, why the fuck don't you climb down, Trooper, so's we can get this show on the road!"

The branches flew out of Green's hands, exploding in every direction at once. He bounced crazily in the harness, staring pop-eyed at Connelly's grinning face. "Shit! Hell! I thought...damn!"

"Come on, you Pennsylvania jackass! Move it! Times a'wasting!"

A flurry of activity. Tugging Green to the ground, releasing his chute, getting him packed up, and running him off like a drunk being evicted from a waterfront dive.

"Let's go!" Pat barked. "Best not keep the major waiting."

CHAPTER TWENTY-FOUR

The sun on my face as I woke. Not really hot yet, but bright. Well above the horizon. My sleeping bag felt damp and sticky.

I unzipped it all the way to let it air and sat up. Rubbing my eyes. Blinking. Looking around.

Colte was already up and dressed, sitting, smoking, with his back against a tree. I spotted Denbeaux coming up the hill toward the camp through the woods, entrenching tool in hand, his white T-shirt appearing and disappearing behind the greenery as he came toward us. Green and Gomez were still asleep.

About twenty yards away, the sleeping hammock hung. Suspended between two stout trees. The sound of heavy breathing coming all the way across to where I sat. Steady. Stentorian.

Behind me Dubois and Connelly were also up and dressed, talking quietly. I stood up, pulling my crumpled fatigue pants out of the sleeping bag and stepped into them. I took my upside-down boots off the two sticks I had inserted in the ground the night before, holding them out and shaking them hard. No uninvited occupants.

I pulled them on and stretched. Still achy. Massaging my shoulders as I stood there. Yawning. Feeling the long stripes of soreness rubbed raw by the harness the night before.

We had all left the DZ as soon as Connelly and I had returned with Green. Colte, leading, setting a stiff pace and staying with it. Laden down with gear. Colte was determined to put a lot of distance between the team and the DZ. Just in case anyone had spotted our chutes coming down.

Five straight hours, with only three rest breaks.

We covered a lot of ground, up and down hills, gradually climbing higher. Moving well up into the deep woods. The chain of woods in our sector covered the hills like a snake that had been severed in several places.

Almost 0300 hours when we finally made camp. I was tired, but feeling better, a lot of the tension of the last few days dissipating during the trip up there.

I looked at my watch. 0830. Hell, no wonder I'm tired. Only about four hours sleep.

Denbeaux tossed his entrenching tool ahead of him like a spear, landing it at my feet, sticking up in the space between our sleeping bags. "If you want to shave and clean up," he said, jerking his thumb back in the direction he had come, "I just dammed up the creek. Nice, clear cold water. We should have a good pool in ten, fifteen minutes."

Bill and I dug out our towels and shaving gear, had a cigarette and headed back down. We waded in, pant legs rolled up, to shave and wash with the water already well above our ankles. The icy water felt good.

Feeling the warmth of the sun on my back as I guided the razor, mirrorless, using both hands to find the way. Beginning to feel refreshed. Drying our feet on the shore and heading back.

"We're due on the air at 0915 if there's anything to send," I reminded Denbeaux. "Let's check with Colte. The major's still asleep."

Colte was sitting, but even as we approached, his hand went to his fatigue shirt pocket and he held out a slip of paper. "Nice and simple," he said. "Arrived DZ 2145. Team intact. No enemy contact. The girls are beautiful. The beer stinks. Cheers!"

Denbeaux and I got out the one-time pad, putting the message into code. Then we picked up the radio equipment and climbed toward the top of the hill beyond our camp.

Before setting up the radio, we picked a likely spot before the trees thinned out too much, and used our compass to locate the direction of Bragg and the message center. Together, Bill and I laid out the antenna, each of us scrambling up a tree to get it hung well up in the air.

With fifteen minutes to go, we swept the dial. Stopping and listening, then sweeping again. There it is! Picking up Base and another team, coming in loud and clear. Delighted. Listening to that traffic, back and forth until they signed off.

Setting the dial now for our own frequency and waiting. Making a few small sweeps to either side. "Here they come, Bill!" A series of V's coming in loud and clear.

"As soon as they stop, Fitz, jump on that key!"

Back down at camp, we found the team sitting around a small campfire heating their food in separate mess tins. Everyone cooking or eating, except the major.

Jesus! The sound of marbles being shaken in a canvas bag still coming from the hammock. Colte looking at us with raised eyebrows.

"No problem, Sarge," I said. We got Base loud and clear. We got a message back, too. A long one. Okay if we eat before we decode?"

"By Jesus, Gunnar, did you hear that?" Pat threw in. "Loud and clear they say. Oh, they didn't screw around when they picked the commo boys, let me tell you. Cream of the crop!"

Colte waved a hand at the circle of eating men. "Haul up a rock and have some chow. The message can wait. Probably only tells us we're friggin' surrounded anyway. Coffee's good, by the way. The real thing. Gomez brought it in, goddamn pot and all."

It was good, too. My empty stomach growling. The smell alone enough to make you swoon. Real coffee. Terrific.

What the hell was that? Jesus. Feeding time at the zoo.

The major reborn. The hammock swinging dangerously as the one leg came out and down. Teetering. Then the other. But he made it. One sock foot at time. The major standing in shorts and a T-shirt. Blinking. Looking over the hammock at the circle of men. Flustered. Hand brushing his mustache. A perplexed walrus looking at his watch.

212

"DAMN!"

He ducked under the hammock and danced three or four steps toward us, very agitated.

He said it again. "Damn!"

Then he pawed the air with one hand in our general direction and raised his voice. "Sergeant! The time! Sergeant Colte! We've missed our morning radio transmission. Damned important. Should have let Base know that all is well. Team safe. All that sort of thing. Damn!"

We were all watching across the rims of our metal coffee cups as Colte rose and went over to the major. "No sweat, Sir. That's all been taken care of. The boys hit Base loud and clear. Message went off on schedule. Everything's fine."

The major's eyes looked considerably less pained. "Ah! Excellent. Good work, Sergeant. Good show!"

He began to pull clothes out of his rucksack, hanging them over the hammock as he got ready to dress. Remembering, he turned abruptly toward us as Colte was almost back to the campfire. "Oh, I say, Sergeant! Any message from Base?"

Colte nodded. "Yes, Sir. A long one in fact. The boys will work it up for you right after chow, Sir."

A split second's pause, but then the words. "No, no, Sergeant. That won't do. Messages from Base are not to wait. Have them work it up right now. Might be important, you know. All communications from Base get top priority. Always! The men can eat later!"

I should have known. I had my can of spaghetti and meat balls half open, almost ready for the pan and the fire.

The major swung back to his hammock to continue dressing. Denbeaux and I got up without being asked and went to get the one-time pad to start decoding.

Fat-ass bastard!

Connelly came over and spoke quietly. "Gimme those cans and your mess kits. I'll get them heated up for you." Stopping our protest with an upheld hand. "No sweat. You haven't had breakfast until I've cooked it. Gimme those."

Denbeaux and I going through to check every five-letter group. Underlining those where we had taken them differently. Shit! Quite a few. Three long pages. The five-letter groups looking like some weird language. "DBONZ RXACT ELGOG." No meaning at all until decoded, and maybe none then, if we really blew it.

In the field we had to keep messages going out as short as possible. We had been warned. So the aggressors couldn't zero in on us. So they couldn't pick up our signals. They had brought out vans with range-direction finders mounted on their roofs for this problem. Short and sweet, that was the byword.

Base, on the other hand, could send all day long without giving the aggressors any clue as to where we were.

"Jesus, Bill! I can't make beans out of this line. What did you get for these five groups? Balls! About half the letters we took on this line are different."

214

Starting to sweat. Working away. Connelly bringing us our breakfast and more coffee. The rest of team sitting around the area, but watching.

"*Peliliter.* Shit, that can't be right, Bill. *Peliliter!* What the hell can that be?"

"Skip it, Fitz. Keep going. We'll get back to it later."

The next two lines are okay.

"*Stapdard.* What the hell does that mean? Follow *stapdard* procedures?"

I stared at it. "Damned if I know, Bill. That's what I got, too. Wait a minute! *Stan*dard! That's what it is. Only two words we still don't have. Hold it. That's *rations,* right?"

Bill pointing. "Now this one again. Not *pelileter. Perimeter!* That's it! Hey, Fitz, I think we got it all. Hey, Sarge! We got the whole thing! Every word."

Colte, stone-faced, taking the message from us. "*Every* word! Big deal. What did you plan on getting, half?"

Barnes was shaving when we went over. Sitting cross-legged on the ground. A helmet full of water beside him. He had an ivory-framed mirror propped against a tree in front of him. Shaving cream still covered his neck.

Colte handed him the message. "Nothing exciting, Major. Pretty much what we expected. About fifteen assignments. Transmission times and frequencies. They want us to set up a joint supply drop with Captain Beasley's team by the middle of next week. We'll need one for rations by then, anyway. If you'd like, Major, Connelly and I can work up some assignment schedules for the men. Line up how we can best cover each job. We can have it ready for you in a couple of hours."

"I think you had better read me the message in full, Sergeant."

The major had removed a tiny pair of scissors from a leather case and was now busy clipping and shaping his mustache. His face was close to the mirror as he concentrated. "After you're read it through, you may leave it here, and I'll go over it and make up the assignment schedules. I'll want you to call a team meeting for 1600 hours, so I can put the men in the picture and lay out the drill."

Well, Colte, old pal! I guess he told you where to get off. *He'll* make up the assignment schedules. Thanks awfully, though, just the same. Then *he's* going to put us in the picture. "Daffy Duck goes to Camp," probably.

Colte got the message, alright. His ears reddened just a trace, and he motioned us to go back while he cleared his throat and prepared to read the epistle from Base to the Major. Barnes stopped us as we started away, sitting back from the mirror for a moment to wave a heavy arm in the direction of the others. Pointing with the dainty scissors.

"Oh, you men! Deveau, Fitzgibbons! Tell the others I said they should...ah...practice their specialties for the day. And...ah...see that everything's working properly and ready for action. I want to see the men working."

Bill and I didn't look at each other as we crossed the clearing. I just hope he spells our names that way on the court martial papers when I tuck the next message up his anal pore!

We delivered his *orders* to the team. The others staring at us. Then looking across to where Colte stood reading the radio message to the major who was now busy grooming his eyebrows.

Dubois was kneeling, scrubbing his mess gear with gravel. He stopped and banged it sharply against a rock in front of him. "He ees right, of course! Hey Connolee. What do you say? Let's start by blowing up heez fuckeen hammock, eh! For prac-tees!"

Connelly squatted down next to Dubois and spat into the dying fire in front of them. "That's the trouble with you goddamn froggies. You think too small. Screw his hammock. Give me five minutes alone with his toilet paper and I'll blow that bastard's ass off!"

Dubois smirked. "Oh, but you are wrong, my friend! I 'ave thought of zat, but take annozair look at ze may-jor. We deedn't bring enough C-3 for a job of zat size!"

CHAPTER TWENTY-FIVE

I was still holding the match to the tip of my cigarette, taking the first big drag when the word rang out from somewhere down the hill below me. Causing me to swallow a great gulp of smoke the wrong way. Breaking out in a paroxysm of coughing.

"AGGREEEESSSSSOOOOORS!"

It was Connelly. Loping up toward us, through the trees.

He yelled again. "AGGRESSORS! Four truckloads at the bottom of the hill! Fanning out and coming this way fast! Go! Go! Grab your gear and haul ass!"

It was the third morning of the problem. I had been out on assignments for most of the last two nights, thanks to the major's planning.

Not five minutes earlier, Bill and I had finished sending out one of Barnes' thirty-minute books. Small wonder the aggressors were in our laps. I was just pulling off my boots to try to grab a few hours sleep when Connelly burst out of the woods with that wonderful news.

Aggressors! My good Jesus!

The camp erupted in furious activity, everyone racing for their gear.

Rolling up my sleeping bag. Slapping it on top of my rucksack, which was already packed. Grabbing my helmet, a stray shirt, and my mess gear. Jamming it still dirty into a pocket of the rucksack. Buckling on my cartridge belt and .45.

Seeing Coy and Gomez already in full gear dashing over to help Connelly and Green.

Shoving my arms into the rucksack's straps and grabbing my M-3 submachine gun, I scrambled uphill toward our radio set up. As I ran, I could hear Denbeaux coming fast behind me.

"Holy Christ, Bill! We'll never get our shit packed up in time! Oh, God! What about the antenna?"

We had the antenna, yards of copper wire, strung out fifteen feet in the air between two trees. Out of breath as I dropped my gear beside the radio. On my knees, throwing stuff into the canvas bags and cases.

"I'll get it," Denbeaux yelped, galloping past me and starting to climb the tree where the near end of the antenna was attached. That's when the idea hit me.

"Bill!" I got out between gasps, "Leave it! Just pull up the lead and tuck that out of sight. Once we get the rest of the gear out of here, they'll never spot that wire up in those branches. We'll come back for it.

Denbeaux pulling furiously until he had the long lead up in the tree. Jamming it away among the branches. A thundering crash and Denbeaux was beside me grabbing the last of the gear.

Our ears straining for noises from the woods below. Not a sound yet except for those from our teammates nearby. We slung the radio gear on top of our rucksacks as we moved out fast.

Heading uphill, feeling like a couple of pack horses. Going as fast as we could up the steep rise. Leaning almost parallel to the ground. Adrenalin pumping. Giving us that extra shove toward the top.

At the crest of the hill, where the trees thinned out, our teammates were waiting. Except for Colte and the major.

Fortunately, Colte had laid out escape plans the first day. Connelly, supply case above his rucksack, bazooka on top of that, light thirty machine gun hanging down across his waist, looked like a science-fiction cartoon. He gave Gomez a wry grin.

"Okay, Doctor. You take Mutt and Jeff and the friggin' radio with you. Head for the Vineyards and hole up. The rest of us will head for the Stockyards. Send one man to Cross Roads Blue for a meet tomorrow night, 2100 hours. We'll see how many of us made it. Shove off!"

Gomez starting off without a word. Down the sparse slope to the left. Heading for the deep woods below in the valley. Leaning back to keep from falling. His short, thick legs leading. Skipping, hopping, sliding. Almost, but not quite, a full run. Denbeaux and I right behind him. Skiers without skis. Skimming down the surface. Feet sliding. Four or five quick jumping steps and sliding again.

Christ! If I fall with this load, I'll break every bone in my body. Keep going. Don't stop.

The trees starting to get closer together again, getting bigger. The ground not quite so steep as we descended into the woods. A much more gradual slope. Staying right behind Denbeaux. Both of us behind Gomez.

We wound our way down toward an open field below. The steady trot took its toll, our chests heaving, permitting no small talk. Uniforms already soaked. Boots landing heavily on the uneven ground.

Just keep laying them down. Stay with Denbeaux. The backs of his legs a blur out to my front. Don't lose them, for chrissakes!

My hands were up beside my ears, my fingers gripping the carrying straps of the radio that was riding on top of my rucksack. Its weight was braced against the back of my head and neck. From time to time when I slipped, my M-3 greasegun would swing out, and slap back hard against my stomach. Shit! I just know if I fall forward that sonafabitch is going to take out my appendix. I just know it!

The ground leveling off at last. We stopped after nearly forty minutes without a break. Standing there at the edge of a big field, about two hundred yards across. Leaning forward. Pulling in great gulps of air. Letting go with one hand at a time to flex my fingers. Swinging each arm, trying to get feeling into it. The three of us blowing like horses.

I was about to suggest that we drop our gear for a breather, but Gomez spoke first. Getting the words out between gasps and jerking his head back in the direction we'd come.

"The 82nd is right behind us. They've only got rifles, no packs. They're over the top of that hill by now, but they gotta stop to poke the bushes. Make sure we ain't holed up back there."

We took that in. "If they spot us, there ain't no way in hell we'll ever outrun 'em. Not with this gear. We got to get across that field and into the woods before they get down here."

Denbeaux and I both nodded, too tired to talk.

"Don't wait for nobody," Hector urged. "No sense in all of us getting caught. Spread out. Run if you can!"

We took off. Into the open field. Denbeaux and Gomez both out ahead of me, pulling away. I just couldn't go any faster.

Leaning into the harness. A steady trot. The ground pounding by under me. Blinking to see. Almost stumbling over bushes. Pushing my head up now and then to make myself look ahead and correct my direction. I had to slow to a walk in the middle, my legs trembling from the strain. Realizing that if I fell, it would be all over.

I spotted Gomez, off to my left, about twenty yards ahead. He was also walking, bent forward as though into a stiff wind. Denbeaux, that long-legged bastard, was out in front of him!

Keep going. Put them down. Jee-sus!

The woods only about fifty yards away. Christ, I'm almost there.

I could feel a tingling at the back of my neck. Where is the 82nd? Can they see us? Can they see *me*?

Three or four deep breaths and I begin to trot again. Got to get there. Into those woods. Out of sight. Bushes now. A tree. Then lots of scrubby bushes. Skirt them. More trees. A lot of trees. Keep going. Oh, baby! Into the goddamn woods!

Denbeaux ahead and waiting. Flagging me down. His gear on the ground beside him. Gomez there, too. Bent over with his hands on his knees, gasping. Moaning.

Stopping beside them. Dropping to my knees. Letting go the gear with one hand. And rolling slowly, falling so that I landed with my back against the rucksack. My trembling legs kicked out in front of me. I was almost crying, it hurt so badly just to breathe.

Gomez was flat on his back, spread-eagled. His fire hydrant body going up and down like a bellows. Opening my eyes, I didn't see Denbeaux, but his gear was dumped on the grass a few feet away.

Without warning, Gomez rolled in one fluid movement up onto his feet, trotting back the way we had come. Startled, I pushed myself up to follow him.

Denbeaux was kneeling behind the bushes. Gomez and I crept up behind him, keeping low, until all three of us were kneeling, looking back across the field. We followed Bill's pointing finger, and saw two, tiny figures walking along at the edge of the distant tree line, steel pots glistening on their heads.

Denbeaux let the words out three or four at a time, still out of breath. "They just came out...while I've been watching. They can't have seen us. They would've sounded the alarm...for sure. They'd be headed over here...right now...on a dead run."

Gomez grinned. "Those bastards. They can't believe we could be this far ahead of them. They think they missed us. Think we're still up in those woods. Look! There come some more now! Over there. See! They're all poking the bushes."

As we watched, the aggressors fanned out along the tree line and along the edge of the field, forming a long line, about ten yards between each man. We watched them turn and start back up the rise, swinging the stocks of their rifles viciously at the bushes as they went.

Balls! We must have just made it out of sight.

Gomez nodded in the direction of our gear. "C'mon. Keep low. One at a time. Keep those bushes between them and us. Don't let 'em spot us now, for chrissake!"

Our rucksacks and the radio gear were soaked with our perspiration. Boy did I hate the thought of saddling up all that crap again.

I'd been in this area two days earlier with Hadley, so I knew where we were. I knew this belt of trees ran along for about eight miles, following the valley to the river. This was the stretch we had dubbed "The Vineyard." Bushes taller than a man and clusters of pine trees so thick that when you crawled in under them they would block out the sun at high noon. We knew that once we got a couple of miles into these woods the aggressors would never be able to find us.

Gomez smiled again. "Let's go, mules! Let's do it! Thirty minutes. That's all we'll need. Then we can hole up. I just hope the rest of our guys got half so lucky!"

CHAPTER TWENTY-SIX

It had been dark for an hour. Gomez and I, lying under a thick stand of bushes at the top of a rise, had been listening to their uphill approach for some time.

We were expecting Denbeaux, but we could tell that at least two men were working their way toward us. Their flashlights flicked quickly on and off as they checked a compass point or landmark.

They were still about thirty yards away when we heard Denbeaux's low call. "Hey, Gomez! Fitz! Wake up, you bozos! Allee allee infree, for chrissake!"

Gomez chuckled, slapped me on the knee and we moved out into the open. "Hey, Denbeaux! Over here. Who you got with you anyways? You capture the 82nd CO or something?"

Gomez picked them up with the beam of his flashlight. Denbeaux and Dubois. Dubois carrying a full rucksack, Denbeaux carrying the rest of Dubois's gear. Bill had only taken a sidearm for the meet at Cross Roads Blue.

"No one knew what to do with this friggin' froggie, so they dumped him on us. We're supposed to keep him out of trouble for a few days, and in return he's supposed to shine our boots and cook our meals."

"But of course, Denbeaux! You collect zee cow biscuits and I weel cook your fay-vor-eet deesh for you. Dung L'Orange."

Denbeux and Dubois taking turns then to fill us in on the details of how the rest of the team had fared. No one had been caught, but if it hadn't been for Colte, Barnes would have been grabbed for sure. Because of his insistence on setting himself up like he'd booked into the Ritz, the good major had been forced to leave half his stuff behind.

Just beautiful. His goddamn hammock! His shaving mirror. The rest of his hoard of shrimp, crabmeat and smoked oysters. That he had been eating each night before dinner, by the way, without offering a smell to anyone else on the team. Lost them all! You can bet that the good old boys of the 82nd peed themselves when they grabbed those goodies.

"But wait," Denbeaux said. "You want the best part? He also lost his .45."

I strained to see Bill's expression in the dark. Was he bullshitting us?

"It's the truth. Dumb bastard had set it down loose somewhere and in the rush to take off, he left it behind. They'd goddamn well court-martial one of us for that."

A sound like a leaky tire being blown up by an asthmatic. Gomez laughing. "Oh, Jesus. His *hammock*. All his friggin' snacks. *And* his .45. Cut it out, you guys! You're just trying to cheer me up!"

Dubois spat on the ground. "Oh, eet ees true alright. But now zat fat walrus, he wants uz to go back and find heez sheet for heem. Eh? 'Ow you like zat, Gomez? What zee 82nd might have meesed, he wants us to go back and find for heem. Instead of Feetz and Denbeux sneaking back alone to get zee antenna, he wants Green,

Teelton and me to go back, too! Lookeen for *heez* merde!"

Bill and Francois filled us in on other details.

It was the radio messages that had T-boned us, but we already knew that. Barnes just wouldn't listen when we had tried to tell him that we were supposed to keep the messages short. What we didn't know was how Colte and Connelly had saved our asses. One look at the messages Barnes insisted on sending, and on their own they decided to take turns keeping watch more than a mile below camp whenever we went on the air. Watching the roads and lowlands with binoculars. It was only because of that early warning system that the team was able to get out of camp at all.

Connelly had taken off to warn us the second he spotted the first truck with its radio direction-finder on the roof, snaking its way through the valley toward us with four troop trucks right on its tail. He knew they'd make their fix before we finished.

Once the rest of us were packing furiously, Colte had sprinted down to the creek to find Barnes. Bill told us that when Colte got there our peerless leader was sitting bollicky, bare-ass naked in the middle of the creek, puffing contentedly on his pipe.

By the time Barnes grabbed his shorts and made it back to camp, he was already in trouble. Colte, his own gear already packed, hustled to get the rest of the guys out of camp while Barnes dashed about trying to dress and pack at the same time.

We had already caught hell from Colte a couple of times if we left anything unpacked that was not in actual use, but the major had his gear spread out like he was running a yard sale. When Barnes began fumbling with the hammock, Colte finally stepped in.

"Leave it, Major! By the time you get that sonafabitch down, much less rolled up, those whores'll be up here! With all respect, Sir, we've got to haul ass *now!*"

Barnes, his face already red from his exertions, exploded. "*Leave* it! Leave the hammock! Don't be ridiculous."

Furiously, he had continued to tug at the knots, but then they both heard it. The crashing sounds of men in the woods below the camp. Still some distance away, but a lot of men and coming fast.

Apparently, Bill said, the sickening realization must have hit Barnes that he had a lot more to worry about than his beloved hammock. Belatedly, he made a rush for his rucksack and carbine.

With Colte leading and Barnes in his wake, they had raced out of camp.

Hector said it for all of us. "No way could Barnes outrun them eighty deuce guys up that hill. *Noooo* way!"

Dubois and Bill laughing. "Fucking Gunnar is one smart bastard, let me tell you," Bill said. "He had already picked out a hidey-hole for just such an emergency. One of those big thorny bushes you couldn't push a hand into. Gunnar cut a path in right under it, just wide enough for a man to crawl in. Ran it right in to the core, too. We could have got four guys in there if we had to. He left enough brush right there next to it so you could pull it in behind you and block the opening. Got rid of the other branches."

I said it before I could stop myself. "He cut a hole in a *bush*! Just in case?"

Everyone laughing. "Yep. Ran the major over there and shoved him in first. Got behind and pushed, with Barnes yelping as he cut the shit out of himself on thorns. But they made it in, pulled the stuff into the opening behind them and stayed there."

Gomez chuckling. "Shit Almighty! I can see Gunnar shoving Barnes right through that shit. That hurt, Major? Good, how about this? Man, wasn't for Gunnar, we'd of never lived that down. Our CO caught right in his base camp, for chrissakes!"

Gomez summed it up. "Barnes! They oughta send that sonofabitch back to England. Maybe then we'd have half a chance, do some good on this problem."

Dubois gave me a poke. "Eef zat fat bastard had kept heez precious hammock and the rest of his sheet packed up, Feetz, zee 82nd, zey would 'ave got zeep, yes!"

Denbeaux, laughing. "*Zeep*, huh! Jesus, I'd sure hate to see them get that. What is this zeep, Francois? Some kind of French social disease?"

All of us laughing, but all of us still pissed, too.

We knew the 82nd was no doubt already having a field day waving that goddamn hammock around, not to mention the rest of the shit Barnes left behind. Not to mention his .45. We also knew that the other Special Forces teams were going to have a circus with all of us once those little tidbits got around. Balls!

****

It was after midnight when Denbeaux, Dubois and I met up with Green and Hadley. The five of us heading back to our old camp area.

A bright, starry moonlit night. A couple of empty rucksacks with us. Hoping! Hoping that just, maybe, they might have missed the .45.

Single file and well spread out, we picked our way through the woods. Separating at the top of our old hill, Denbeaux and I peeled off to try and find the antenna, if it was still there, the others heading down to our old camp. Bill and I moving carefully, quietly, stopping to listen. Not a whisper of any one else around.

It took a little while in the dark, but we found the spot we had used to set up the radio. Was the sonafabitch still up there, or not?

We could identify the two trees, all right. Denbeaux shinnying a few feet up one of them and feeling with his hands. Waving at the empty air. Shit! Climbing a little higher. Flicking his light on and off quickly, once, a cloth over the front, the dull glow disappearing as fast as it came on. But it was enough.

"It's here! It's here, alright. They never saw it, Fitz! We're in business!"

Both of us really excited. I made my way to the other tree and scooted upwards. Bill got his end loose first and I could feel the weight of the copper wire pulling down as I finally got mine free. Bill hanging on to the other end as I used the spool and walked toward him, winding up our wire. Beautiful. Antenna recaptured. We moved cautiously to rejoin the others.

More than an hour at our old camp, with the five of us on our hands and knees searching the whole area where Barnes had set up his hammock. Hooded flashlights close to the ground. Using sticks to scrape around and under the bushes. To turn over the loose brush and leaves. Green beside me, waving his stick. A whisper. "If Barnes thinks I'm reaching *my* hand under a bush, shake hands with some snake, he's crazier than I thought."

Poking, scraping, looking. Not a goddamn thing. Not even a baby shrimp.

"Looka here, guys!" It was Hadley! We all circled over to look. He was holding up a tiny leather case. The major's mustache scissors. "Must have dropped it when he was throwing stuff in his rucksack. Well, at least he'll know we looked alright. And in the right place. And, I can tell you this. His goddamn .45 ain't here. No, sir. No how!"

His sterling silver scissors turned out to be the only prize we found. We wondered how Barnes would take the news that, indeed, his .45 had been picked up by the 82nd.

We split up and went back to our area. Gomez was waiting at our camp when Bill, Francois and I dragged in close to dawn. He

231

listened impassively to the results of our search. Then he said, "OK, now. Since the major ain't here with us today, you know that it's my job to take over, do things the way he'd want. So before you guys turn in to grab some shut-eye, I want to see some practicing in your specialties. Practice is the key to this whole friggin' problem. C'mon, chop chop!"

He was out of breath but still laughing when Denbeaux, Dubois and I finally caught up to him and threw him in the bushes. The thorny bushes.

CHAPTER TWENTY-SEVEN

Take a break. Pass it down the line. Fifteen minutes.

Jesus! Swinging the case of radio equipment down from behind my neck to the wet ground. Sitting down heavily on top of it. My rucksack braced against a tree behind me. Using my thumbs to pull the straps away from my bruised and aching shoulders.

Christ, was I tired. All around us the rain poured down, beating its steady tattoo on my helmet, running in rivulets down my poncho. Useless goddamn thing. Drenched anyway. Sweating so much under the rubber cloak that I wondered why I bothered to put it on in the first place.

After a moment, I brought my hands out through the slots and began rubbing them together, flexing the fingers painfully to try to get some circulation going. Across from me, Green ran a meaty thumb slowly along the toes and sides of a boot, bringing it up loaded with mud. He stared at his prize impassively for a second or so, and then flung it into the bushes behind him.

Five hours in this good-for-shit rain. Up and down the goddamn hills. Slipping and sliding in the mud. Working to stay behind the man in front of me, mile after mile.

This was the fifth time the major had changed our team location in nine nights.

Asshole! He doesn't ask Colte or Connelly what they think. Oh, no. Just passes out the orders like he was goddamn MacArthur. *Now*, of course, the dumb shit is convinced the friggin' woods are full of the 82nd and that radio direction finders are behind every hill. Every time we send a two-minute message, he has us saddle up, moves the whole team twenty mother-humping miles.

Jesus! Listen to that thunder. It's raining harder now than when we started. Can't even have a goddamn smoke, for chrissakes. Not when it's coming down like this. Look at friggin' Hadley. Lucky bastard.

As I watched, Coy's hands came out of his poncho, his jack-knife open in one, and a thick, oblong of chewing tobacco in the other. The tobacco looked like a bar of dark, sweet chocolate as he hunched over it, and the truth is it looked goddamn delicious as I sat there dying for a smoke, watching him.

Coy hunched his shoulders a little more to keep the rain from splashing directly on his hands, and went to work with the knife. Slowly, carefully, he sliced into the thick bar. A good-sized wedge separated. He lifted it to his mouth, letting it ride on the blade, under his guiding thumb, the way some people eat apples.

I watched, fascinated, as he popped it home, sliding it over between his molars with his tongue. I could see the bulge in his check as his teeth clamped on it. Leaning back with a sleepy, dreamy expression on his face, Coy began to grind his teeth on the chaw in a slow, circular motion.

The knife and tobacco were still in his hands, but Coy was obviously oblivious now to his surroundings. Head back, soaked boots sticking straight out in front of him, he chewed blissfully. Thoughtfully. A man at peace with the world.

Watching Coy, I felt like Saul blasted from his horse by the biblical bolt of lightning. I felt a sense of overwhelming illumination. It was inconceivable that I had never understood something so glaringly, patently obvious.

See, I had always considered tobacco chewing to be a singularly repulsive habit. With a few childhood memories of spittoons in Dorchester barbershops, chewing tobacco, to me, had always been on a par with pricking blisters on my feet and watching the pus run out. But that, of course was before this moment of revelation.

Tobacco chewing, as I could now see, as any fool could see, was a rare and precious boon, offered to suffering humankind by a gentle and compassionate deity. At that moment, with certainty, I knew I was viewing what had to be one of the greatest pleasures a merciful God could bestow upon his cloddish creations.

The skills required of the artful practitioner were testimony to the value of the undertaking. The plying of the knife. The lifting off of the "just right" wedge. Its balanced ride to the mouth. The solid, chewy morsel gripped in square, manly jaw. The peaceful, contemplative quietude induced. My God, it was magnificent! Marvelous. I just had to try it.

I looked up and found Coy's eyes on me. His jaw continued to grind away in pleasurable cycles, but he had correctly read my fascinated absorption with his labors.

He smiled and winked at me, then turned his head to one side to spit expertly across the narrow trail and into the woods beyond. The small brown missile left his mouth neatly, a pea out of a blowgun. "Hot damn, that's good," he said, and grinned across at me, his jaw still working. Then the knife tapping the top of the delicious-looking bar, he raised a questioning eyebrow at me.

There was the slightest, almost a fleeting pause, before I nodded my assent. I mean, what the hell! If I didn't like it, I could just spit it out.

My mouth was literally watering as Coy's knife dug into the chocolate colored bar, and he lifted the second wedge toward me on his blade. I shoved forward on my knees, mouth open to receive the blessed communion. He dropped the slice on my tongue. "You take keer now,'an don't swallow that juice! Just you chaw on it nice and easy, and spit when you has to, y'hear!"

I shoved back to my sitting position, feeling the smooth, solid lump of tobacco resting against my left cheek, between my molars. I felt it give slightly as I clamped down hard and began imitating Coy's cyclical jawings, surprised at the toughness of the chaw. Trying to look relaxed as I grinned back at Coy and began to work in earnest.

The first thing that surprised me was the hardness, but the second thing was the juiciness. As soon as I started to chew, it seemed as though every slight movement of my jaw caused an immediate flood. I had a mouthful of the stuff in seconds. Kind of foul tasting stuff to tell the truth. And it was all over the place. Under my tongue. Next to my cheek. A mouthful in nothing flat.

No problem. Just spit it out.

The thing is, that was when I remembered something rather important. As a spitter, on a scale of one to ten, I happen to be a minus eight. That's the truth. And the thing is, I *knew* that! I had known it for years! How I had ever forgotten so primary a fact I will simply never understand.

When we had moved back to Dorchester at the end of my first year in high school, I had found myself immersed in the company of expert spitters. It was one of the few things most of the guys who hung round corners in those days ever studied seriously. They had been practicing and developing the art for years. As spitters, those guys were non-pareils. They could hit a fly in the air. They could let loose long floaters that sailed away spreading disease and pestilence for miles. They could spit small round pellets through a keyhole without wetting the door.

To my everlasting chagrin, it was an art I simply couldn't master, despite hours of lonely practice at the end of subway platforms and on the three-decker back porches in the dark of evening. All I ever got for my trouble was a wet chin and soggy goobers on my shirtfront.

The memories of my many early failures came back to me with a rush as I sat there in the mud on that rainy, godforsaken day in the hills of North Carolina. With a mouthful of poison tar and a suddenly worried expression on my face.

I leaned forward and splashed a great sea of the vicious liquid out of my mouth in the poorest imitation of a spit anyone has ever seen, groaning as it ran down my chin and splashed across the front of my poncho.

Coy's explosion of laughter came just as I heard the words "saddle up" barked from somewhere up in front of me.

I had already decided to spit out the chaw as soon as I could turn my back on Coy long enough to do so discreetly. Somehow, I didn't quite make it to that point. Even though only a second or so had passed since I had loosed the previous river of brown effluvia down the front of my poncho, I found that my mouth was already full again.

Somewhere between shoving forward to stand and turning my head to try to spit out the sonofabitching thing, an awful realization hit me. I became aware that a great gulp of that elephant-killing liquid had somehow slid to the back of my mouth and was just beyond the point of no return.

Too late! The foul globule dropped with a devastating rush straight down into my stomach. The precise feelings generated when that organ greeted the unfamiliar visitor are hard to describe. One who had inadvertently stumbled into an uncovered cesspool might have an inkling. If he had stayed to drink!

I do know that my stomach leaped to repel the wretched invader, and very successfully sent it and the rest of its unsorted contents rocketing right back up the tube with a force that has permanently widened my esophageal passages.

The next three or four minutes are mercifully lost to me, which is just as well. I do recall at some point being aware that I was on my hands and knees in the mud with several of my team members watching with great interest. I do recall Coy laughing and laughing. I recall heaving and retching as wave after wave of otherwise nutritious foodstuffs vacated my bodily premises, apparently not liking the company I had suggested they keep.

Jesus, was I sick!

The next hour or so, as we made our way to the end of that evening's journey became a personal nightmare. Some good soul picked up the extra radio gear for me, and I know someone else took my grease gun.

I staggered along the trail with the rucksack on my back, a drunken Quasimodo without benefit of a bell rope to hang on to. I couldn't get the ghastly taste out of my mouth. Every now and then I'd drop off by the side of the trail and make another small contribution to the replenishment of the local topsoil, but the poisonous juices simply refused to disappear.

When at long last we stopped, most of the team, despite the wet ground, lay down with their backs against their rucksacks to try to catch some sleep. Still nauseous and light-headed, I slipped off my rucksack and lay down, too, flat on my back, feeling the rain on my face. I did not intend to sleep. I was just waiting for a little strength to return so I could get up and get out my entrenching tool. So I could open it up and fix the shovel end in the axe position. So I could crawl over to where Coy Hadley was already sleeping and cut out his tobacco-blackened heart. With just such pleasant and inspiring thoughts did I drift off that night into soul-replenishing sleep.

To this day, I might add, just the sight of some country bumpkin strolling out to the pitcher's mound with a tobacco-filled cheek is enough to make me retch. That sight alone would cause me to walk out of a World Series game in the last of the ninth with the bases loaded. *Sorry about this folks. An old army injury kicking up. I'll be in the bar across the street having a double scotch. Neat.*

CHAPTER TWENTY-EIGHT

The start of the Free Legion problem had been just short of a disaster for our team. Almost captured in our own team area. The 82nd running around in triumph waving the major's abandoned booty overhead like Julius Caesar returning from Gaul. This wasn't good. For one thing, it's never good to encourage those bastards.

The aftermath, especially the affect on team morale, was palpable.

The turnaround for us came during the fourth week. That was the night we had to abort a supply drop from Bragg because of aggressor activity near the DZ just as the plane arrived. It was also the night we lost Barnes.

Well, we didn't really lose him. I mean we knew where he was. We all knew that.

It's strange how a small disaster can completely dissipate the dark, all-enveloping cloud left by a larger one. Our team renaissance began with another small disaster. For three nights in a row we had been trying to set up a badly needed supply drop. Rations were very short and we also needed special equipment to perform certain tasks assigned by Base to our team. It was essential that we arrange and complete a successful airdrop.

Each night at dusk, four of us would set out on the three-hour trek across our sector to the field we had picked out as a DZ. The coordinates, alternate dates, drop times and code checks for the three nights had been radioed to Base earlier and passed to the flyboys, but we had those three nights to pull it off or we had to start all over again.

The first night, in intermittent rain and clouds, the plane had found the general area, but we couldn't bring it home. Once or twice we heard it circling way off in the distance, flying low and looking for us, but we couldn't raise them on the radio.

The second night, about half an hour before we got to the DZ, it started to rain really hard. By radio contact time, we were sloshing around in mud, with thunder crashing and lightning turning night into day every couple of minutes. We got the plane on the radio this time, but after one low pass, playing tag with crosswinds and downdrafts and rain flooding in their open door, the gods who fly big bird in sky said bye-bye and headed home, leaving us to pack up and slog all the way back to camp, empty-handed again.

Bill and I, as the radio operators, had to be there every time. The others, at least, could rotate the nightly journey. Barnes, however, did not slack off on the daytime tasks assigned to Bill and me. He expected us to carry our full share of the intelligence activities of the team. At that point in the problem, that was basically how we were spending our days.

Information gathering was an obsession with Barnes. His daily comments were full of references to the brilliance of the final report he intended to file with Base. Out we all went, usually starting before dawn, to our widely scattered observation posts, to positions that changed daily. From these we were to observe, note, photograph and document copiously much more than the comings and goings of the 82nd and their law enforcement cohorts. Rather, as the major made eminently clear, it was our specific job to describe in detail every structure in our sector, and to document the travel path of every single moving thing that passed through the area. *Thus spake Barnesthustra.*

As the days dragged by, rebelling no doubt against tramping all night and alertly observing all day, I confess that more than one imaginary truckload of oddments made its way into my reports. "But that's what the lettering *said*, Major. 'Irish pig's knuckles.'"

No one escaped this onerous duty, except for the good major himself, of course. Our leader, by choice, never left our camp in the deep woods. What he did all day we do not know, but in the late afternoon as we filtered back, he was always at work on his final opus, which grew thicker by the day. He was chagrined, of course, that he could only send nuggets of his accumulated wisdom to base by radio, since all his messages now were kept under two minutes, which he made us dry run for him while he timed us.

We tried to explain, with Colte's backing, that given the remoteness of our present location, and its steep, uphill woodsiness, he could safely send messages of up to four or five minutes with no danger. Five minutes or less would simply not allow the aggressors to pick up the transmission, zero in, get a fix on our position, *and* get their troops to us, but Barnes dismissed such reasoning, waving a meaty finger under out noses and replying, "Get me caught once, shame on *you*. Get me caught twice, shame on *me*."

Colte also suggested that letting us observe in pairs, so one could sleep while the other watched made sense, but Barnes would have none of that. *Four* reports a day instead of eight! Unthinkable.

Connelly summed up my feelings on the sector-encyclopedia the major was hell-bent on writing. "He figures they see his report at Base at the end of the problem, they'll forget about his minor derelictions. Like leaving his .45 under a goddamn bush."

The major had not been a happy man since our "run for your lives" frolic. An unattractive stammer began to intrude into his speech. I think he even suspected that some of us might be laughing at him behind his back. Pure paranoia. We all admired him something fierce. When a sleeping bag was included in an earlier supply drop to replace his lost hammock, it wasn't us who pinned the note to it. The one that read, "For Major Barnes. Do not use during training classes."

It was after our second unsuccessful attempt to induce the great silver eagle to shit that a clearly irate Barnes marched over to where Bill and I had just sat down upon our return to camp. With the whole team looking on, he stood over us. "This won't do," he snapped. "It simply will not *do*."

Bill and I got to our feet, not at attention exactly, but not at ease either. We were kind of stunned to find ourselves the object of his wrath after working our butts off all night. "If you men don't have the training to do the job properly, you shouldn't be out here. It's a simple task. Get on

244

the radio, get on the right frequency, contact the plane and direct it to the DZ we've selected. It's a clear text operation. It's *voice!* It's not even in code."

Connelly, who as it happened had made both trips, was on his feet and beside us before the major had finished. "It was not the radio operators' fault," he interjected with some heat, leaving off the "sir," as we all noticed.

Pat took a breath and continued. "We had one hell of a thunderstorm over there tonight, Major, in case you hadn't noticed, *Sir.* And these guys still made contact. They had the plane, loud and clear. But with the rain, which was torrential by the way, you couldn't see crap out there. It was the pilots who pulled out and left." A pause. "*Sir.*"

No one can pause before "Sir" like a senior non-com with a burr up his ass.

Colte, although I hadn't seen him coming over, was standing beside Connelly and he spoke before Barnes could respond. "You know, Major, I have a thought."

That got the attention of the whole team. He damn sure had mine. "Maybe it would help, *Sir*, if you went along for tonight's drop yourself. You know, to get a first hand look at what we're up against. See, that way, you could give us all the benefit of your superior experience. *Sir.*"

The major got the pause, and the intonation, too, no question. He stared at Colte, his face flushing. But, again, before Barnes could speak, before he could utter the refusal we were all sure was on the tip of his tongue, Colte added, sticking it in up to the hilt and giving it a nice half-turn. "You do understand what I'm suggesting, Major? I mean like actually *leave* the camp yourself, Sir. Actually go out with the men, Sir. Personally."

The major's head had tipped so far back on his neck that one of his chins disappeared. A long pause while he looked down the length of his nose at Colte. The suggestion lying out there in front of all of us like pigeon shit on a blue suit.

Three or four seconds on the clock. Your move, Major!

False start, then bluster, then the major got it out, the stammer back and very marked. "Wh-why, of course! Of *course!* Ca-capital idea. J-just what I-I was about to, uh, sug-ge-gest myself!"

Ivory appearing under the caterpillar. The major shaking his fist in the air. "Absolutely! Time to t-t-take the reins, g-get the d-ducks in a row, r-r-rally the troops."

The mustache was going in and out on his upper lip six to the dozen. His eyes, though, were unable to conceal his fury as they darted around the half circle of men. The major rocking on his toes in the silence. I could see that the concept that it really was his idea in the first place was growing on him. *I dare you to say nay!*

Only a few hours of sleep, a quick supper of C-ration beef stew and three of those crackers that you could use to jack up a truck, and it was time to saddle up and tiptoe off to meet the flyboys. Five of us going this time. Four plus Barnes.

We made the trip without incident, Connelly in the lead and, maybe, I couldn't swear to it, finding two or three extra hills to climb just for the major's edification. The darkness didn't help our progress either. The cloudiness had remained, and the night had brought with it that near blackness you sometimes got in those hills.

We plodded along, Connelly, then Green, then Barnes, with Bill and me bringing up the rear. We had the radio gear, but except for a few flares and DZ panels used to bring in our manna from heaven, the others all had empty rucksacks. It would be nice if for once we returned with them loaded, even if it did mean the major would attribute this to his special know-how. The footing was still slippery from the heavy rains and if we hadn't made the same trip twice already, it would have taken us even longer.

As it is, we made it to the DZ, a good-sized open pasture with woods on two sides, at about 2300 hours, almost an hour before our scheduled contact time.

Connelly checked out the wind to determine which way he wanted the plane to come in, so they could drop the bundle into the wind and we wouldn't have to run eight miles chasing our goodies. Bill and I set up the radio near the edge of the field, but far enough out in the open so that we could get good flashlight contact with the plane once it was in range. Connelly and Green taking the reflector panels and flares well out into the field about forty yards away from us. The major helping. Tap-dancing near the radio and giving us a time-check every fifteen seconds. With twenty minutes to go.

Connelly and Green waited until about ten minutes before the scheduled contact and then laid out the panels with the long base of the "T" pointing across the field in the direction Pat wanted for the drop. Then they placed the flares to light the "T", sticking them in the ground, ready to light as soon as we got the plane in close.

"Remind them to drop the fucker low," Connelly had told us just before he had headed off with Green, testing the wind by dropping a leaf and pointing to it to estimate speed. "Tell them we got a fifteen to twenty mile breeze blowing east to west."

With any wind across your DZ, of course, the lower the drop, the better your chances of keeping the bundle out in the open, out of the trees, and away from large rocks, stumps and other DZ junk that might transform our goodies into a dog's breakfast. Some of the pilots were so good you could practically reach up and touch the superstructure as they zoomed in to shove your stuff out the door. Others were nervous types who wouldn't come in low, and couldn't hit a clear spot if you used the Sahara for a DZ.

It's when the chutes are in the air that the fun starts. The team racing out to douse the flares and roll up the panels, even while the bundle is still coming down above us. Then, as soon as it hits, running to break it open, grab everything and bug out before the aggressors catch us in the open carrying enough weight to cripple a camel.

Now we wait.

CHAPTER TWENTY-NINE

At 2350, Denbeaux and I were leaning over the radio, headphones on, keeping the dull glow of the radio dial lights covered with a light cloth except when Bill had to lift it to sweep the dial. I was on the generator stool, the double-handled crank in front of me. Denbeaux sweeping back and forth across the assigned frequency, both of us listening.

At Denbeaux's nod, I began to crank. Every few seconds, the mike cupped and held right at his mouth, Denbeaux tried for contact. His hushed words seemed loud, the only sound in the darkness. Again and again. "Sky Rider Four, this is Bushel Basket. Do you read me? Over. Sky Rider Four, this is Bushel Basket. Over..."

The time creeping toward 1200 hours, but still nothing.

Barnes, leaning over us now, hands on his knees, his moon face right at Denbeaux's shoulder. Giving us more help. "Try it again, dammit! Are you *sure* you're on the right frequency? You *can't* be on the right frequency! Try it again!"

The blast almost blistered my eardrums when it came. Making me grab for the headset, to pull it away, to ease the pain. Bill's hand shooting out to the dial, turning down the volume as quickly as he could. Both of us hearing the lazy, folksy, country-boy voice coming in. Those beautiful words. "Bushel Basket, this is Sky Rider Four. I have you loud and clear. Do you read me? Do you read me? Over."

While I continued to crank steadily, Denbeaux's softly spoken response, right at the mike. "You are loud and clear, Sky Rider Four. Can you give us your present position? Where are you now, Sky Rider Four? Over."

Barnes, beside us, was hopping from foot to foot like a kid about to pee himself. "I can hear it!" he bellowed. "I can hear the plane! Bring it in! Bring it in!"

Flicking on his flashlight, Barnes ran a few steps toward the middle of the field, waving the beam above his head from left to right as he shouted toward Connelly and Green. "We've got it! We've got the plane! Light the flares! Light the flares!"

Connelly, coming on a dead run out of the inky dark, almost slammed into us, jumping at the last moment and just clearing the generator, and banging head-on into the startled major who was running back to us. "Turn off that fucking flashlight! Those are goddamn trucks you hear, Major! Trucks!"

Trucks! Jesus!

Headlights! Coming toward us. Weaving downhill through the trees on the old dirt road that came over those hills. Less than half a mile away. Coming fast!

I continued to crank furiously as Denbeaux cracked out the warning, throwing gear into our radio bag with his other hand at the same time. "ABORT! Sky Rider, this is an ABORT! Do *not* drop, Sky Rider. Do *not* drop. Do *not* drop! Over and out."

Leaping off the generator stool as though it were electrified, I pulled the handles off the motor and threw it in its pack, collapsing the seat as Connelly and Bill threw the rest of the equipment into the two cases. We had them on our shoulders in record time.

Barnes already off and running. "This way," we heard him yelp. "This way!"

He took off on a dead run toward the middle of the open field, heading for the woods on the other side. Toward the woods a long way across on the other side.

"Shit," Connelly snarled. "Alright, follow him. Move!"

The three of us running after Barnes and looking for Green, out there somewhere.

A figure looming up ahead of us. Green, his rucksack full of panels and flares, was now galloping after Barnes.

The roar of truck motors to our rear, getting louder by the second. Barnes, Connelly, Denbeaux and Green all in front of me. Their longer legs eating up the turf. Disappearing into the gloom. Out of sight. Pisser! Running faster.

A heavy figure ahead and to my right. The major. I'm gaining on him. He is thudding along, blowing hard, as I came up beside him. I don't even look at him as I pass, but I hear him dropping further behind me as I run on.

Can't hear the others in front of me. Bushes! Chest high. *Slow down*. Watch it now! Stumps, too. Don't trip for God's sake!

"Over here! Over here!" Connelly's voice ahead of me, low but carrying. I change direction and head for it. More bushes, closer together. "Down!" Pat orders, and I see his darker bulk ahead, next to the dark blob of a bush. "Get down. Hit the ground."

Making a baseball slide under a sizable bush next to his, dragging the bag of radio equipment behind me, my rucksack keeping me upright in a sitting position.

Rolling onto my stomach. Heart thumping. Chest heaving. Again I hear Connelly's "Down! Down!" The major thuds past and crashes chest-first into a heavy bush a few feet beyond mine. Then he, too, drops to the ground and rolls in against it.

Christ! How far had we run? Well over a hundred yards. Closer to two. But we're still only about halfway across the open space. I picture this pasture as I saw it once in the daytime. Remembering fences, gullies, small hills and wooded patches pock-marking the long open space, but not a clue as I lie there in the dark as to where any of that shit might be. Sucking air into my lungs in great gulps, then peering back into the dark like the others, trying to listen. Are they there yet? Are they in this field?

I hear them now alright. And I see the headlights. Two trucks grinding to a halt, braking and skidding where the dirt road meets the edge of the pasture. At the end of the field we had just come from. Two searchlights shoot out toward us, playing across the open space, over the deep grass, seeking out bushes, stumps and the rotting remains of fallen trees. These objects jumping into the lighted circles and disappearing as the beam moves on. Good thing we had all blacked our faces with burnt cork before we got to the pasture. Damn glad for it now although I hated the ashy smell of the stuff.

Belligerent voices at the other end shouting directions.

"Hold the light there! What's *that?* Aw, shit! Friggin' stump. Nothing."

The voices thin above the deeper throb of idling truck engines, but carrying clearly to us. All of us flattened on the ground, pushed in at the base of a bush, as the search light beams move along, move apart, meet, join and separate again.

One voice, higher than the others, floating out to us, causing my stomach muscles to tighten. "But, *Lieutenant*, they *must* be here somewheres. We *seen* the light. I seen it. *Some*body was here!"

A general babble. The truck motors churning unevenly, sounding annoyed.

Connelly, slithering on elbows and knees to the major. In a voice so low I could just hear the words. "We've still got too much open ground between us and the deep woods, Major. If they decide to run one of them trucks past us, we got no chance. They'll be on us like crabs in a whore house."

I heard the major grunt. His breathing was still so loud I was afraid they'd hear it across the field. "We gotta bug out right now, Major," Pat said. "Go for the woods."

Even in the dark I could see Barnes, lying on his stomach, his head going up and down as he nodded his agreement.

Connelly, in the same low voice I had to strain to hear. "When I tell you to go, you take off one at a time and go for those woods. Green first, then Fitz, then the major, then Denbeaux and I. With our long legs, we'll catch you guys in the woods. Keep low."

All of us getting in position to come up running. "Whoever makes it, head for Horse Biscuit Hill. We'll meet up there. OK, Green! Take off!"

Green rolled up on his feet and was off. I rolled onto my knees, starting to hike the radio equipment bag back onto my shoulders, but Connelly's hand shot out and he grabbed it. "Gimme that, Runt! Now take off!"

I was up and running in a crouch, out of the heavy brush and into the open rolling pasture on the other side, trying to keep the bushes between me and the corner of the field where the trucks were pulled up. Despite the dark, I was really picking up speed. Without that half-ton sack of radio equipment, I felt like I could do sixty miles an hour.

Dark as hell! No sign of Green. Where *are* those goddamn woods?

Jesus, keep going straight, whatever you do, don't get turned around. A few small bushes. One fair-sized tree. Christ, it seems like I've run miles! A denser darkness straight ahead. A horizontal line of heavy blackness getting taller as

I ran toward it. The woods! Oh, beautiful. Maybe thirty yards ahead.

On the ground! Right in front of me. A thick black stripe of some kind. Asphalt? A road? What the hell? Braking down to a trot, and then skidding to a halt. Jesus! Just in time.

A goddamn ditch!

It ran off on both sides as far as I could see in the darkness. At least three or four feet across, and I couldn't tell how deep, but an easy jump.

I backed off a few steps, then a quick run and I was across. Running full out now for the tree line. The heavenly smell of damp pine needles greeting me.

Lots of tall trees in front of me. Nice full branches, thick with leaves and pine needles. Oh, baby! I made it.

"Fitz! Over here." It was Green, a low whisper.

I trotted over to where he was kneeling and dropped down beside him, pulling in two or three big breaths. Not even winded, though. Not without that sack to haul. Both of us looking back in the direction we'd come from.

Green, beside me. "How about that sneaky goddamn ditch? Sonafabitch almost aced me good. I thought it was a friggin' path!"

Laughing nervously, but just then we both heard it. A man running. A big man from the sound of it. Off to our left somewhere, not yet in view. Definitely a big man.

"There he is!" I pointed across Green's shoulder. A huge figure, legs pumping. "Jesus, is he over that ditch yet?"

Green cupped his hands to his mouth, trying to call a warning without being heard across the field. "Watch it, Major! Watch the ditch!"

Gone! The great black blob was there one moment, sailing toward us out of the darkness. Then, just as suddenly, it was gone.

For one long, long second, nothing.

Then KA-BLAM! KER-PLOSH!!

The second sound, I realized, was that of a geyser of water shooting up out of the irrigation ditch. That first terrible slam had been the major hitting bottom.

Green and I were frozen in place, staring blankly at the sudden emptiness.

The search party, having found nothing but an empty pasture, had been climbing back into their trucks, on the point of departure. Now a renewed tumult broke out and shouts carried to us clearly in the still night air.

We were up and sprinting back toward the ditch, to where we had last seen the figure. At the same instant two more blobs appeared out of the darkness, coming up fast but skittering to a halt on the other side of the ditch just as Green and I got there.

Connelly and Denbeaux.

Pat dropping to one knee and peering down into the pit between us, from which there issued the unmistakable sounds of a water buffalo giving birth.

The trucks were roaring to life, their wheels skidding on the gravel, and behind Denbeaux and Connelly searchlights again flared, reaching toward us across the field.

Dropping to his stomach, Connelly stretched an arm down into the ditch and flicked on his own flashlight. The trench was eight feet deep, give or take, with about a foot of water in the bottom.

The major was sitting there. Leaning against the side, the water barely covering his hips. Blinking up at us. He was moaning, but his face did not reflect pain. Instead, it held a surprised, almost bemused expression.

One of the major's legs was straight out in front of him. The other, however, was somewhere under him, and under the water, except that we could see the heel of that boot poking up at an odd angle near his hip. Not good. Not good at all.

The trucks were in the field now, a siren howling, the clang of metal getting louder as they bounced across the ruts and gullies.

It was the major who broke the silence.

Staring straight ahead, almost as though talking to himself. "Heard it snap, you know? The leg. Oh, yes, yes. A clean, sharp break. Oh, my, yes, yes."

He then began making clucking noises with his tongue. The kind that used to be spelled "Tch! Tch!" in the Joe Palooka comic strips. He alternated between clucks and moans, as though expressing his sympathy to the twisted limb.

Connelly flicked off the light and stood up. "Let's go," he growled. "All of you. Into those woods and keep going. Don't stop no matter what. Take off, you bastards!"

Behind Connelly and Denbeaux I could see the headlights of two trucks wheeling and bouncing hard as they came toward us. They couldn't speed on that uneven ground, but they were not wasting any time.

None of us moved. Denbeaux said it. "You just going to *leave* him here?"

Connelly spun on Denbeaux. "You got a block and tackle in your rucksack, Asshole? Get your ass moving, right now! MOVE!"

Denbeaux jumped the ditch and the three of us took off, running all out again. At the tree line we stopped to look back. Connelly had flicked on his flashlight and set it down on the ground, right beside the ditch above where the major lay, pointing the beam toward the oncoming trucks. As soon as one of the trucks changed direction and headed toward the light, Connelly leaped the ditch and came running after us like a gazelle.

I ran through those woods like my pants were on fire, my weapon up to ward off small branches, ducking under big ones, going uphill until my lungs were bursting and then racing down the other side in great leaps and bounds. I could hear but not see Connelly as he caught up and passed me, some distance off to my side. He passed me before I was a quarter of the way up the first steep hill after we entered the woods.

Trotting, walking, loping down hills, plodding up others, it took me a good two hours to make my way to the top of what the team had dubbed "Horse Biscuit Hill." I had not seen or heard anything of our pursuers, thank God, and only the occasional stumble or muttered swear from what I felt sure was one of my team members, moving in the same direction some distance away. I could hear one lone figure from time to time a little behind me

The clouds finally opened a little and a sliver of moon and a few stars were now visible.

"Pull up a stump, Shorty. You seen Green?" A voice out of the dark, no warning.

Jesus! Connelly. It's hard to talk while you're having an acute myocardial infarction, but I managed some kind of answer as soon as I had pulled the most important parts of my body back together. He and Denbeaux had been sitting quietly, watching me make my way uphill for the last five minutes.

I dropped down beside them. "I'm pretty sure I heard Green just a little behind me," I told them. And I was right.

After Green arrived the four of us sat there, smoking, taking a breather.

"We had deep woods right behind us," Connelly said after awhile. "A fucking jungle thirty yards from where we were set up. It's pitch dark. You can't even see your fly, you need to piss. We separate, spread out, run in them woods and sit still. That's all we had to do. Fuckers show up by that pasture in trucks, woods running on forever, they couldn't find us if they looked for five hours. But *he* takes off across four hundred yards of open field. Whyn't he wear white ducks and ring a fucking bell, while he was at it?"

No one had anything to add to that. Especially me. I was thinking, *Shit, that was where I had planned to run anyway!*

After awhile, Denbeaux broke the silence. "I wonder if they've gotten Barnes out of there by now? It must have taken some hauling and shoving to get a man his size up and out of that ditch. Christ!"

All of us stunned when Connelly murmured: "Wendell Fucking Barnes! Remember that name, men. The luckiest bastard that ever lived. Oh, yeah. He is one lucky sonofabitch, Wendell Barnes."

Bewildered, I tried to see his face, but it was too dark to read his expression, especially with the burnt-cork browning out everything but his eyes. Green spoke first. "*Lucky?* How do you figure lucky, Sarge? That poor bastard broke *one* leg, I know of. And maybe his hip, too, for all we know. And you call that lucky?"

Connelly stood up and looked down at us. Even in the dark his eyes glistened with fire. "You're goddamn right I do," he answered. "Think about it. If this had been a real problem, I'd have been required to shoot the prick!"

260

CHAPTER THIRTY

Colte was waiting for us outside the empty barracks. Everyone else had already taken off for morning classes or for other training assignments, but our team had been given the word at morning report. Stay put. Fall out at 0900 hours in the company square to greet our new team leader. Captain Roger Rozzelli.

"What's a Roger Rozzelli, Gunnar?" Green, asking what we were all wondering.

"He's gotta be Eyetralian," Hector Gomez added. "I don't trust none of these people that didn't come over on the Mayflower, *Senors*."

Personally, I didn't care if he were Hindu as long as he wasn't another Barnes.

"Just so's he don't carry one of them swagger sticks?" Hadley threw in. "I ain't sure I can handle another swagger stick, Gunnar."

Denbeaux, a big grin. "C'mon, Colte! What's the word on this new bird? You can give it to us straight. We've already had Oliver Hardy. Who did we draw this time, Stan Laurel?"

Colte ignoring our questions. "Okay, okay, knock off the bullshit and fall in. TEAM, Ten-Shun! RAAAT--FACE! FO--ERD----HAAR! Double time, HAAR!"

Trotting in single squad formation to the orderly room. Bringing up the rear, I didn't bother to get my hopes up.

In the last two weeks of Free Legion, we'd really come alive. With Colte and Connelly at the helm, we didn't miss a single target or

261

assignment, a reassurance we all needed after Barnes.

Everyone in the Group seemed to know about our fuck-ups with Barnes, but no one gave us a hard time about it. They knew it wasn't our fault.

Hey, Colte! You want I should carry that M-1 out to the range for you today? So's you won't lose it? What do you keep in that pistol holster, anyways? Milk duds?

Hey, Fitz! How come your radio messages were under forty minutes today? You guys losing your nerve?

What do you say, Dubois? Got time for one more beer before you head back to your comfy little sleep hammocks? Oh, right! You lost all them in the woods, didn't you?

Oh, it had been a great two weeks since the end of the problem, all right. A million laughs.

And now we get this Roger Rozzelli. Never heard of him. We couldn't get one of the really good guys, like Beasley, or Scagnelli, or Bucky Walters. *Noooo.* We got to draw someone who wasn't even here for the Free Legion problem. Probably an ROTC officer who made captain in Korea because he was off taking a crap when his outfit got hit.

"Column...raaaattt...HAAAAR!...Teaaaamm ...HALT! Leeffff FACE! Paraaade...REST!"

Colte disappearing inside the small building, then sticking his head out to wave us in the door. "Fall out, men. At ease. Come inside."

We went through the outer room and on into the CO's office. Eight of us, crowding in to stand around the walls.

Captain Rozzelli was sitting on the front edge of the desk, wearing a rumpled sweat suit and sneakers, and drying his face with a towel as we entered. Tall and lanky, he had a lean, muscular build with black, curly hair that was slightly longer than you were used to seeing on an airborne post. His nose had been broken at some point and his eyes had a sleepy, half-lidded look as he watched us filing in. To me, based on a quick glance as I passed, he had the look of a Hollywood star that had been severely beaten by his producers for repeated failures at the box office.

Bringing up the rear as usual, I had to cross right in front of Rozzelli to shove in between Denbeaux and Connelly. When I looked up, Rozzelli's Great Dane eyes were following me. Then he looked at Colte, an eyebrow lifting. "They brought their kids?"

Jesus, don't tell me they actually gave us someone with a sense of humor.

Connelly grabbed me by the back of the neck. "Don't you worry about Ol' Fitz here, Captain. He's a holy terror in the field. Only problem is he has to be home when the streetlights go on."

The meeting itself was brief but it went well. If we expected Rozzelli to give us a rundown on his background and experience, though, we didn't get it. After the initial introductions, we all moved outside to the exercise field in back of the orderly room.

Mostly Rozzelli wanted to know about the Free Legion problem. What we thought of it, and how we had done. Kind of a sticky issue since we had no idea what he had heard about Barnes, but we let Colte and Connelly do the talking.

Connelly opened the Barnes can of worms after a little general talk. "You should know that we screwed up pretty badly one time early on. The 82nd nailed us with their radio direction-finders, almost caught us napping."

Rozzelli, chewing on a blade of grass, took that in. "Stay on the air a little long, did you?" His eyes flicked over to Denbeaux and me.

"Yeah," Colte cut in before we said anything, "but it wasn't the radio operators' fault. They tried to tell us, keep 'em short, but we didn't listen."

"Who's we?" Rozzelli asked. "You and Connelly, or Major Barnes?"

I started to say something, but Connelly slipped me an elbow that re-arranged the ribs on one side of my body, so no one answered that. It just sat there. Then Colte continued. "Water over the damn now, Sir. Point is we were lucky we get our asses out of there. And, we might as well put it all on the table, Captain. We had to leave some gear behind. You'll no doubt get the needle good on that from your fellow officers as soon as they hear you've got this team. Figured you'd better know."

Rozzelli was looking over out heads as we sat in a half-circle on the grass facing him. "What kind of stuff got left?"

"All kinds of crap. A sleeping hammock. Cans of shrimp and oysters and whatnot. But the worst of it, Captain, was a .45."

Connelly added, "Bad enough it got left. Worse, the eighty deuce picked it up."

Rozzelli gave a soft whistle, and we saw the wide toothy grin, which would soon become very familiar. "Shit! A .45. Dare I ask which one of you that belonged to?"

Colte, not looking at any of us. "Not really important, Captain, who left it. We left it. Your team left it, and it shouldn't have happened. Pat and I, we just didn't want you to get blind-sided. Figured you'd better know."

Rozzelli looked around the group. "Anybody else want to give me some kind of clue. Someone leaves a .45. That's kind of important, isn't it?"

None of us said anything. We followed the lead of Gunnar and Pat.

Rozzelli nodded, "Well, I would guess you've all been taking a bit of heat for that one, all right." He reached under his sweatshirt and pulled out several sheets of typed paper and dropped them on the grass in front of us. "They gave me the Group's report on this team, on your performance on the AFFT problem, when they assigned me to you guys, and I was just reading it again when you arrived."

We all stared at the paper. "Most of it's pretty good, as a matter of fact. Turns out, since none of you apparently know, that the .45 returned by the eighty deuce is registered to an officer. By the way, that guy has been transferred out. When he gets out of the hospital, that is. He's going to Maryland, to an army intelligence posting. I must say, though, the guy filed one hell of a report on the team members and on the team sector while he was in the hospital. Never saw anything like it myself. Over fifty pages."

We all looked at Rozzelli. Afraid to look at each other. "In his evaluation of the team," Rozzelli continued, "that unknown officer did name the man who lost the officer's .45, the man who had been given it to clean. But the officer asked that the poor slob not be prosecuted, which I think was damned magnanimous of him."

We stared at each other, thunderstruck. Colte rolling up to one knee, about to speak, but Rozzelli held up a hand. "*That* report, by the way, has been ash-canned. Totally. And there are no copies. None. I was there when Bank himself threw the only copy into his wastebasket. I mean he *threw* it in there. He'd saved it just to show me what you guys had been up against. Now, don't quote me on this, because I don't want to speculate on the actions of my commanding officer, but he was bloody irate, and I had the feeling that as soon as I left he was going to take that basket outside and piss in it."

All of us falling apart, roaring with laughter. I couldn't hold it in. "I'll bet I know who he named," I said. "It was either Fitzgibbon or Deveau, guaranteed."

Connelly chirruping, "*Deveau!* I knew it was him. Had to be. That guy Fitzgibbon couldn't lift a .45, much less clean one."

The barest pause after we finally quieted down, another blade of grass moving up and down in the corner of the captain's mouth.

"Writing long reports," he said, a bemused look on his face, "even very long reports, that hardly seems like a good reason to break your team leader's bones. I asked for a proper investigation of that myself, but I have a feeling my request went into that same waste-basket."

Connelly jumping in on that one. An evil grin. "You can lead a hippo to water, Captain, but you can't make him swim. All we know is Major Barnes was running for the woods, Sir, when a drainage ditch attacked him. Now it's true that Fitz here was trying to push him under the water with a stick when I finally got there, but none of us would allow that. No, Sir. Not with witnesses approaching."

Colte nodding. "It was a tough decision, Captain, to just take off and leave him there, drowning, but I'm told the men wanted to get back to their camp in time for chow."

Rozzelli, the crooked teeth showing again. "Was it hot chow?"

Without waiting for an answer, he added, "Because, I mean, if it was hot chow I could understand it. But *cold* chow? I mean this outfit has to have *some* standards!"

****

Rozzelli, to the general approbation of the team when we heard about it, was taking Colte to dinner somewhere off post. It was a couple of nights after that first meeting. To get to know his right hand man a little better, we suspected, and probably to get a more detailed run-down on the rest of his team. Colte got dressed in civvies for the occasion, amusing all of us. When he came

267

out of the room at the front of the barracks that he now shared with Connelly, he was wearing a chalk-stripe blue suit, a wide red tie, a dark grey shirt, and highly polished white and black wing-tip shoes.

The look was startling, almost bizarre, at least to me. In those clothes, that he had probably only worn five times since their purchase around 1948, he looked like an early forties Chicago gangster out of an Edward G. Robinson flick. It was a rather forceful reminder that Colte, and many of the other senior non-coms around the Group, had done their coming of age entirely in the military. They had no other home, really, since the mid-forties, and they lived largely apart from the civilian community they protected. When it came to non-military attire, their fashion choices seemed to be dictated by the tough-guy movies of the forties.

I kept my opinionated musings to myself, however, when Gunnar came down the aisle and stopped beside my bunk, looking remarkably sheepish for him, and holding an electric blue tie up in one great paw. "What do you think, Fitz? The red or the blue? What goes with this grey?"

Well, I was the right guy to ask, all right. Although I had brought with me a number of quality sports shirts and a couple of pairs of slacks from Kennedy Brother's Men's Store on Washington Street when I entered the army, I had owned exactly one real suit in my life before I was drafted. My high school graduation present from a caring aunt. "The red, Sarge," I told Gunnar, with limited choices but absolute confidence. "The one you're wearing is perfect."

I was genuinely surprised, even touched, by the look of mixed pleasure and relief that washed over his rock-like features at my pronouncement. "Thanks, Pal," he said. "I figured the red was right, but I decided I'd better check it out with Boston."

He grinned then, heading back to his room, passing other teammates who nodded and added their approval. Only Gomez, leaning against a bunk, tried to stop him as he passed. "Hey! What is this? You don't want my opinion? We Latinos are the kings of fashion."

Gunnar waved him off, the manic smile showing. "Boston knows," he said, ending all arguments.

We stood in the dark of his room like proud parents, sneaking looks out the window until the captain's long, green Buick swung in to pick him up on the main company street.

"Now, see," Hector mused, saying what we were all thinking in our own way. "That's classy. The captain taking old Gunnar out to a real dinner, get the ice broken over a coupla good steaks, coupla drinks. Shit, guys, I got hopes for this friggin' captain."

In those days fraternizing between officers and men was actively discouraged by the regular brass but the team concept, so fundamental to the Group, tended to break down such artificial barriers.

Dubois watching at the window with the rest of us. "Strange," he commented, "een all zee times he take me to deenair, Major Barnes, he navair peek me up at zee barracks."

The rest of the team went out that night to celebrate the selection of our new leader. Afterwards, walking back together from the beer hall in the sticky evening air, we were all admittedly a little trashed from the quantity of beer we had managed to disappear in the space of four hours. All in all, though, I know I felt better than I had since the day Wendell Barnes had first tromped out and stood looking down his nose at us. Already that seemed like a millennium ago in army years.

"Hey, Pat," Coy asked, you ever been to the Blue Ridge Mountains? The place they're sending us for Operation Cleo?"

The North Georgia problem was due to start at the end of July, and would run right through August.

"Yeah, I've been through there. As far North as you can go in Georgia. Mountains that won't quit. We'll have to learn to sleep standing up when we go in there. Ain't a flat space in that whole damn forest big enough to lie down in. Beautiful country, but nothing but rocks, snakes and friggin' pine trees."

Coy lighting up at that. "Snakes, huh? Glad Barnes won't be on this one. I'd need three, four of them big old rattlers make that fat bastard a belt."

Green, a raspy laugh. "Only take a small one, though, make him a noose."

"Forget Barnes," Pat told us. "He's not our problem anymore. Bucky Walters told Gunnar and me in the briefing we got yesterday that there's going to be a shit pot full of the eighty

270

deuce down there this time. Full companies. They're still pissed about all the crap we pulled off on the AFFT, and they'll be gunning for our scalps this time."

Green grunting. "Seemed to me like they went all out last time. And we still fucked them good on the wind-up."

"I loved Scagnelli's story," Denbeaux chuckled. "You guys weren't there but he stopped by last week while Fitz and I were working the radio down by the mortar range. He stopped to shoot the shit with us. He said we should have seen the look on that 82nd colonel's kisser when Scag's team did the Clark River Bridge. The colonel shows up, his jeep and six trucks full of troops behind him, all ready to cross the river and catch Scag's guys out in the valley. The umpire steps out, blocks them, tells them, 'You'll have to turn around, Colonel. I know you think you see a bridge here, but it's been blown since 0600 hours, courtesy of the 10th Special Forces.' Man, was that sweet."

"That's what I mean," Pat emphasized. "That colonel, and a lot of the other officers who got caught napping, they are pissed. They want to catch us, skin us, roast us over an open fire this time. They've learned and they'll post guards on the key bridges for sure. And they'll expect us to hit their regular convoys and supply runs. We're not going to get easy pickings like we did on Free Legion this time."

"Are they really gonna have the local badges with them, too?" Hadley asked.

Pat snorted. "The eighty deuce advance team is already down there setting that up. By the

271

time we jump in, they'll already be working for them. All the sheriffs, constables, game wardens, even the damn cattle inspectors, all out beating the bushes and looking for us. Feds are paying them cash, to be on the aggressor team."

"No shit now," Gomez demanded. "What happens if they catch us, Pat? They lock us up, ship us back here, or what?"

"There's been talk about hanging the Mexicans," Connelly said, moving just in time to avoid a swipe from Hector. "You'll get all this at the big meeting on Friday, but basically the deal is this. First time you're caught, it's twenty-four hours in the local slam, two meals of bread and water, and you get an hour's head start to get out of town before they come after your ass again. Second time, same deal, but it is forty-eight hours in the lock-up. Anyone gets caught a third time, they're off the problem, sent back to Bragg. Probably, you're on the way out of the Group. Walters told me the eighty deuce wants to send back at least half of our guys, teach us to fuck with them."

"Me," Hadley said, "they ain't gonna catch my ass no way, no how. Them local hoosegows in them itty bitty towns, Georgia, them are not places I want to spend two hours, never mind twenty four."

"Jails are jails," Denbeaux said. "They all stink."

"You wait," Coy told him, "till you see one of these. Those buildings been up since before the Civil War. Got those big old brown recluse spiders. They bite you, you'll be lucky you don't die. Roaches big as dogs. If you can ride one of them roaches for eight seconds, you get a prize. Mattresses are full of crabs and lice. And they stink of piss and vomit from all the drunks they lock up every Saturday night after they put away a jug or two of white lightning."

"If you do get grabbed," Pat added, "one thing, don't give those local sheriffs any shit. My cousin, a few years ago, went up there above Atlanta somewhere to play in a college football game. Won big, too. He and three of his buddies got thrown in the local jug that night for being drunk and disorderly, and the sheriff come in about midnight with an axe handle and beat all three of them senseless. Seems it was his old team they had whipped. Told the court in the morning they were acting up, taking his jail apart, so he had to take steps. Judge gave them extra fines for that. My cousin, he's in no hurry to go back there for some reason."

Dear Mr. and Mrs. Fitzpatrick. We are sending your son home from the Blue Ridge Mountains. This is the first package. More to follow. Shit!

"Hey, guys. Loosen up. We got two weeks of training left to get ready, and then we're gonna go down there and tear hunks out of those bastards. This Operation Cleo is gonna be fun. Guess what Walters says the eighty-deuce brass started calling our outfit since Free Legion? Bank's Bandits! How about that, huh? That ain't all bad now, is it? And who were you with in the army, Pal? *Bank's Bandits.* Hell, I like that."

CHAPTER THIRTY-ONE

Rozzelli in front of me. His hand coming out of the dark, while he still stared ahead. Fumbling near my face. His fingers finding, digging into my left shoulder, his other arm pointing.

Moving up to peer past him.

Above us, twenty yards away. A guard! Sitting back against the metal plates of the railroad bridge. The bottom half of his face flaring into light and disappearing as he puffed on a cigarette cupped in his hands.

Rozzelli tugging away my M-3 submachine gun. His mouth at my ear.

"Go under the trestle, up the other side, and be ready."

He tapped the watch on the inside of his wrist, and pointed to mine, before again whispering in my ear. We had all synchronized our watches before we started.

"Fourteen minutes. 0140 on the dot, I'll throw a rock on to that bank. When he turns this way to look, come across that trestle and take him down. Hold him quiet until we get up there."

Swell. Whyn't I just wrap him up in tissue paper, mail him parcel post, I'm at it.

I moved around Rozzelli, feeling bareass naked without the weight of the greasegun in my hands. *Take him down!* Empty-handed, for chrissakes.

Moving past Green who had been out ahead on point as we moved up the riverbank for the last half hour. Slipping by Anston, my knees shaky.

Heading for the grillwork of the trestle, looming above me like a burned-out building.

It isn't fair. Sending me instead of one of the real bone busters back there.

Me, for cryeye. A hundred thirty-five pounds carrying a case of beer. *Put him down and hold him until we get there!*

Halfway up the bank on the far side of the trestle, on all fours, feeling my way upwards in the dark, thanking God for my dark-blue, ankle-high sneakers. One foot at a time. Hands touching the ground, propelling me forward. Monkey walk. Don't start a goddamn avalanche, for chrissakes.

Stopping to use my sleeve to wipe off the sweat running into my eyes. A glance at my watch. 0134. Still plenty of time.

Maybe the guy's a midget. Hey, I'm not the only half-portion they grabbed for this goddamn army. Maybe he'll faint when I jump out and go for him. Just a little further. Slowly. Ease up now, have a quick look over the edge of the trestle.

Damn! Paul friggin' Bunyan! Oh, yes, I'm going to die, alright. This black stocking cap will be a big help when they're looking for my head, after it comes down in Cleveland.

All those other bozos spending *hours* throwing each other around like goddamn beanbags. Me, I'm on the radio sending and receiving, my brain turning to sawdust.

Sweet. After this jerk up here pulls my head out of my asshole, they'll say, "Oh, by the way, let's give the *surviving* radio operators some of that judo karate crap."

Stupid fuckin' army.

I look at my watch. 0139 and the second hand moving! Less than a minute.

0140.

THUMP! The rock!

The guard jumping up and spinning! His back to me!

Oh Jesus mother of holy god Peter, don't turn around.

My feet digging into the gravel as I make my dash.

One heel striking steel as I vault over the tracks.

Take him low! Tackle him. Drive him over the edge.

Balls! They guy whipping around! Facing me! The whites of his eyes like poached eggs in the dark. My hands are out, reaching for him as I leave my feet.

His rifle coming straight out and up at me! The end of the wooden stock of his M-1 slamming me in the upper chest, the metal trigger guard catching me right in the face! A loud whooshing sound. The guard sucking in air, and my breath rushing out.

Hammered upright by the rifle, straightened up but still in the air, driving forward, off my feet. Awful, rib-cracking pain.

The guard going backwards. Jumping back! Out into space. Falling backwards over the yawning edge in front of me. The ground crashing up into me. My knees, and then my face and chest, hitting and sliding, grinding through gravel, the stones ripping and tearing at my face. The top of my head thudding hard against something solid.

****

"Pisser! Just pisser. Is he dead?"

Rozzelli's voice, somewhere above me.

A beefy hand rolling me onto my back. Gomez.

My eyes watering. Agonizing pain when I try to breathe.

Water splashing my face. Gomez is holding his canteen over me. He and Rozzelli leaning down, only the whites of their eyes showing under their black, stocking hats, oval holes in their blacked faces. The tips of Hector's stubby fingers flicking at my nose and mouth, knocking off lumps of dirt and gravel.

"Got a nice egg, the top of his head and he done his nose real good, Captain. And a lot of skin's scraped off his forehead. Lemme see if his ribs are broken."

Hands trying to use my chest for a bellows. Air returning first, then sound. "AAAAGGGHHHH! Leggo, you sonofabitch...leggo!"

"SSSSSSHHH!" Gomez, one thick finger across his lips. "Shh! Well, guess he kin breathe."

I proved him right, taking another breath. Less painful. Another. Even better.

Warm, sticky wet stuff oozing all over my lips as I sat up. Blood. Nose full of it. Flowing heavily out of one nostril, splashing down onto my shirtfront.

Sitting all the way up. Head feeling hollow, like a brittle glass sphere.

Gomez reaching in his pocket. A tearing sound. A pad pressed up against my nose between his fingers.

"Hold it there, Fitz. Breathe through your mouth. Don't blow out. Let it clot."

Gomez and Rozzelli lifting me to my feet. Standing. Feeling the ground swaying under me. *May I have this dance?*

Green just over the edge of the bank, busy with the guard. Finishing up. Trussing him to a metal girder. I can see the gag sticking out of the guy's mouth above the tape. He looks like he's in shock.

I hope he feels better than I do. What the hell! Some day he might want to add up a column of figures, or write someone a postcard. Simple things it was clear I'll never be able to do again.

Connelly and Dubois coming out from under the bridge where they had been setting their mock C-3 charges, wire running out behind them as they headed across the bank and into the woods with the detonator.

Green coming up the bank, his greasegun in one hand, the guard's rifle in the other. On tiptoe as his boots touched gravel. Toe-dancing over and peering into my eyes. A hoarse whisper. "I think you got the wrong idea about these here

278

war games, Fitz. See, you're supposed to be a Special Forces trooper, not a friggin' mortar shell—got it?"

Rozzelli shushing him and pointing to the other end of the bridge. But smiling as he did so. The rest of the team grinning, too, as they came up and passed me.

I fell in behind them, heading across the bridge. Walking started my nose bleeding again. Not easy trying to walk quietly with my head tilted back and the gauze pad pressed against my nose.

Terrific. Another swell day of fun and frolic in the boondocks.

Jeez, but I love these exercises. We jump off of railroad trestles. *Ain't that grand!*

****

Waking early, barely light, despite being up most of the night on that problem. Too irritable and frustrated to sleep. Crawling out of my sleeping bag and feeling about as low as I'd ever felt in the friggin' army.

My forehead felt like it had been sandpapered by an angry carpenter. My nose was all puffy, full of black, clotted blood. A red welt ran from the bottom to the top of my chest, hurting even when my fingers brushed across it buttoning my shirt. Gomez had checked me out when we got back, in the dark, but he was sure nothing was broken. And he was right, if you didn't count my pride.

It wasn't the physical pain that was bothering me. It was the shame of it. The humiliation. *And* the injustice of it.

Not one goddamned class in hand to hand combat since I'd joined this miserable outfit. Not one! Not for the goddamned radio operators.

All the others had spent hours bouncing each other around on mats like friggin' India rubber balls. We'd trot by and see them working with rubber knives and wooden handguns. But us? We got ditty-dum-dum ditty, day after friggin' day.

With the blood in my nose, my cigarette tasted like I was sucking an open wound. I remembered the day Green came strolling up to me as he came out of the mess hall while I waited in the chow line. It was a couple of days before we went in on Free Legion. Big smile, his hand extended for a shake. As soon as my hand touched his, he jerked me forward off balance, then reversed, and spun me around and over. I sailed through the air and landed flat on my back on the thick spongy grass beside the sidewalk. Stunned! The whole line of men roaring with laughter.

Leaning over me, Green had pulled me back to my feet, grinning. "Ain't that the damndest thing you ever saw, Fitz? Works every time, too. Shit, man could throw an elephant with that one."

And he strolled blissfully on his way, swallowed up by the sea of laughing men. Terrific!

But not for us. Not the goddamned radio operators. We were supposed to learn that shit by osmosis.

Jesus, did I feel low. But the worst part was, I was convinced that last night's little escapade had finished me for all time with Rozzelli. That's what really hurt. The idea of having to leave the team. The Group. My friends. Of washing out. Damn, I wondered if I'd be cut before I even got a chance to go in on Cleo.

Even though it was late when we all got back, no one wanted to let it go. It was just too good a story. Gomez and Green telling the guys who didn't get a good look all about my unique 'take-out' tactics. Connelly, too, jumping in the air next to the campfire to demonstrate. "Ain't this the way you done it, Fitz? Ain't this the way you flew across that trestle? I don't think I got the flap of the arms just right, have I, Hector?"

With me laughing, of course. Joining in. All the guys taking turns. Except Rozzelli. I'll give him that. He didn't jump on the corpse. The only time he came over to me, in fact, was when Gomez was checking me out. I'll give him that, too. He did hold the flashlight and made sure Hector checked me out good.

Everyone turning in at about four in the morning. Denbeaux coming over to sit beside me to finish his coffee. Dubois joining us. They knew I was down, of course. Denbeaux examining my face in the dying light of the campfire as he got up to head for the sack. Clucking his tongue. Trying to get a laugh out of me. "Hey, I said we all got to eat a pound of *green* before we go, Little Brother, not *gravel.*"

As I sit here now, watching the sleeping men, smoking a cigarette, the humiliation still weighs on me like a wet poncho. Shit! Why didn't I tackle the bastard around the ankles? Why didn't I go in feet first? Anything, for Christ's sake, except what I did. With all of them watching. With Rozzelli watching. Watching his badass trooper charge across that trestle and cold-cock himself.

God, how I hate this friggin' army.

****

"Rozzelli wants to see you."

It was Colte bending over and prodding my shoulder. I had fallen back to sleep against the tree. When I opened my eyes, I saw the rest of the guys were all up, sitting in a half circle under the trees finishing their morning chow, drinking coffee.

Rozzelli was in the middle of the group sitting on a stump, blowing on a steaming cup of coffee. He looked sour and half asleep like he always did in the morning.

Rozzelli pointed to the ground beside him as I came up. I could feel everyone's eyes on me, all ears cocked. I know my face was red. "Grab a rock, Fitz. Sit down. We're about to have a team meeting."

I lowered myself gingerly to the ground. Rozzelli continued to blow and sip on his coffee for another minute or so. He wasn't waiting for the team's attention. He had that. Finally, he set down the metal cup, and looked around the half-circle.

"Last night, we had us a kind of a little fiasco over there at the railroad bridge. Came out alright, this time. Except that Fitz here almost had his rib cage turned into a bunch of kindling."

Rozzelli picked up a handful of dirt and let it trickle through his fingers before he continued. "The thing is, see, I made a mistake, and Fitz paid for it."

The lop-sided grin came and went. "See, my problem was, I believed all that shit in the handouts they gave me when I got back here after my mountain-climbing stint in Colorado. From the prep school they sent me to after I first reported here last fall."

Well, now, that's interesting. Rozzelli *had* been here before us. Here and gone to Colorado. That means he was among the first. One of Bank's handpicked choices.

"See, I had no idea that some of you guys hadn't had any unarmed combat training as yet. Shit! Until yesterday, I was afraid to give Fitz here any crap for fear he'd catch me alone and they'd send me home to my folks in one of those black bags."

Rozzelli began to laugh softly. "Well, okay, we all had a lot of laughs at Fitz's expense last night, and it didn't seem to bother him any, either, I noticed. But there is something that all of you might want to think about, okay? Fitz had absolutely no friggin' idea whatsoever what he was supposed to do when he got up on that bridge, and that is the God's truth. But, see, the thing is, when I gave him the tap, he *went.* You all got that? He *went!* What's more," Rozzelli started to laugh again remembering, and the whole team ended up laughing with him, "when that bell rang, boys, old Fitz came out of the chute like Joe Louis going after Maxie Schmelling in the rematch. Result was a little different, I admit, but the charge across the ring was the same."

Damn! Sonofabitch. He's *not* gonna dump me. I'm still on board!

Rozzelli took a last, long sip of coffee, before adding, "We go back to the barracks this afternoon, but we're coming back out here next week. Five days. Our last field training before we go in on Cleo. We're going to use that time to teach each other some of the basic techniques of hand-to-hand. Taking down a guard. Taking away a knife or a gun. What to do with a rifle to make the guy sorry he has one. We can't do it all in a week, we all know that, but we can make a damn good start. And we will. Some of you, Pat, Gunnar, you're pretty good at this shit already. Your job, next week, with me, will be to make certain we don't see any more human cannonballs on this team. If we're gonna wipe blood off our shirts, let's try and make sure it's the other guy's."

CHAPTER THIRTY-TWO

Out in the field with Rozzelli. The uniform of the day, sneakers, khaki shorts and loose fatigue shirt partially buttoned. Rozzelli, his hands up in front of him like a boxer, except that the hands are open, palms forward, circling slowly as Colte stalks him looking for a chance to move in. Colte had told us the night before that at the end of his tour in Korea, Rozzelli had studied jiu jitsu and judo at the Kodokan in Tokyo for six months, so we were looking forward to this.

Rozzelli, on his toes, bouncing a little on the thick, spongy grass in the corner of the meadow near the marshy creek. The next best thing to a mat we could find. Jesus, but Rozzelli was fast! Surprising all of us.

Colte rushing in, both hands grabbing for an arm, one hand missing, the other catching a piece of a sleeve. Temporarily.

Rozzelli's left foot rocketing up, catching Colte high on the chest, driving him backward. Making him lose his balance and his grip on the sleeve. Gunnar, falling backwards, trying to recover. Rozzelli dropping down and grabbing both of Colte's ankles, jerking them up in the air, toward his own waist.

Colte landing hard on his back and shoulders. Rozzelli dropping one foot and grabbing the other by the toe and heel and spinning it like a crank. Gunnar flipping over on his stomach. To keep his ankle from snapping in two. Rozzelli's right elbow and knee both hitting Gunnar's back in unison, along the spine. Not hard. But hard enough to bounce him off the ground. Holy shit!

Just demonstrating, you understand. Just showing us the way. Four or five days, and Gunnar probably won't hurt at all anymore.

More demonstrations. Connelly with his arm twisted up between his shoulder blades as he goes over Rozzelli's hip. Gomez gasping for breath with his windpipe caught in the crook of Rozzelli's arm. Rozzelli's open hand smacking Gomez in the kidneys, barking, "Stab! Stab! Stab!" And me, I'm thinking, *run, run, run, while you can still walk, walk, walk!*

Anston Green's turn. *Whoa! Hey, Anston, I didn't know you could fly!*

All of us pairing off at Rozzelli's direction. After he had manhandled the big guys enough for us to get the message. *Pay attention, guys! This jiu-jitsu shit works!*

Rozzelli, Colte and Connelly all instructing. Taking turns. Teaching us to fall first. Teaching us how to break our falls with a forearm and hand as we land. Teaching us to relax as we fall so we don't hit and break into pieces.

Simple leg throws next. On to hip throws and shoulder throws. In that order. Going slow, but working to get the moves right. A whole day on basics. Forty minutes of drilling, twenty minutes to recover and think about what you had learned. Up again.

Second day, second hour, Green facing me with an M-1 rifle at port arms. The trestle like a bad nightmare between us. Rozzelli supervising. Telling Green, "Knock him down with the rifle when he rushes you." Rozzelli having spent the previous hour showing me what to do.

I charge straight in, pause just as the rifle thrusts out at me, then grab it with both hands jerking Green toward me and stepping past him, sweeping my right leg around to take his legs out from under him. Following through and jerking the rifle free in a quick rotating move as he lands hard and flat on his back. *Oh, yes! Oh, baby! Sweeeeet!*

Change partners, men. Let's go! Let's see some action!

End of the second day, and all of us except the terrible three, Rozzelli, Colte and Connelly, sore and achy from all the tumbles. From the shoulder throws. Landing hard again and again on the spongy turf, and, as the day wore on, getting up a little more slowly each time. Rozzelli watching us wind down like cheap alarm clocks, taking mercy on us. The last hour, hand grips and arm locks. No throws. *Don't grab wrists, guys. My niece can break a wrist hold and she's only six. Grab the fleshy part of the thumb, the drumstick. Get that, you got control.*

The end of the third day. My bruises feel permanent now.

We all wake up crippled in the morning. Rozzelli has us line up and do stretches and then takes us on an easy, two-mile run to shake it out. When I was a civilian, a two-mile run would have triggered a wake, prayers and a quick burial.

Breakfast. Half an hour's break, then down to the pasture again. Sore spots as big as a hand all over our backs and hips. The excitement of a good throw quickly taking away the pain.

Day four. Discovering my problem. With the giants like Colte, Connelly and Denbeaux, and even Gomez who was as strong as a draught horse, I did fine as long as they kept their backs to me. *Advantage, Fitzpatrick.* Dropping my knees hard into their calves to buckle them. Gabbing a hand and elbow and stepping across in front of them to throw them down across my leg. Fine, no problem. Spinning their wrists up into the small of the back once I had the drumstick. Great, no problem.

Face to face, however, they were able to parry my every move, laughing at my frustration.

Heading straight for Pat, my legs driving, arms pumping, both arms reaching for his ankles. Jumping instead, going up into the air and kicking out with both feet. A slamming stop. Pat taking both of my sneakered feet on the upper chest without moving, his hands out to the side, grinning. I ricochet off backwards, crashing onto my head and shoulders at his feet. All the wind knocked out of me. Lying there like a pile of dirty laundry. My sadistic, bastardly teammates all convulsed in laughter.

Rozzelli, too, the whore! He just couldn't help it.

I get two more runs at Pat, and since I'm ready for it this time, at least I don't crash in a heap, but I still end up on my ass or eating dirt. I slink off to let others take their turns. I know one thing now that sucks worse than being in the army. Taking hand-to-hand combat with gorillas, that's what.

That afternoon, Rozzelli took Denbeaux and me off by ourselves while Colte and Connelly drilled the rest of the team. Rozzelli trying to work around my problem. "I wish I had one of my Japanese teachers here, Fitz. Those guys could throw a truck on its back from a standing stop."

Rozzelli giving me a few more moves. A few alternate approaches for Denbeaux and me to practice. His tip of the day. "Last winter when I was being bounced all over those Tokyo flower gardens, the most important thing I learned was to use surprise. Do the unexpected."

Demonstrations. An hour of practice. Some new ideas. Rozzelli leaving us to keep at it. Later, just before we knocked off, Rozzelli returned to our private field, trotting toward us. Without breaking stride, he charged right at me. Arms wide, yelling as he came. *Jesus!*

Automatically, I grabbed him by the shirt-front with both hands, dropping down to the seat of my pants, and kicking up as I rolled backwards. Pulling him over, one foot in his stomach, the other on his chest as I rolled and kicked out as hard as I could. Just like he had shown me two hours earlier.

Holy Shit! Rozzelli sailing over me! Heels over head! Landing flat on his back a good three feet behind me with a tremendous "THU--WHUMP!"

A long groan as he lay there, his eyes closed

Denbeaux was laughing quietly as Rozzelli opened one eye slowly and looked up at us, noting my cretin-like dance of celebration.

His voice was tiredly sardonic. "Denbox, old buddy, I greatly fear we're creating a Frankenstein here. Oh, the nippos would love this little shit. A year in Tokyo, they'd make him emperor."

****

Thirty minutes later. Heading up through the woods to the team camp. Following Denbeaux. My whole body hurting from the misses as much as the hits, but on a high, too. My throw of Rozzelli like a cold beer in August. Denbeaux stopping me just before we came in sight of the camp. A suggestion. A Denbox special! Oh, yeah. I liked this idea.

Going ahead of him. Limping. Grimacing painfully. Hobbling into the clearing. Denbeaux right behind me, looking grave, calling to Rozzelli across the camp. "Tough luck, Captain. I think our 'cut and slash' man has popped a hamstring. Better have Doc Gomez take a look. I think your hired killer here is all through for a few weeks!"

Swinging one leg and limping toward Gomez. Starting to pass Connelly. Like everyone else, he was watching me, looking disgusted at the news. He was just starting to tap out a cigarette when I reached him.

An astonished expression on his face as I rose up in front him like a demented Irish genie popping out of a bottle. One split second as my knees came up to my chest and my feet shot out to catch him high and right below his collarbone. Everything I could dredge up went into the effort.

Connelly went over backwards too fast to keep his feet. A halo of cigarettes spewed out into the air above his head like spent shells from a heavy .30. He landed on the seat of his pants but continued to roll well up onto his shoulders, his feet straight up in the air. He continued over backward as a bellow of rage exploded from him. In a flash he had rocketed back to his feet, heading for me like a polar bear after a sea lion.

The whole team convulsing. Even Rozzelli. Especially Rozzelli.

Leaping for my life. Jumping to get Gomez between us. As Pat sent Hector flying to the side, I made it to a tree and around it. Pat, circling it too wide in his rage to get at me, crashed into a bush as I dashed back across the camp. A desperation run for Rozzelli, jumping behind him, my captain laughing too hard to interfere. Connelly chasing me around Rozzelli like we were two spokes of a wheel.

Pat's grasping hands snatching at my sleeves, swiping at my legs.

Rozzelli, at long last grabbing Pat by the back of his belt, then wrapping his arms around him and pulling him away. Connelly beginning to laugh. *Oh, thank Christ! He's laughing!* Dropping to the ground and holding his sides he was laughing so hard.

The team loving it.

Connelly, out of breath, all anger finally gone, pointing a finger at me. "Fitzpatrick, you little turd. I just hope your folks find a good use for that ten grand they're going to get in a week or two. First time I catch you alone. I'd hate to think your death is going to be useless as well as painful!"

Rozzelli patting me on the head. "Now, now, Patrick! Let's have none of that. No corporal punishment for the children."

He gave me a slap on the back. "Run along and play now, Jimmy, my lad, and keep up the good work. When we go in on Operation Cleo, I'm going to buy you a knife."

CHAPTER THIRTY-THREE

The flying boxcar dropping down like a roller coaster through the heavy winds and downdrafts coming off the mountains. Rain rattling across the roof and sides of the metal plane body. The small windows above our heads awash. Water teeming by the open doors at the tail of the plane, splashing in from time to time in icy sheets.

The jumpmasters at the open doors in the tail, kneeling and leaning out into that churning sea for thirty to forty seconds at a time looking for the DZ, pulling themselves back in like turtles, shaking their sopping heads. Clearing faces and eyes with soaked sleeves. Drenched to the crotch. Leaning out again. Where *is* that friggin' DZ?

Over an hour since we took off from North Carolina. Pitch black sky around us and a solid bank of dark rolling thunderheads below us when we got down here. Like flying above filthy, exploded bales of cotton.

The pilot dropping down through them for a look every few minutes. Abrupt, swooping, elevator falls. The noise of the motors alternating between a whine and a screech. Hurting my ears. My stomach jumping. Breaking out below into the pouring rainstorm. Flashes of lightning cracking the night open for seconds at a time. *What the hell is that? Mountains! Shit! We're flying up the goddamn Grand Canyon!*

The whole world lighting up and then disappearing again in the rain and darkness.

Goddamn! Look at those sonsabitching mountains!

Water splashing past the jumpmasters and into the tail as the plane banked sharply to the left.

You'd better friggin' bank, Baby! Looking like we were about to ram the peaks in front of us.

Climbing again. Sharply. The motors roaring. All the way up through the clouds. The plane leveling off. Two or three minutes, droning along.

Oh, my Christ, here we go again. Plummeting once more.

We had been doing this for twenty minutes, at least. Diving down and back up through those goddamn clouds. My stomach trying hard to keep up with my body. I looked down the tightly packed plane at the faces of the men banked against the fuselage in bucket seats, at the rise and fall of the doors beyond them. Half the guys already turning green. Wondering whether I looked as bad as they did.

I was at the very end of my stick, sitting near the front of the plane, just before the steps that led up into the cockpit. At my elbow, the crapper. The infamous square box, out in the open. The flat lid covering the hole beneath.

From my immediate left, a harsh, retching sound.

Hadley! Right next to me, cheeks puffed out. Pulling his helmet off and separating the steel pot from the plastic helmet liner. Leaning forward over the steel pot. Letting it all come up.

Noses crinkling all around us as the foul odor wafted through the plane. The helmet full of a lumpy orange-custard mess.

Across the aisle from Hadley, a few seats down, Mullins had his head tilted back and his eyes closed. One terrible groan and his head snapped forward. *Whoosh!* A geyser shooting out of his mouth as his body jackknifed forward. Spewing it all over the floor in front of him. All over his boots and pant legs.

"USE A GODDAMN STEEL POT, YOU ASSHOLES!"

Sergeant Casey Killian, looking like a belligerent bulldog, barking at all of us as he came down the aisle. "If you're going to hurl, use your helmets! And pass it down to the commode. C'mon! Get that shit into that hole before we all die from the smell!"

Hadley passing his contribution to me. Another barfing explosion, a second helmet, brimful, passing from man to man down the aisle. To me!

Others, jaws working, holding it back and pulling their helmet liners loose from their steel pots at the same time.

Holding my breath and keeping Hadley's potfull at arm's length as Killian arrived in front of me.

Holding the helmet above nose level and reeling from the awful odor. *Alas, poor Yorick!*

Killian pointing past me to the commode. "Bang them out for cryeye, Fitz! And then give 'em a fast rinse in that sink before you pass 'em back. C'mon, goddammit! *Move!* You ain't no friggin' statue! That stuff is going to stink us out of here!"

Swell. Pisser. This was all I needed.

Emptying the dripping headgear. *Yeecch!* Pumping the faucet to produce a few spurts of yellowed water. Swishing that around. Banging it again.

"Hurry up, goddammit! You ain't no friggin' autoclave. Here's another!"

"HEY!"

Looking up at Killian, my arm stopped in mid-air. *What?* What *now* for chrissake? Casey pointing to the crap still dripping off the helmet. Leaning toward me his eyes wide.

"You saving some of them large hunks, Fitz? Figure it's gonna be a long time till breakfast or what? *Rinse* that fucker clean!"

The steel pots coming and going. The box awash with all manner of disgusting flotsam. Screw it! Let the flyboys muck it out later. A nudge at my elbow. Jesus! Another one.

Rozzelli, up near the doors, pulling off the headphones he'd been using to communicate with the pilot, then coming down to where our team sat. Stepping gingerly over Mullins' dinner on the way.

He hung onto the static line over his head by one hand as he bent over to talk to us. Bouncing up and down with the motion of the plane. *Haven't I seen you at the zoo, Captain?*

Cupping his mouth with his free hand, so we could hear him above the roar of the motors. "Pilot thinks he's got our DZ located now. We can jump or we can go back to Bragg and do it another night. We've been circling, hoping it would clear off a little, but that's not going to happen. The pilot needs a decision now. They way this plane is loaded, it's drinking fuel like a bloody camel. Myself, I'd rather jump than fly this cesspool all the way back to Bragg! But you guys got a say in this. So, how about it?"

Colte yelling over the motors. "Let's go Captain. Let's get our asses out of this friggin' outhouse!"

Connelly, "GO!"

Gomez, "GO! GO!"

Rozzelli moving toward me. All the answers the same. "GO! GO! GO!"

Are they *shitting* me? Jump out in *this* kind of crap? Can you *do* that? Right in the middle of a goddamned thunderstorm? I don't believe this.

Rozzelli in front of me. Everyone else on the team had already voted. It was down to me.

What do I want to do? Shouldn't I stay here and clean up this commode? We don't want the flyboys to think we're piggy!

Oh, crap. I heard myself barking it out through my phony grin. "GO, Captain. Let's do it!"

The word "go" had exploded from me with surprisingly loud but entirely manufactured enthusiasm. Well, you friggin' hypocrite, I told myself, there's still one chance we won't have to do this. We could still crash into one of those peaks.

The three other teams watching as we stood up, snapped our static-lines into place and shuffled past them. A symphony of colors staring up at us. Perspiring red through pasty white to sickly green.

See you later, fellas! They *found* our DZ. They *think*. Lucky, lucky us. I'm so thrilled I just might pee in my boots. *Dear Mr. & Mrs. Fitzpatrick. We regret to inform you we found your son in a Georgia tree-top. We located him by the stink!*

"GETTT ----REEEEEAAADDDYYY!"

Rozzelli at the door behind an equipment bundle that came up to his chin. His other hand already clamped on the outside of the door. Down by his knees, the soaking wet head and shoulders of the jumpmaster popped back in.

"GO!"

The static-line cable giving a fierce jerk in my hand as Rozzelli, pushing the bundle, leaps out. Jerking again and again as others swing into the door and vault out. Shuffling forward, last in the stick, staying right on Hadley's backpack.

Faster, you bastards. Move it! Jeeee-sus, not a chance I'll hit that DZ, I just know it.

Crowding Hadley. Sailing out the door on top of him. Riding him out. Spun away by the roaring wind and off into the stinging water. Eyes squeezing shut as a thousand icy needles jabbed at my bare face and hands. Tumbling to my left.

Jeeee-sus God Almighty! Sweet Georgia Brown! I'm coming home!

CHAPTER THIRTY-FOUR

"Now don't go getting big-headed on us, Fitzpatrick, but that suggestion of yours about the chickens might just be moronic enough to work."

Rozzelli was sitting with his bootless left foot propped up on a stump in front of him. He had twisted it when a loose rock turned under him the night before, coming back from another drop that never happened. The ankle had begun to look like a hippo's thigh, but Gomez was sure nothing was broken.

Rozzelli had that bemused, faraway look in his eye with which I was becoming all too familiar. It gave me a queasy feeling in the pit of my stomach. The same feeling Napoleon's men must have gotten when he started muttering about Moscow and passing out snowshoes. Will I ever learn to keep my mouth shut?

What Rozzelli called my 'suggestion' had really been a simple passing remark. A gripe, really. As soon as I saw that look on his face, I was sorry I had ever mentioned those miserable chickens.

The 82nd troopers had been running our asses all over those damn mountains for almost two full weeks. Every day, from early light until after dark. One search and sweep operation after another, determined to flush us out into the open.

We had been pretty much forced to hole up and stay put during the long days, so our habit of supplementing our rations with goodies bought from the locals was for the moment cut off. We were down to one can of C-rations per day for each man and, without a supply drop it looked like it would stay that way. Rozzelli had already sent three of our men to another team area to try to set up a joint drop some thirty miles away. God only knew when they would make it back with more supplies.

The night I made the gaffe about the chickens, it was almost midnight. We were camped in a clearing high enough up on the mountain so that we could risk a small campfire. Even if they did spot it from the valley below, which was unlikely, it would take them hours of noisy scrambling through pitch-black woods to get anywhere close to us.

I was by the fire watching each team member arrive. Watching each one go over to where Rozzelli had hung the rucksack with our remaining rations. The choice had been the same for days and we all knew it. Nothing left except sausage patties and corned beef hash.

These were always the last selected, with good reason. The hash was perfect if you needed cement to fill in a stone wall, and any self-respecting house cat who would pass by one of those sausage patties without burying it, wouldn't know a turd if he coughed one up.

Still, each guy would approach the rucksack hopefully, reach in, and take out a single can. Turning it over slowly, he would read the label by the light of the fire. As though one that said "Sausage Patties" on one side might still say "Franks & Beans" on the other. In the condiment selection tonight, just to flesh thing out, we have jelly disks! I think I'll eat mine right after I smoke these 1942 Camels. Wonder why no one snapped these up? Says right on them, "Finest blend of turkish and aromatic goatshit."

It was against this background that I opened my big mouth about the chickens.

The six of us were sitting there with our feet stretched toward the dying fire, concentrating mostly on keeping the slop we were swallowing going in one direction at a time. The quiet firelight was conducive to the formulation of those great and profound revelations that every soldier has experienced, and to which we occasionally gave voice.

"Jeez," said Gomez, "These friggin' C-rations sure do make you fart."

The thought being father to the deed, as it were, he promptly rolled up on one cheek and fired off a salvo that almost blew out the campfire. From our reaction, you would have thought Gomez had been flown in by the USO to entertain the troops.

"You know what really frosts my ass?" I said. "We're up here boiling our muddy socks to make soup, and the eighty-deuce is down there bellying up to a full chow line night after night and going back for seconds."

Connelly nodded. "That's for sure. The lucky bastards."

"Yeah," I said, "and Sundays are the worst! Then they're gorging themselves on huge chicken dinners!"

I went on to tell them that at noon on the previous Saturday, when it had been my turn to man our observation post with a view of the valley and the river below, I had spotted a two-and-a-half making its way through the woods on one of the back roads. It was loaded with live chickens destined for the 82nd's Sunday dinner pail. The truck had aroused my curiosity because military traffic generally did not use the back roads on their regular runs.

To my surprise, the truck pulled over and stopped. The two drivers hopped out, went down under a bridge and proceeded to pile bareass into the river for a leisurely swim. Understandable, since it had been hot and humid for weeks.

"Can you imagine," I had told my team mates, spooning the last greasy dregs of sausage patty into my mouth, "a whole truckload of plump, juicy chickens. If only I had been closer! Like in that cornfield next to the road. By Jesus, I could have grabbed one of those crates and screwed back into that field before those sonsabitches could even blow the water out of their noses!"

It was only a daydream, but Rozzelli snapped it up like a bear catching salmon. "*Tomorrow* is Saturday," he reminded us, "And it's almost guaranteed to be another scorcher. If those ugly ducklings took to the water like that last week, what makes you think they won't do the same thing tomorrow!"

Rozzelli's excitement was infectious. He pulled himself to his feet and stood over us, leaning on the crutch Gomez had made for him. He had that lunatic grin that must have given opposing linemen the screaming fits when he was chewing up all that yardage for Purdue a few years earlier. "Well, men. Let's have it. It's got to be up to you, because I sure as hell can't go chicken stealing with this ankle. Do we sit it out up here eating sausage patties until our crap comes out in links? Or, do a couple of you guys hump your asses down there before dawn like Fitzie says and bring us back some chickens?"

Like Fitzie says! Oh, terrific!

Shepherding us off on our long downhill trek with empty rucksacks. Rozzelli waving his crutch at us like a crazed Long John Silver. Gomez, too, beside himself with excitement, giggling the way he did when he got nervous. Slapping each of us on the back. Saying over and over, "Oh, Jesus! Live chickens! Bring back some plump ones!"

Connelly jumping on it. "Guys," he said, "I knew it. Friggin' Gomez has a thing for plump birds. That's why he goes off in the woods alone like that. He's been screwin owls!"

Typical. Urged on by a lunatic, one-legged officer and a dancing Mexican, we disappeared into the darkness.

CHAPTER THIRTY-FIVE

We were in the cornfield next to the bridge in plenty of time. Taking up our positions across the road from where I had seen the truck pull off the week before. Hidden by tall rows of corn. Ready to wait it out.

As it began to get light, we crept out to the edge of the road one at a time to get a long look around and familiarize ourselves with the terrain. Up close the river was a lot wider than it had looked from up on the mountain. The bridge itself was narrow, but long—at least fifty yards across.

The bank down to the river was also a lot steeper than we had expected. It looked damn slippery. Connelly was insistent, though, that we follow through with that part of *his* plan, "Hey!" he assured us, "piece of cake!"

None of us had any experience driving trucks. We decided to go with Denbeaux as the driver after he had assured us that any goddamn fool could put a truck in gear. "Don't worry, guys," he had chortled, "I'll double-clutch that bastard like Barney Oldfield in the 500."

After a pause, Bill added, "If not, I hope you suckers can swim, because I'm liable to go right off over the side and drive that mother straight down river to Atlanta!"

It was a long, steamy uncomfortable wait, but we knew the hot sun increased our chances of success. The shade disappeared as the sun rose higher. Ants paraded across us. Flies kept zooming in to examine our nostrils and flit in and out of our mouths. A very long morning.

Patience, however, was rewarded. A little after eleven, a truck chugged to a stop and the sound of cackling chickens was music to our sun-blistered ears. Out and down underneath the bridge trotted our two blissful sheep, little knowing how costly today's skinny-dipping would be.

As soon as they disappeared under the bridge, Denbeaux and I ran out and across the road heading for the truck. Green stayed where he could see us and still watch Connelly. While Denbeaux climbed up into the cab behind the wheel, I, very quietly, opened the door on the passenger side and left it that way.

Holding our positions for about ten minutes. Denbeaux and I could hear the two guys splashing around. Connelly waited until they were well out into the river, on their backs, playing seal. Then he signaled Green, and then us.

Denbeaux started the truck.

Until then I don't think I ever appreciated just how noisy those big bastards are. The engine kicked over with a deafening roar. Connelly and Green were off like a shot. They dashed down the embankment and under the bridge. They raced across and scooped up the clothes and boots of the startled truckers. Arms full, they came scrambling back up the bank again on the other side. All without a pause.

For maybe four or five seconds our swimmers just stood there, the water up to their chests, watching the whole thing in horror. Taking in Connelly's, "Hi, you fuckers! How's the water?"

Then, with howls of anguish the truckers exploded into action, trying to yell, swim for the bank, run across the water and fly all at the same time. Jesus, what an uproar!

In the truck, Denbeaux was revving the engine and bellowing at Connelly and Green, "Come on you bastards! Run!"

Connelly and Green looked like they were coming up the bank in slow motion, their arms full of gear, their feet going out from under them on the slippery rocks. Stumbling. Laughing and swearing at the same time. I leaped off the truck, ran over and grabbed Connelly by the shoulders as he neared the top. Hauling him up. Then I did the same for Green.

Jesus Christ! I could hardly believe my eyes! The taller of the two truckers, a big rangy, black guy, who clearly knew what running was about, had already rounded into sight and he was eating up the distance as he started up that bank in great bounding strides. His howls of rage must have been heard back at Fort Bragg!

By the time I got a hand onto Green, pulling him up onto the flatter surface of the road, Denbeaux had the truck in gear. It was already rolling. Heading out and onto the bridge. Beginning to pick up speed. Green, gasping for breath but breaking into nervous laughter as he looked back over his shoulder at the furious, naked man swarming toward us and nearing the top of the bank.

Connelly had one foot on the running board and was trying to hop to keep up with the truck while he threw in the stolen clothes and kept his balance. Jumping aboard and shouting, "Hold it...hold it, Denbox, you dumb bastard! *Not so fast!*"

Denbeaux hitting the brake too hard. I saw Connelly disappear headfirst with one great crash, landing inside on the floor under the dashboard. A pile of ass and legs.

I leapt on then, trying to keep the open door from slamming into me as I turned half around. Letting out a squawk of surprise! That naked trucker was coming fast! No more than twenty yards behind Green and charging like an enraged bull.

The truck, in fits and starts, was only going about ten miles an hour and we were only about a quarter of the way across the bridge. Green was running headlong right at me, clutching his armload of clothes.

"Oh, my Christ, step on it!" I yelped. Hanging onto the door with one arm, and making a desperate grab for Green. Catching him by the shirtfront and jerking him toward me, pulling with all my might.

All I remember is falling backwards into the cab on top of Connelly, with Green on top of me, clothes and boots flying everywhere. Bedlam. Denbeaux slamming down on the accelerator and yelling as we surged forward, "We're off, we're off!"

Tires squealing, motor roaring, and above everything else, the squawks of a truckload of terrified chickens! We careened across the bridge like a great mad thing. I know Denbeaux had the accelerator right on the floor because in no time we were disappearing up the road on the other side. The door finally slammed shut with a crash!

Denbeaux, hanging onto the wheel and laughing uproariously, was cheering the truck on.

"Yahoooooo! Roll, you mother humper, roll!"

The trucker who had come closest to catching us was left stumbling in our wake. He staggered to a stop halfway across the bridge, standing there alone as we roared off, his curses lost in the swirling dust and general uproar.

Oh what a sweet feeling it was! When I finally righted myself and leaned out the window to look back. I could see him way back in the distance. Shaking his fist. His mouth working soundlessly. All I could hear was our own laughter, Denbeaux whooping and the steady throb of the truck engine. In addition, of course, to the delicious din from our captured booty.

CHAPTER THIRTY-SIX

Gomez had been up on the mountainside taking in the whole operation through his binoculars. He told us later that the guy chasing Green had come within inches of grabbing the back of the truck as we took off. Fortunately, the way Denbeaux was careening around, with the dust and dirt flying everywhere, the guy just couldn't see to get a grip on anything.

Gomez said he'd never seen a more dejected pair than those two bare-ass GI's standing beside that road in the middle of nowhere, watching their truck disappear into the Georgia mountains.

Apparently, they spent one hell of a long afternoon hiding under that bridge, waiting for it to get dark, and they had to be careful because those hills were full of bible belters. If they ran out naked and tried to flag down the wrong people, they could end up with an ass full of rock salt. Or worse.

As we got the story later, they had to wait until well after dark, after they had practically been eaten alive by mosquitoes, before they could make their way across the fields. They picked up enough clothes from a scarecrow to cover the essentials. Then they headed down to one of the main roads and eventually flagged down one of the military vehicles out searching for them. We would have given a lot to hear them explaining that one to their CO and fellow troopers.

Our plan, in the meantime, was to get those chickens off the road in a hurry, hide the truck, grab a few choice birds and turn the rest loose in the Georgia woods. We would radio Base with the map coordinates of the truck's location later. A few miles down the road, we turned off on a lonely dirt trail into the foothills, just big enough for the truck. It was still before noon when we stopped, with a hard four hour hike back to our team area ahead, but still leaving plenty of time to get there by dark. We would have to cross some pretty tough terrain, but we'd picked our route with care so that we wouldn't lead the eighty-deuce from the truck to our doorstep.

By the time we stopped the truck, we were still pretty high on the excitement. Laughing like loons and teasing each other, recounting just how screwed up everyone else had been. As a result, it was later than we intended when we finally got started on what turned out to be a surprisingly long and tiring job.

One by one, we hauled the crates off the truck, broke them open, shooed off the chickens, smashed the crates into small pieces and threw the pieces back into the truck. Damn, but there were a lot of those boxes. And even more goddamn chickens. We had assumed that the chickens would scatter as soon as they were freed, but instead they milled around us, refusing to leave. When at last we were ready to move out, we started off in two pairs, each carrying a crate of chickens between us.

We headed into the woods with our crated chickens squawking and cackling loudly in protest. The noise, and our clumsy passage through the woods, seemed to create an attraction of singular fascination to all the other chickens. They promptly began following us, scurrying along the ground, flapping through the underbrush, and even fluttering in short bursts from bush to bush in our wake.

By the time we had gone a few hundred yards or so into the woods we knew we had problems. To begin with, a crate of live chickens turns out be a lot heavier than one would imagine. And going up and down hills across difficult terrain was no easy task with those crates. We kept switching sides and hands, but it was tough going.

There was a worse problem. No matter how many times we stopped, set down the crates, and tried to shoo them off, the freed chickens would only strut angrily away, swearing noisily, and then come flocking back into our wake as soon as we started off again.

Two hours of slow going and our feathered flock was still with us. We were hot and tired and it seemed like the whole world was alive with chickens. God, did they make a racket. We started worrying that the entire countryside must be following our progress--the Pied Pipers of feathers.

Tempers were already short when Green, who knew as much about chickens as I knew about coalmines, got *his* bright idea. Our best bet, he told us, was to wait until we got to the top of the next rise. Then, if we took off downhill at a full gallop, we could flat outrun our feathered friends. According to him, we'd be long gone and up the next rise before the chickens knew what happened.

We were all so tired, no one even argued. We sat and had a smoke, gathering strength.

Up and ready, we took off. Four looney troopers in two pairs, galloping downhill swinging crates of live chickens between us. Their weight alone propelling us faster and faster. We were up to a good 20 mph, with disaster looming, when Denbeaux and I finally chucked it in, dropping the crate and sliding to a long ass-burning halt.

That was when Connelly tripped over the bush. We watched him rolling over and over in front of us like a child's hoop. Until he hit the tree. He slowed considerably after that. Which is more than I can say for his partner, Green.

Green, before our awe-stricken gaze, continued on! Down the hill in great hurdling leaps and bounds! Jumping over and between bushes. The rope handle of the crate of chickens was still clutched in his sweaty left fist, as the crate itself bounced and ricocheted of every rock and bush along his path. At last it struck a large dogwood broadside, spewing live chickens and wooden slats all over the countryside.

Green, spinning around like a drunken top, at last came to a halt. A diving, falling, watery, headfirst halt into the creek at the bottom of the gully.

For one cheery moment, I had hopes he had been killed, but the fates were against that. Green pulled his muddy face out of the gurgling water, and waved the remains of the chicken crate at us in a weak salute.

In the brief silence that followed, Connelly sat up slowly, groaning and rubbing his stinging shins. That's when I noticed that some of the chickens, quite a few actually, were already on the other side of the creek ahead of Green. The others were all over the hill, pecking away in total unconcern.

Denbeaux did not turn his head. He sat hunched forward, his chest heaving, but his eyes slid over and met mine. "Golly, gee, whiz," he said. "What a swell idea that was! Remind me to kill Green tomorrow."

We gathered ourselves together and resumed our weary passage, bruised but no wiser. No further suggestions for ridding us of our feathered battalion were forthcoming, so we plodded on. With dusk closing upon us, we finished the last mile or so of the steep climb back to our team area.

I still have a vivid memory of the started looks on the faces of Rozzelli and Gomez. They had been watching our progress up the last few hundred yards. Watching as we climbed steadily, leading our crack guerilla force of about two hundred flapping chickens.

Gomez, in particular, was flabbergasted, open-mouthed, as a disgusted Denbeaux drew abreast, chickens flapping all around us. "Well, you wanted a plump one," Bill said. "Help yourself. You'll damn sure find one in there somewhere!"

Two days later, the rest of the team, our would-be rescuers, made it back at last, heavily laden with the goodies they had lugged for three backbreaking days over the mountains.

"Good Christ," said Colte, looking around in astonishment. "What the hell have you guys done? Gone into the egg business?"

The next few days were glorious indeed. Rozzelli's sprained ankle improved dramatically under the continued ministrations of Gomez and we were eating chicken in about every way that the imagination of man could devise.

We had fried chicken. We dug holes and heated rocks and had baked chicken. We put cooked chicken in a rubber bag and kept it in our icy mountain stream and had cold chicken. When it rained, we had wet chicken. But we didn't even make a dent in the chicken population that had followed us up to our forest hideaway.

God only knows what the chickens ate, or why they even stayed there. They seemed to thrive, but I soon became convinced they must be about the dumbest creatures on this earth. Every night the whole flock would scatter squawking and screeching as "Cookie Gomez" used his special surgical field training to dispatch half a dozen for our evening's repast. But, as soon as he was through, with blood still running from his tree-stump chopping block, back they would come every damn time.

Cookie explained to us, in the technical language of the trained field surgeon, that he always let the headless chickens run free, because it helped to "pump out the bad stuff." Watching Cookie work, I sometimes came close to pumping out a little of the bad stuff myself. But I didn't. After our steady diet of C-rations, chicken, even three times a day, tasted pretty damn good to me.

CHAPTER THIRTY-SEVEN

It was the Wednesday after that lovely coup that the first storm warnings came drifting in about the 'Great Chicken Grab.' Denbeaux and I, of course, were the first to know.

Some bird colonel back at Bragg had gone ballistic when he found out that a whole group of 82nd troopers had been deprived of their premium rations and had to make do in the field with vegetables and omelets for their Sunday dinner. The chickens in question had been paid for with 82nd currency and he was furious that his men had to go without just because of some smart-ass, fancy-britches, Special Forces hooligans. *Stealing trucks! Stealing army chickens! What in the hay-ell was the U.S. Army coming to?*

Apparently, this colonel knew all about *our kind*. He'd heard all about Bank's Bandits. As far as he was concerned, a general court martial was too damn good for the lot of us.

Without consulting either his superiors, or ours, he enplaned for Georgia likes an avenging angel. I can imagine him during the flight down, poring over his army manual and redlining every breach of regulations involved in our caper.

The message we got from Base was brief, but reading between the lines, we got the picture. This colonel had flown in unannounced to the local field headquarters of the Military Intelligence officers assigned to referee the problem. He had stormed in and demanded, *ordered* in fact, that he be taken immediately to the camp of those 'goddamn chicken thieves.' He wanted *names*.

315

Base had agreed to the visit only on the condition that it would be *outside* the problem, and only if the colonel agreed to return to Bragg without communicating our whereabouts to his troops in the field. His reply was simple. "I don't give a damn *where* they are, I just want the name, rank and serial number of their commanding officer. I want the names of the men who left my two troopers naked in the field."

I don't know if any civilian can appreciate what it feels like to be a dog-ass private first class in the United States Army, who has just taken a radio message that says, in essence, that there is one red-faced, bullshit, full-bird colonel out after his ass. It certainly jangles up the juices.

As Denbeaux and I trotted down from our lofty radio position to the team area, the guys could tell by the speed of our approach that something was up. My trembling lower lip may also have given one or two a hint.

By the time we got to Rozzelli, most of the team was present and accounted for. By the time Denbeaux and I had made it clear that Colonel Ballbuster P. Hardass was even now bearing down upon us, we had their undivided attention. Even Connelly, I noticed, a cool hand if ever there was one, had begun nervously eyeing the hordes of stray chickens pecking about our campsite and roosting in the lower branches of the trees about us. I saw Colte picking stray chicken feathers from his shirt and pants and stuffing them deep into his pockets.

Only Rozzelli seemed totally undisturbed.

We had found him lying against a tree, dozing quietly in the afternoon sun. When we clustered around, he opened one eye sleepily while we gave him the news. When we finished, his tanned face split with that distinctive, lunatic grin.

With that, he dropped his cap over his eyes and settled back. Before he dozed off again, without lifting the cap, he asked, "What time is this gooney bird supposed to get here?"

Around 1800 hours we told him.

"Ah! Dinnertime," he replied. In the few moments of reverent silence that followed, I distinctly heard him starting to snore.

So there we were at 1800 hours with the light just starting to slip away. All of us helping ourselves to a huge pan of fried chicken, when way off in the distance we heard a jeep tooling along. It came to a stop well down below us on the only dirt road that came that far up the mountain.

We all looked over at Rozzelli nervously, but he just gave us that same crooked smile. In a stage whisper, he said, "...and the condemned men ate a hearty meal." He then leaned over, blew a resounding fart, and burst out laughing.

I began to wonder if it was too late to call my mother.

Fifteen, twenty minutes. Coming into sight on the narrow, twisting path below our clearing. The colonel and the umpire. The silver bird dressed to the teeth in his class A's, his tie still knotted in place, leading the way. His face was flushed from his exertions, but he was coming at a brisk pace, and he looked in pretty good shape. Angry as a hornet trapped in a water glass, though. Having to leave the jeep and walk up the last few hundred yards had not sweetened his temper either.

He was still a good thirty yards away when he snapped out, "Alright! Let's have it! Who's in charge here? Who's in goddamn charge here?"

Rozzelli rose in one easy movement, setting down his mess gear as he did so.

"TEAM, TEEEEENNNN—SHUN!"

I mean he really barked it out good and loud, and we all jumped to a brace.

Then Rozzelli stepped forward, looking every inch the soldier himself. Facing the colonel, his right hand snapped upward in a salute. "Captain Rozzelli, Sir! 10th Special Forces! Welcome to our team area, Colonel!"

There was only one small thing that may have spoiled the picture a bit, and I don't' mean to sound picky. But Rozzelli was still holding a chicken leg in his right hand when he snapped off the salute.

The colonel, caught by surprise at seeing us all rise and brace to attention, had stopped dead in his tracks to return the salute. That's when he saw he was being saluted with a chicken leg and he looked almost apoplectic.

Before he could react, however, Rozzelli immediately switched the chicken leg to his other hand, and said, "Oh, sorry about that, Sir! You did catch us while we were eating. Come right on up. Nice to see you!"

The colonel couldn't quite figure that one out. Was this just some stupid bastard who never should have been commissioned in the first place? Or was this the freshest, most insolent son-of-a-bitch he had ever run into?

Before the colonel had a chance to make us his mind, Rozzelli waved him into the area with a courtly bow. "Come in, come in. Bring the major. How about some dinner, gentlemen? We're having a treat tonight. Fried chicken!"

While all this was taking place, no one could miss the fact that there were chickens goose-stepping at our feet, chickens roosting in the trees, chickens everywhere. The colonel, observing this, struggled for control. "I didn't come here for dinner, Captain. I came here about these goddamn chickens!"

Rozzelli stared blankly at the colonel, a startled look of boyish wonderment on his face. "Chickens?" he answered, politely. "Do you mean *these wild* chickens, Sir?"

That remark was followed by one of the longest and deadliest pauses I have ever witnessed. I was aware of drops of sweat running down my nose and splashing onto my shirt. Blip, blip, blip.

The colonel's eyes bulged, then receded into two fiercely burning coals and his upper lip rolled back like a maddened canine. His hand went into his breast pocket and a notebook and pen appeared. When he spoke, it was through clenched teeth. "Captain. I want the names. The full names, ranks and serial numbers of the men who stole these chickens. And I want them *now!* Do I make myself clear?"

Rozzelli walked forward then, not hurrying. He didn't stop until he was about a foot in front of the colonel. The grin was gone, and he looked the colonel square in the eye. To do this, he had to look down slightly, since he stood almost a full head taller than the colonel.

"Colonel," he said, taking his time about it, "You can certainly have my name, rank and serial number, and welcome to it. And let me assure you that I was really shocked and saddened to hear that some guys had gone and stolen your chickens. Took them right away from your badass 82nd troopers, is what I gather. That right? And a truck, too."

Rozzelli continued. "Way I get it, *somebody* in charge of that operation was pretty damn slipshod, wouldn't you say? Men parking and swimming and leaving a whole truckload of chickens unguarded in enemy territory."

Rozzelli and the colonel continued staring directly into each other's eyes.

The umpire coughed nervously, started to say something, but thought better of it, shutting up as Rozzelli flicked one hard glance in his direction.

"Now, as for your report, Colonel, I really wish I could help you out. Truly, I do. But, see, the reason I picked this area for our camp should be obvious. I took one look at all these wild chickens here, and I told my men, 'Stop right here, boys! Don't go another step! We have found the promised land!'"

The famous Rozzelli grin split his face then, and he added, "Ain't that right, Connelly? Weren't those my very words?"

All heads swung to Connelly except the colonel's. His eyes remained fixed on Rozzelli.

Connelly rubbed his chin. "Uh, no Sir, Captain. Not exactly. What you said was 'Goddamn! Look at all these mother-humping chickens!' I think *that's* what you said, Sir."

You could almost feel the tension evaporate within the team with that exchange. We knew then it was alright. Rozzelli wouldn't give this guy dick. The colonel was way out of line and we all knew it. It was *his* guys who had screwed up. Big time. And that was *his* problem, not ours.

The only question now was what he would do to save face. First he wrote several notes on his pad. Not an easy task since it was getting darker by the moment. Then he jammed the pad back into his pocket. Spinning on his heel, we all heard the words "insolent bastards" muttered as he stormed off down the path. The umpire, falling in behind him, looked back once to give Rozzelli a quick wink.

At the last turn, before the path disappeared into the woods, the colonel stopped once more to yell back at us. "You'll hear from me, Rozzelli! I'll get those names. You can count on it. And I have *yours*, all right. It's in my book!"

We were still watching their disappearing backs when Colte suddenly stood up from behind a bush a few feet from the path. In the deepening gloom, he clasped his hands over his head, giving us a victory salute.

It had to be a full ten minutes after that when we heard the colonel's voice explode from the now pitch-black woods below. "Alright, goddamn it! That does it! Where's my fucking jeep?"

CHAPTER THIRTY-EIGHT

"Come on, you leetle turd! Gad off and geeve some won else a chance to ride. Come on! Gad off! You gad all zee fun and we gad zeep."

I braked the tractor at the end of the row and lifting my oversized and silly-looking baseball cap, wiping my forehead with a grimy sleeve. Denbeaux was following along behind the tractor with Dubois, tossing green peppers into the long, low wagon. Denbeaux mimicking Dubois, "Come on, Feetz! Gad off before this Froggie bastard gets mad and geeves *you* zeep. You get that friggin' French zeep, you'll be sorry."

Bill ducked as a plump pepper sailed past his head. I climbed down, leaving the motor idling for Dubois, who went past me to take his turn at the wheel.

Beyond us, twenty yards from the end of the pepper field, Green emerged from the back of Cummings General Store, wiping his hands on his baggy apron. Leaning on a push broom, he yelled across to us, giving us his best imitation of the kindly plantation overseer in action.

"Hey, y'all! What's all this yere stoppin' and moppin'? Let's get that there wagon movin,' y'hear. I don' want to see nothing out in that field but assholes n' elbows! Pick, you humpers! Pick!"

Ducking back inside fast as a hail of peppers landed around him. The screen door slamming. We could hear him laughing as the peppers splattered against the back of the dilapidated building.

Dubois turned the tractor, lining it up to start back across the long field. All three of us heard the two vehicles at the same time. A jeep and a truck leaving the asphalt road beyond the store and coming across the sandy gravel. They ground to a halt next to the gas pumps. Immediately, a squad of troopers with M-1's jumped down and came trotting around the building, stopping to squint into the sun in our direction. Spotting us, they broke into a run, fanning out, four or five on each side of the field.

Their sergeant ran straight toward us. On his heels, a lieutenant wearing the white armband of an umpire. They stopped just beyond the tractor, and the sergeant gestured up at Dubois. "Turn that sonofabitch off!"

Denbeaux holding up a hand before Dubois could reach for the switch. "Y'all talkin' to us, Cap'n?"

A long pause as Bill walked toward the sergeant. Trying to put as much drawl as he could into his words when he spoke again. Dipping them in Southern Comfort. "You ain' got no call to speak to us like that, Cap'n. We ain' none of us in your dang fool Yankee army. Now you git, y'hear! We got wuk to do. An you take them tother boy scouts with ya!"

For just one second, maybe only half a second, the sergeant was taken aback. His eyes batted, and he hesitated. But then he looked us over again, all three of us, and when his eyes went back to Denbeaux, he knew. Oh, he goddamn well knew alright.

His jaw came out a fraction of an inch and he stood there, staring up at Denbeaux, feet spread apart, hands on hips.

"Country boys, huh? Just a bunch of pepper pickers, huh? Well you just stay put until the Captain gets out here, farmer boys, and we'll damn soon see about that. And *you*..." He raised his voice and looked up at Dubois without moving his hands from his hips. "You got three seconds to turn off that friggin' motor or my boys here are a'goin to come up there and turn *you* off on your goddamn head!"

Oh, yeah. He knew.

Dubois cut the motor as all of us stood there. The motor chugging, coughing, wheezing, falling silent. The half-circle of troopers edged closer, surrounding us. My mouth felt like it had been dried with a blowtorch.

THU---WAAANG!!

The back screen door of the store swung open, smacking to a stop against the weathered shingles.

Green came out, followed closely by a burly trooper who had a grip on his elbow and wrist. It was clear that Anston could leave anytime, as long as he was willing to leave that particular limb behind.

Behind them, an eighty-deuce captain appeared, the silver railroad tracks glistening at the front of his blocked fatigue cap. Behind him there was another umpire, a major in army intelligence, his heavy-set stomach pushing over his fatigue pants belt. He had to hurry to keep up.

Green was bareheaded. He wore a red and black-checkered workshirt, dungarees and sneakers. His baggy grey grocer's apron flapped at his knees. He broke into a forced and unsuccessful grin as he was hustled toward us. "Hey, Will-um!" he called his voice rising nervously, but playing the game. "Hey, Will-um! These yere fellows think ahm in their aaah-meee!"

Back at the doorway, Mr. Cummings stepped out. Looking worried. Wiping his hands on his apron, he looked as nervous as we did. He knew the rules, but he didn't like them. His nephew, Henry, only about sixteen, came out also, looking angry as hell. *Where did these damn Yankees get off pushing around his pals?*

Three or four customers followed, looking confused and upset. *Them men ain't really goin' to hurt them boys, now is they? Land sakes! Them boys ain't done nothin' at all!*

Two or three more uniformed troopers came through the door, standing with the onlookers, watching. Rifles at sling arms.

The troopers behind us crowded in as the captain marched toward us. A hard shove at my shoulders, propelling me forward, almost losing my balance. Almost falling. Feeling a rush of anger as I caught myself. *What the hell?*

I started to spin around, but I was grabbed before I could do so. Three or four hands shoving me roughly. Bill and Francois getting the same. The three of us were pushed into a line facing the Captain. The umpires moved up to look over shoulders.

Green looked around, blinking at the captain. "Say, General, are you in charge hee-ah? What seems to be the trouble? Hell, if I short-changed someone in the store, I'll make it good!"

The captain, looked us over, ignoring Green. His hand came up to point at me. Always *me*, for chrissakes.

"Let's start with the half-pint. Fairfield! Benson! Bring him along, and follow me. Hold the rest of them here for now, Sergeant, and those men are not to do any talking among themselves, understand? Separate 'em. Sit 'em down, let 'em wait until I send for 'em."

Walking behind the captain between the two troopers he called Fairfield and Benson. Trying not to march. Just a country boy! Feeling the icy trails of sweat running down my sides to my belt line. The heavy-set umpire trotting along with us.

Jesus! My cover story! Get it right now, for chrissakes! My mind a blank. Damn! *Why me?*

They frog-stepped me around the corner from the field and stopped in the shade beside the store. The captain pointed. One of the troopers spun me so that my back was up against the building. Hard, banging me against the wall. The back of my head, shoulders, and rump hitting at once. A sharp stinging smack.

"*Hey!* God Dammit!"

Before I even got it out, there was a beefy hand flat against my chest and a second hard shove. Another slam into the building. This time making my head ring.

"Shaddup!" The guy on my right, leaned in. Hoping I wouldn't.

The captain, his back to us, was looking off at the horizon with his cap in his hands, casually wiping the inside with his handkerchief. The umpire was turned half away, but his eyes flicked over to me, then away again. Pretending not to hear or notice the rough stuff.

So, that's the way its gonna be, huh! A little rough stuff is okay, but don't kill anybody! Alright you whores! Just don't be surprised if I give one of you a kick right in your cultured pearls, you friggin' bastards! Angry as hell now, glaring back. The leering troopers standing on either side of me.

"Name?"

"Huh?"

"WHAT'S YOUR GODDAMN NAME?"

The captain spun around to fire that first question at me, catching me by surprise. He stepped in, shoving his face in at me from no more than a foot away, shouting the question the second time.

"Uh...Farnum, Sir. James A. Farnum."

Shit. Why did I say "sir?" Jeez. *Watch it. Watch it.*

"YOU'RE A LYING BASTARD!"

A bellow. Right in my face. But ready for it this time. Alert.

"Guess you'd know what a bastard is, Corporal, being a damnyankee!"

An observer would have missed the short jolt he gave me in the solar plexus entirely if he weren't watching very closely. A quick jab with his stiffened finger tips where the ribs parted. It shot the wind right out of me. Brief, fierce pain. The two troopers, each kept a hand flattened against my shoulders to stop me from doubling over. To keep me flat against the building with the rough shingles digging into my back.

"I.D.! Let's see it. Now!"

The words came at the same moment as the jab and the captain's hand lingered right in front of my stomach, palm up. Waiting. A long gurgle as I struggled to get my breath back. I fumbled in my back pocket, pulling out the old wallet I borrowed from the Divens family the week before. I was a little sick to my stomach from the jab, but determined not to show it.

The wallet was good. Nice and shabby, like it might have been discarded before the Civil War. Inside I had three dollars, a much-folded hand-written letter to "Dear Jimmy" from "Your Ma," with Atlanta, June 10, 1953 at the top. There was also an old, yellowed, I.D. card that had been given to Mr. Divens years before. It probably came with the wallet but had never been filled out until recently.

Mr. Cummings had taken all the papers we wanted "fixed" to a lawyer and had them typed up. We had all kept our real first names, ages and other data whenever possible, to make memorizing our cover stories, easier. My card read:

James A. Farnum

1027 Peachtree Street

Atlanta, Georgia

D.O.B. 1-20-33

Occupation: Farm Worker

My story was that I was born and brought up right in that part of Atlanta, and had never been away from that city until I came up here to live with the Divens family and work the farms. More important, I was clearly not a Rhodes scholar.

The captain's eyes lit up. "Atlanta, huh? Benson! Go get Cogsworth. Bring him over here."

Benson trotted off. My hand moved up unconsciously to rub my still sore stomach. Bastard. I watched the captain studying the card.

"Age?"

"Twenty." No "sir" this time. Glaring at him, but an inner voice warning me. *Be careful.*

"What's the population of Atlanta?"

A shrug. "Don't rightly know. Lots bigger than this place, though. Must be way over five hundred people live there."

The umpire suppressed a smile, the Captain's neck reddening.

Two troopers rounded the corner and trotted over. Benson and his cracker friend, no doubt. The captain nodded now at the umpire. I could read his mind. *Watch this, you dink!* The umpire moved up a bit closer.

"More than five hundred, eh? Teach you that in high school, did they?"

"Never went to no high school."

Touche! Didn't like that one, did you, Captain Asshole?

The captain walked away, dragging Cogsworth with him. A consultation. The captain nodding his head. Coming back in three minutes. Cogsworth stood beside him, leaning in. The umpire moved in even closer, standing right beside the captain now.

"Now, then, Farnum, or whatever the hell your name really is, when I ask you a question, I want an answer *fast!* You got that? Any stalling, delaying, screwing around, your ass is heading for the clink. That's the rules. Confirm that, Major, if you please."

The umpire nodded. He coughed once. "Uh, the accent, that we don't count. But if he answers in a way so as to raise a question about his truthfulness, if he's, uh, well, just being evasive about something that he ought to know, well, that's enough."

"Damn right it is," the captain added. And then he began firing the questions at me. Five full minutes. Where did you go to school? What are the streets that cross Peachtree between your house and the school? Where is the nearest fire station? There's a trucking company a few blocks away from the address in your wallet. What is it? His voice gradually got sharper and more frustrated.

Giving him back the answers. Talking as slowly as I could, but answering. Parrying a few I didn't know with, "Cain't rightly say!" Or, "Never heered of that." The umpire giving the captain a "that's not fatal" shrug, and a nod telling him to keep going.

Cogsworth was leaning in the whole time, listening carefully. His eyes were wide, staring at me. The captain's eyes flicked back and forth between us. Furious as most of my answers were followed by Cogsworth's quiet, "Raht! That's raht!"

The captain finally spluttered to a halt. Cogsworth turning to look up at him. "Sheet, Captain! This here boy sure do talk funny, but he sure is from Atlanta, ain't he?"

"*Atlanta!*" The captain spat the word and turned on his helpmate as if it were all his fault. "Can't you hear that goddamn Boston accent, Cogsworth? Atlanta, my *ass!*"

The major from Intelligence gritted his teeth to keep a straight face. The other two troopers looked disgusted. Cogsworth now confused and embarrassed. His feelings were clearly hurt and I knew what he was thinking. *Sheet! That's what you get, trying to help out a pissyass, goddamn Yankee officer!*

The captain spat. Jerking his thumb toward the corner of the building. "Alright, goddamn it! Take Rhett Butler here back and bring me the next one. Let's try the big stoop this time. What was it they called him? Willum? Swell! Don't run off, Cogsworth. This one's probably another good ol' Atlanta boy, lived right across the friggin' street!"

CHAPTER THIRTY-NINE

As my escorts hustled me by, we passed Mr. Cummings, young Henry, and the other concerned faces. I gave them a fast wink. Feeling elated, I dropped to the ground a few feet from Dubois as one of the troopers barked at the others. "Watch him!"

Benson and Fairfield went over and grabbed Bill, jerking him to his feet and starting him off at a trot between them. Bill looked back over his shoulder, over their heads to catch my eye, an eyebrow raised. I nodded and winked back just as Fairfield caught him looking and gave him a short, sharp blow in the stomach with his rifle butt. There was a great grunt from Bill, then a few seconds silence. Bill was doubled over between them as they hustled him off. We heard Bill's voice. "Why, thank you, Son! I needed that. I *love* pain!"

Another 'thump' as they rounded the corner out of sight.

All my work with Mr. Divens had paid off hugely. He was the head of our team's adopted family. The lived about three miles up in the mountains from the general store, but he did have a cousin who lived in Atlanta. On Peachtree Street, in the same ten hundred block I used for my cover story. Mr. Divens and his family visited there for a couple of weeks every year.

We had made a game of it, picking their brains. Mr. Divens and his kids. Getting them to tell us everything they had seen and could remember about that few blocks of Atlanta. Then, as extra ammo for our cover stories, we did some other digging. Reading the Atlanta Constitution, other local papers. Picking up other facts and local color. The name of the mayor. The location of the city hall.

We sat in the hot sun waiting. Dubois was a few feet away, looking sour, but he flashed a quick smile at me. The thick, black mustache that he had been growing since we left Jump School had begun to curve up impressively at the ends. A product of his constant, patient, twirling. Anston was sitting beyond him chewing a blade of grass, still playing the country boy to the hilt. He looked up at the three troopers towering over him. "Sheet, Frenchie! They sure do pile the *merde* up high round here, don't they?"

A "shut up!" and the crack of a boot kicking him in the ankle rang out together.

Green exploded in pain. "Ouch! *Shit!*" He rubbed his ankle furiously. Subsiding. Still smirking.

Another five or six minutes sitting in the hot sun. Then, quiet again. Around us we could hear flies buzzing, boots shuffling. We could hear the captain's voice in the distance rising in anger. Annoyed murmurs among the troopers. One of them saying, "Shee-it! Give me five minutes alone with anyone of these assholes and I'll get you friggin' answers, alright."

The younger umpire, the outsider in this group, pacing back and forth nervously. Everyone waiting. Here they come! Denbeaux and the Katzenjammer kids. Trotting back. So far so good!

Dubois was next. Denbeaux dropped to the ground, pulled out his shirt and reached a hand inside to rub a sore spot on his chest. Where he'd gotten thumped good. Grinning. A couple of our keepers were smirking down at him. Denbeaux leaned forward confidentially, still rubbing his chest. "Fleas, y'know."

I knew Dubois' cover story almost as well as he did. Supposedly, he was a French Canadian from Quebec, where, in fact, he had spent some time. According to his story, he was working his way through the American South on a sightseeing tour. He even had what purported to be a Canadian Army medical discharge card in his wallet. Supposedly issued for a bad heart.

We had been taking turns back at camp giving each other the third degree. Dubois had collapsed us all when Bill prodded him about his medical discharge. "Eet waz becuz of, 'ow you say eet, my condeeshun. I am, what you zay een thees countree, queer!"

I hoped he wouldn't run that one by the good captain and his helpmates. They might not laugh quite as hard as we did.

Dubois returned, running stiffly between his guards. We got a quick glimpse of the captain pacing angrily back and forth beside the building. Looking bullshit.

Up and at 'em Anston, baby. Your turn. Tuck it to 'em, pal. Watching Anston being run off. "Hell, boys! I tole the general I'd give him back his goddamn nickel." THUMP! They were almost to the corner. "What's he want...a dime?"

THUMP! THUMP!

The last wait, while our confidence rose and the frustration of the troopers increased. Then we all heard it, loud and clear. "Alright goddammit! Take him back. Get him out of here before I knock his smart-ass teeth in!"

Anston and the wart hogs came around the corner. Good old Anston. Couldn't shake him up. The troopers around us now looking thoroughly disgusted and grumbling. "Shit, man! You call this friggin' game fair! We got ever one of these bastards cold, we still can't run their asses in! *Shee-it!*"

The captain and the major came out from behind the building, following Green and his escort. The captain looked pissed to a fare-thee-well.

Bill, Francois and I stood up as Green approached. The captain, stopped Green while he was still about fifteen yards away. "Hold it there, Buddy. Hold up one second. There's something I've got to say, and I'm going to say it right here in front of all of my men."

Green, obviously surprised, turned back to look at him. The captain was actually smiling. He walked up, holding his hand out to Green.

"I gotta say it, Son. You are one hell of a soldier. You and your buddies over there. You beat me fair and square."

He pumped the hand of our astonished teammate, and slapped his shoulder. "I'm going to personally write a commendation to Colonel Bank on the job you guys did here today. What are your names, Son? For my report."

Denbeaux, Dubois and I, our mouths opened in horrified unison. Too late! Green's proud answer rolled out. "Private First Class Anston Green. 10th Special Forces! And those guys are Denbeaux, Dubois and Fitzpat..."

Maybe he saw the explosion of joy in the captain's eyes before he finished. Maybe that was what stopped Anston. Maybe it was a belated bell going off somewhere inside his head. But it was too late. He had said enough.

The captain could not contain himself. He gave a jump and clicked his heels like Hitler in Paris in that famous newsreel. "You *heard* that, Major!" he bellowed. "*You heard him!* We've *got* them! We've got the *sonsabitches!*"

With a roar that dropped all of our hearts into our boots, he ran up to point at us. "*Arrest* them! Arrest those men, Sergeant! Make them *priz --nars!*"

Exultant troops all around us. Cheering. Hands grabbing us and rushing us toward the truck. Everyone wanting to grab some part of one of us. To be in on it.

A jostling, plunging, riotous run toward the truck. My Chicago Cubs baseball cap sailed off, lost forever. The sergeant was getting nervous. He was afraid his boys might rush us right on past the truck and get on with the lynching. He had to shout to be heard. "Okay, okay! Easy now. We've got 'em. Put 'em in the truck. First squad in with 'em. Hold it now! *First* squad only, I said! Kelly! Get your ass back out here! That's it. Second squad stay here for now."

My shins were scraped painfully on the bed of the truck as I was half thrown, half shoved in. The civilian workshirt I had borrowed from Mr. Divens the week before was ripped at one shoulder. We stood while the handcuffs were passed up from the cab and as our hands were secured behind our backs. The four of us were pushed roughly to the floor. Jammed all the way back against the cab of the truck. Facing the exultant troopers.

Green was devastated. In shock! The other three of us were disgusted. We had been home free. It had been so close. So goddamn close.

Our Pennsylvania coal miner looked almost ready to cry. He tried to mutter an apology. "Goddammit, I thought...can they *do* that? Aww, shit!"

I was so angry myself that I didn't dare look at him. As the truck rolled away from the store, the rest of the troopers crowded around cheering. The jeep fell in behind us, then moved out to lead. Peacock captain proudly sitting next to the driver, giving his troops the two-fingered Churchill greeting as they drove past.

Denbeaux, who was sitting beside Green, gave him a nudge with his elbow. "Hey, forget it, Pal. You got suckered is all. Just forget it."

Rolling toward the Georgia slam. Denbeaux spoke again. "Truth is, I've been dying to see one of these goddamn jails. Besides, this is where old Farnum here will come into his own. Show us how he used to trap them cock-a-roaches back in Atlanta. Bread and water, my ass. With ol' Farnum along, we'll eat like kings!"

CHAPTER FORTY

Jumping down from the truck. Having trouble with our hands handcuffed behind us, but we managed to do it without falling. We got no help. We found ourselves standing in the center of a small town that none of us had been in before. Until then it had only been a dot on our maps. And, as we looked around, none of us very sure which dot.

An old barn of a house stood directly in front of us. It sort of leaned to one side like it was still looking for a place to rest after standing there for close to a hundred years. White clapboard, but the paint looked fairly fresh. Butted up to it on one end there was a two-story stone structure. Ugly is as ugly does. The lock-up for this end of the County.

"INSIDE! MOVE IT! THINK WE GOT ALL DAMN DAY!"

A boot answered the sergeant, catching me flush on the buttocks, and making me bellow in surprise and pain as I staggered forward. Trying to turn and get a number, but other hands pushed me forward toward the door. I passed the grinning captain who was looking innocently down the street. I tried to get a leg out to kick him in the shins as they ran me by, missing and hitting the side of my sneakered foot against the heavy doorframe. Excruciating pain. *Ain't this grand?*

The Sheriff's office was on the left inside. A knee slammed into my rump as we got through the door. Just to aim me. The others got the same. The four of us were red-faced and disheveled when the hands finally let us go. All of us were in some pain, our shirts pulled out. About ten troopers were crowding around us. *Go ahead, hotshots! Try something.*

The sheriff was sitting in his chair, his feet up on an open drawer of his battered old wooden desk, a few files in his hands. The room smelled of pipe tobacco, now mingled with the pungent body odor of the men pushing in.

The sheriff sighed, dropped his feet to the floor, put down his paperwork and turned to face us just as the captain came through the group to stand at the end of his desk. "Four of 'em this time," he said. Like the sheriff couldn't count. Like they did this two or three times a day.

The sheriff's hands rested on the desk. He looked like he could pick it up with one of them. He had on a tan shirt with a badge over the left breast pocket, but no other insignia. He was wearing blue dungarees and yellow work boots.

"Good morning, men," he said, addressing the group. He looked at the captain. "*Four*, you say. Shoot, all these men in here, their rifles at the ready and all, I thought maybe you'd gone and captured a whole company of these here spy fellas."

The captain didn't like that at all. Not one bit. Before he could speak, however, in that same slow drawl, the sheriff added, "Suppose you could clear some of your fellas out of here, give us a little room to breathe? Jest keep enough in here, Captain, so's you feel safe."

The captain's face went from annoyed white to an angry red, and he looked at his sergeant and jerked his thumb at the door. "Everybody outside. Wait by the truck. You can stay, Clark, you got the keys to the cuffs."

Sergeant Clark repeated the order, shepherding everybody toward the door. I fell in with the troops and had one foot out before he saw me. "Hey!" he yelled, then grabbed me by the neck and half-threw me back toward the desk. Denbeaux, Dubois and Green all laughing. The sheriff smiling. The captain growling, "Smartass."

Sergeant Clark slammed the door harder than he had to and crossed to stand at the other end of the desk facing the captain. His right hand rested on the butt of his .45.

The sheriff looked us over as he took a yellow legal pad from his desk and dropped it in front of him. He picked up a short stubby pencil and licked the tip, his brow wrinkling in concentration. "My name is John Henry Simpson," he told us. "I'm going to need a name and a address from each of you. It's the law."

He pointed at me. "Whyn't we start with our escapee here. Would you tell me your name and address, young fella?"

"Farnum," I began. "James..."

The sergeant leaned past Green to whack me in the stomach, hard, with a backhanded fist. "That ain't his real name, Sheriff. That's the stupid cover story they made up. Now you give the sheriff your real name, Buster, and your army serial number, or I will personally knock you right on your ass!"

Getting my breath, but the sheriff spoke before I could. Unruffled, but a harder tone to the soft drawl this time. "Any hitting takes place in my office, Sergeant, I will be the one to do it. There will be no more of that. Is that clear?"

Looking right at the sergeant. The sergeant looked across at his captain. The captain deciding to assert himself. "These are army men, Sheriff. A poor excuse for it, I'll grant you, but we know how to handle them. You can't baby 'em, Sheriff. Take my word. A good Corcoran jump boot up the ass, time to time, would do these wiseasses a world of good."

The sheriff stood up. Good Christ was he big. My eyes were even with the third button down on his shirt. He put both hands flat on his desk. "Did you two both hear what I just said?"

The sergeant and the captain fell silent. The captain was grinding his teeth.

"Well, fine. As long as we have that clear."

The sheriff sat down again and looked at me, pencil poised again. "Now then, Farnum, what is your real name and address?"

"Temple, Shirley," I said, braced for another punch, but not getting it.

The captain, nodded vigorously. "I *told* you!"

"Address, Mr. Temple?" the sheriff continued, writing the name in block letters.

"Hollywood, California, Sheriff."

He wrote down the words. "Occupation?"

"Movie starlet."

The sheriff wrote again. "Didn't recognize you, Mr. Temple, you've taken to wearing them long pants and all." Pointing at Dubois. "Name?"

"Shorge Washeenton, Shereef. I leev in Virshinia and I am a founding fazzair."

The paperwork finally done, the sheriff came around and unlocked the door into the cellblock and swung it open. "When the sergeant uncuffs you, go inside and wait for me at the stairs. No place to run to in there, boys. Even the rats has to come to me, they want to go home for a holiday."

One by one, we were uncuffed and stepped inside. Rubbing our scraped and sore wrists as we waited. The sheriff stepped in, closing and locking the big door behind him.

"Upstairs, men. Case I have to lock up a noisy drunk or two tonight. Or a axe murderer. It's quiet up there and clean. And I've put extra blankets on those beds."

He took a ring of keys off the wall and followed us up the stairs. We saw six large cells, three on each side with a corridor in between. All the doors were open. "Pick anyone you want boys, they's all the same, pretty much. No radios, no tellyphones, no women in the rooms after six. Otherwise, you men are in the lap of Georgia luxury."

We walked in to the middle room on the left and the sheriff closed and locked the door behind us. Big key. Big lock. Solid stone walls. Bars that would keep a gorilla caged, no problem. One open toilet in the corner. Six bunks. Plain metal frame, two rolled blankets on each and one pillow, no pillowcase. A pot-bellied stove with a pipe disappearing into the ceiling. Couldn't get a head through that opening, never mind a body. One small barred window you'd have to stand on a cot to look out. Steel mesh outside the glass. Like wearing a belt and suspenders. Oh, we were in for the night, alright, and no mistake about that.

The sheriff outside kicking a foot against the bars. Nodding to the toilet. "Not much privacy, but it do work. You want room service, just flush. I know it'd be tempting to send Mr. Temple out for help that way, but he might not like the trip. I'll be up later, boys, with your supper. Catch yourself some shuteye, you feel like it."

Great. Welcome to the slam in North Georgia. Price you pay when you screw up. All we needed was a harmonica solo and Jimmy Cagney being dragged past the door by the screws.

As if reading my mind, Green crossed to the bars, grabbed them in both hands and yelled, "You've got to let me go home, Warden—my ole Mammy's dying of the clap!"

CHAPTER FORTY-ONE

An endless afternoon in our cell. The second floor of the jailhouse was stifling with not a breath of air coming through the small window high up on our wall. Our stomachs were rumbling. We'd all eaten a good breakfast before heading out this morning for our respective jobs, picking peppers or working in the store, but that was a long time ago now. We had already been hungry and looking forward to lunch when Captain Marvel and his creepy cretins had rolled in.

"Peaches," Green advised us. "I had them all picked out to start my lunch off right. The big can, in sugared water. I can taste 'em right now."

Dubois, was standing on tiptoe on the bunk and looking out the window. "Forgat zoze peaches. What we should have done, yes, was eat zoze peppers, a dozen each. Zen, just about now, we could all av backed up to zee cell door and blown eet off eet's hinges."

It was getting on toward four o'clock. Metal clanged downstairs and we heard footsteps clumping up the stairs at the end of the corridor. It was the sheriff, holding a metal tray in one hand and stopping in front of our cell. Four tin cups of ice water, four large hunks of unbuttered bread. At least they were big.

"Early supper, boys. I have to go out for a few hours tonight so I'll give it to you now. Wish it was more, I truly do, but rules of the game."

He held the tray so that each of us in turn could take a cup and a hunk of bread. "Bread's good and hearty, leastways. Wife bakes it fresh ever day." Looking at me with my mouth already full of delicious bread. "Don't have to rush, Mr. Temple. They'll be another whole hunk like that in the morning."

The sheriff stopping again at the top of the stairs. "Shore wish someone would explain these here war games to my wife. She like to bit my head off when she seen me with this tray. Mimicking his wife's voice. 'You spects growed parashooters to live on that, John Henry? Boys what are servin' our country. Them boys'll *die*, John Henry! They'll jest plain keel over and die!'"

The Sheriff, as he went down the stairs, still doing his wife's falsetto for us. "John Henry, ah swear, you must be the *meanest* man in all of Jaw-juh!"

Two hours later, we were even hungrier. The bread we'd received earlier had only whetted our appetites. The clanging of the metal door again. Quiet steps on the stairs this time. Pat, pat, pat.

All of us pushed up against the bars as a different head and shoulders come into view. A mass of salt and pepper hair with an almost bird-like face below it peered down the corridor between the cells.

She came into view then, one step at a time. Full country skirt to the floor. Starched apron with flowers and rabbits on it. A tray in her hands with a white linen towel draped over what? The towering alps! Her voice was shaky when she spoke.

"Now, boys! What ahm doin' here is somethin' terrible. *Terrible!* An' John Henry will plain hang me out to dry, 'n he ever finds out. He'll be just fierce, ah know it, an him usually slower to boil than a ice cube you boys hungry?"

Her last words ran together with the others just like that, without a breath, turning into a question before she finished. Mrs. Simpson bent over then and placed the tray on the floor, out of breath, but more from fright, I think, than her exertions. Our four, "Yes, Ma'am's," came out as one clear statement, all of us staring at the covered tray.

"Now, boys, I has to know. Kin I trust you? Will you each give me your solemn word, as God be your witness, that if I open this cell door you won't none of you try to run off? 'Cause it would be the end of me, boys, if'n you all escaped."

Down the line, every one of us, right hand raised, the other on our hearts. "Our word! Our solemn oath. We swear it." Parashooters, yes, but stupid, no.

Dubois put the keystone block in place. "On my 'on-aire, Madame, as a gentleman of France."

The last word, of course, sounded like "fronce," and Mrs. Simpson repeated it in awe, staring straight in to the limpid Gallic eyes of the speaker. "*Lan* sakes! A gennelman of Fronce. Oh, my, my."

The lock turned and we all pulled to swing the heavy door back. Mrs. Simpson turned to pick up the tray, but Francois got there first. "But, Madame, you must allow me, s'il vous plait!"

Mrs. Simpson, her face shining, "Why mercy, mercy, mown soor." She turned to the rest of us. "I seen that in a book onct. It means 'thank ye kindly.'"

Following Francois into the cell, the rest of us rushing to clear the small table of cigarettes and the big metal ashtray that had been left for us. Like an accomplished conjurer, Mrs. Simpson paused for several seconds with her fingers on the edge of the towel, before she at last swept it away.

A huge, towering bowl of fried chicken. Two covered pots, steam rising from them, lidded only until her hands could sweep in and lift them high. A rolling thunderhead of mashed potatoes with a brown gravy lake in the middle. Fresh-shucked green peas with about half a stick of butter melting quickly on the top. Four deep bowls, one on top of the other, with four large spoons in the very top. A half a loaf of her bread.

Four huge red napkins came out of her apron pocket. "You boys eat," she told us, "ah'll be back in a jif. Don't hurry none. The Sheriff is gone now to meet them army fellas clear acrost the valley, an he won't be back until after seven for his supper. Put the bones and anything else right in the stove as you finish. Dishes and spoons, too. I'll git them all later after they sets you boys loose, and John Henry none the wiser."

Her tiny form disappearing as we served up and dug in. There is a God. A kindly old gentleman. A wise God. One who clearly hates the eighty-deuce and loves Special Forces.

Don't do the crime, you can't do the time. Oh, I can do *this* time.

Food never, ever, tasted better. We threw the bones into the open stove door like Henry the Eighth feeding his hounds. One last, fat chicken leg left. Denbeaux and Green offering it to each other. *No, you Alphonse. No, you Gaston.* Dubois' hand snaked out and it was half-eaten before they knew it was gone.

Footsteps sounded on the stairs. Mrs. Simpson strode in confidently this time with another covered tray. She turned her back to us concealing something in front of her. "POP!"

She turned back with a coke bottle in one hand and a cork in the other. Mrs. Simpson watched Francois' face as she held up this prize. Her voice was a whisper. "It's wine, boys. My own dandelion wine, what I make every summer. It ain' much, but I thought, him being from Fronce and all..."

Her voice trailed off, her confidence waning, but Francois was on his feet, his tin cup in hand, and quickly beside her. A courtly bow. "Allow me, Madame, s'il vous plait."

In a thunderous silence, he carefully passed the open bottle under his nose several times, his nostrils quivering. "Aaaaah!" he said, nodding and closing one eye thoughtfully. Slowly he tipped the bottle over his metal cup, just a splash, swirling it about and studying the cup. Deliberately he poured the liquid in to his mouth, where he held it, sloshing it about noisily for several long seconds. And then he swallowed, eyes closed, long Gallic nose pointing at the ceiling like a hungry swallow. Slowly his left hand rose, the thumb and index finger making a circle in the universal sign of approval. He spoke one word that sounded a mile long the way he said it. "*Mag-nee-feek*!" And then, translating. "Magnificent!"

Mrs. Simpson seemed ready to lie down on the spot and go straight to her reward. Both hands on her chest. She spoke in a voice we could barely hear, "It *did* win fourth place at the fair two years ago, but Lan Sakes, they was only six entries."

Francois pouring out the wine all around, each of us with about two fingers in the big cups. Giving mine a tentative taste. Hey! This isn't bad at all! Ol' Froggie wasn't kidding. *This is good!*

Thick apple turnovers were on the second tray, still warm from the oven. And beside them she had placed a tall metal coffee pot. Shades of every western movie I'd ever seen. Eating the turnovers while Mrs. Simpson gathered up the empty dishes and pots. 'Long as I'm here, I'll jest take these right out with me. Put the coffee pot in the stove, 'n you're through, and I'll get them bones later, don't you worry."

All of us rose as she stood wiping her hands on her apron before picking up the tray again. "You won't never tell a soul now, you promise?"

Francois stepped forward and took one of her hands, lifting it to his lips. Her eyes followed this Gallic tradition in astonishment. "You 'ave our sacred word, Madame. No one een zeez century weel ever hair of your great dedeecation and of zee reesks you 'ave taken to 'elp us in ow-air fight for justeece."

She was almost to the stairs, her tray held high, before Francois spoke again. "Madame! WAIT! You 'ave forgot to lock us een!"

CHAPTER FORTY-TWO

It was a short ride in Sheriff Simpson's battered old station wagon. The tailgate door, which no longer fastened securely, rattled in our ears the whole way. The sheriff drove us to the outskirts of town. The sun was almost straight up above us, hot enough to melt your belt buckle.

Sheriff Simpson got out with us by the side of the road. Pulling out his pocket watch and rubbing the tarnished cover on a pant leg before he snapped it open. "Looks like about five of eleven, boys. Ah tole your friend, fella that brought y'all in, that ah was a-goin to let you boys loose at noon for yo-ah one hour head-start."

He looked over our faces as he slipped the watch back into its pocket. "Fact is, and ah know its silly of me, but I don't completely trust that man. So ahm lettin' y'all go jest a mite early."

He nodded at the woods on the side of the road where we had parked. "At noon, ahm a-gonna drive out here, pull up that dirt road, y'know, like ah was here to drop y'all off. Jest in case they is somewheres aroun' here watchin'. I've got some dummies dressed up to put in the seats from when I've done this afore. They ain't the only ones kin play games, as I see it. And then when I get in the woods, I'll toss them in the back and head home for lunch."

He pointed across the road at the long flat fields on the other side, the mountains beyond them. "Ah was you boys, ah'd head off thatta ways. Try to get over to them mountains, or close as you kin get, before noon. One o'clock I'll be out here lookin' for you, beatin' the bushes. Course, I'll probably start with these woods over here first. But ah will be lookin', boys, that's my job."

He reached in through the window of the station wagon, opened the glove box and pulled out an extra-large Hershey bar. The kind it took two men to carry. He sniffed it, pulled a face and looked disgusted. He then walked over and set it on the edge of the grass. "Seems like chocolate don't last hardly at all in this weather. Jest bought that an hour ago an' it smells like it's gone bad already. Course I might be wrong."

He started round to the driver's side and was halfway back in the car when I got to him. "Sheriff, I'd like to shake your hand if I could."

Sheriff Simpson got back out, brightening. "Why, thank you, Mr. Temple. I take that right kindly. Shore didn't recognize you with your curls cut."

The others, laughing, crowding around to do the same. Simpson shook cach extended hand. "And good luck to you, Mr. President. And Mr. Rockefeller. And Mr. Hardy. I sure do miss your movies, Oliver, I shorely do."

Waving the Sheriff on his way as he u-turned to head back. It was just eleven o'clock.

Green scooped up the chocolate bar and stuck it in his shirt pocket. All of us trotted across the road and into a field of corn, the stalks reached above our heads. We ran like that for about half an hour. At the end of the first field, we crossed a dirt road and went right in to the next. Finally, we ran out of cornfields and started up the hills Beyond them, the mountains looked much closer already. We took a breather. Green divided up the chocolate and handed out the pieces. Mine gone in four delicious bites.

We moved out again, checking our watches. Making for those mountains. None of us were familiar with this area. Our own operational sector was miles away from the town they had locked us up in. We decided we'd figure out where we were later, once we got well up into the mountains. For now, just getting distance between us and Captain Crunch and crew was our only goal. We remembered their faces only too well as they had thrown us headlong into their truck.

It was almost 2000 hours and the dark was closing in around us before we decided to call it quits and get some sleep. We were exhausted and hungry. It was already starting to get goddamn cold. We all broke off short branches from the smaller trees to cover ourselves with, to hold in some warmth.

Each of us was sitting back against a tree, covered up with branches and leaves. The sound of tinfoil unwrapping. It was Green bringing out *his* allotment of chocolate. Bastard *saved* his! Holding it up for all of us to see in the last of the light. All four of his large squares. Denbeaux spoke without a pause. "Jesus God almighty. Lookit, Fitz! That chocolate has gone *wormy* ..."

Green putting the first square on his tongue. "I *love* wormy chocolate, Denbox. Love it. Adds that extra protein." Denbeaux subsided.

The talk turned inevitably to that wonderful meal, to our feast of the night before. Going over every morsel that was served, tasting it all again in our hunger. At one point, finally, I said, "And what about the Sheriff's wife? Taking chances like that for guys she doesn't even know. Mrs. Simpson, hell, she was even better than the food."

Dubois' voice now, coming out of the almost total darkness. "You hear zat, Denbeaux, you big, fat ox? All you can talk about is zee food, zee cheeken, zee mashed potatoes, and zo on. But Feetz here, he knows what is really important in zees life. He eez a man of true sensiteevity, yes?"

And then I added, "And how about that wine, eh, Francois? Was that wine great or what?'

There was a silence of maybe two long seconds, before Dubois replied. "But, alas, poor Feetz, his taste in wine, eet eez in his azz."

CHAPTER FORTY-THREE

We had been in Georgia for almost six weeks when Colte got his brainstorm. At that point, we were open to anything that promised a little action. After the way those 82nd guys had bounced us around when they threw us in the slam, we were also in favor of anything that gave us a chance to even the score.

We were still gathering intelligence on a daily basis, and clocking everything of importance that moved in and out of those mountains.

We would still take turns after doing our day tasks, sitting at various posts where we could watch the 82nd going about their business. Under the protective dark of night, we were still trudging back and forth through the woods and swamps setting up supply drops and exchanging information and supplies with other teams. We had even passed two Air Force officers, acting as downed pilots, across our sector without incident, and right under the noses of the eighty-deuce.

Colte and Connelly, however, had been bridling under the lack of action. Sending those two into the field was like sending two kids into an unattended candy store.

Up to this point, their natural instincts had been held in check by the duties it had fallen our lot to perform, but the fact that a couple of their rivals on other teams had managed to pull off a few small coups tended to rub salt in their wounds.

Casey Killian could hardly wait to dangle his team's prize in front of us--a field radio he had captured from a jeep in broad daylight. Killian had dashed out from behind a gas station to grab the radio even as the men's room door had closed behind an 82nd Lieutenant, and he had then disappeared into a huge cornfield while the gentleman in question was still relieving himself. He would have grabbed the jeep if the guy had left the keys.

Cappadonico's team had also had their moment. When the encampment in their area was being replaced by a new group driving down from Bragg, Cappy's team had temporarily switched the road signs at three key locations, sending the convoy almost eighty miles the wrong way into the mountains before their drivers finally smartened up. By then it was long after dark, and it took the convoy hours to find its way back.

On this night, it was almost dusk and our whole team had gathered to chow down. That was when Colte brought his plan to Rozzelli. He and Connelly had already worked out most of the details. The tough part was convincing Rozzelli that the operation in question was within the "rules of the game" at this stage of the problem.

Overt offensive actions were technically only supposed to take place in the last week or so, coordinated with similar attacks by other teams. It was one thing to have part of your team captured or "killed" during a necessary mission as part of the final wind-up. It was something else to lose men in the earlier weeks of a problem on some lark of their own. Rozzelli was very much aware of this distinction.

There was an out, however. "Targets of opportunity" were always fair game. That was a basic maxim for Special Forces field operations.

I can still remember the look on Rozzelli's face when he said, "Now let me get this straight, Colte. You want to take three men with you. And your target of opportunity is...?"

Colte, spread those tree-trunk arms of his and answered. "The whole goddamn detachment, Captain! The whole friggin' mother lot of them!"

We'd all learned a lot watching the 82nd detachment in our area. The genius of the escapade Colte had in mind lay in the way the 82nd operated in the field in those days. The seven years that Colte had spent in the 82nd were about to pay off handsomely for us.

The 82nd has always been one of the best outfits in the Army. Well-trained, well-disciplined, always ready to fight, they could saddle up and move out in nothing flat when needed. That was unlike a lot of the regular "leg" outfits in those days that could take three days after an alert just to find their underwear.

In this case, the 82nd had been in the field for several weeks before we even got down there, and they never knew what phase of operations we were in. It was true that they had managed to capture some members of our outfit from time to time, but most of their attempts to find us came to naught. Night after night in sweep after sweep, their boys came up empty-handed, and that takes a toll.

They'd spot chutes in the sky from time to time, but we were always gone when they got there. Sometimes they had reason to believe they had foiled a planned drop, but most of the time when that happened, they didn't even know it.

After weeks of chasing shadows, even their officers began to feel a little silly on occasion. Not that they quit, because they didn't. Not the eighty-deuce. But, inevitably, the basic drill becomes more and more like a routine exercise. As the high hopes and initial enthusiasm with which they started off begins to wane, they begin to let up just a little and their guard begins to drop.

And that, of course, was just what we waited for. That slow slide into routine, into numbing regularity, which has been the Achilles heel of every occupation force from the Romans in Gaul to the Nazis in Normandy.

One other ironic thing about the 82nd. Their own pride in their reputation as crack troops could actually work against them out in the field.

"Did you see them line them tents up in that encampment?" Connelly chortled. "The first soldier made them stretch a line and hold it taut. He had them make sure the every front tent pole touched that line! Whyn't they just bring in trucks, pave the whole area, for chrissakes!"

Special Forces teams love to find things all in a line. That was great for us.

"Lookit how they've policed up that area," Gomez pointed out. "There's nothing left to trip over in the dark out there, you want to sneak down, leave a bomb in the CO's boot."

There is a point when orderliness becomes predictability, but in the field that becomes a liability. Airborne troops took pride in not scattering their tents willy-nilly among the trees like some crumby leg outfit. They picked a large and open area, or they picked a spot and *made* it large and open. They cleared it.

At one end, they placed the headquarters tent and a company assembly area large enough for formations and chow lines. Then, the two-man pup tents, in two straight lines, the length of the encampment. At the far end, at least fifty yards from the last tents, and at the opposite end of the encampment from any stream or water supply, would be the field latrine area.

In the 82nd there was even a fixed procedure for where your gear was to be placed inside the two-man tents. Ponchos on the ground first, sleeping bags on top, head to foot. M-1 rifles to each man's left, on its side, bolt up, the muzzle toward his head. The edge of the poncho pulled in toward the sleeping bag, covering the rifle, keeping it dry for the night. Shirt and trousers in the bag to keep them dry. Jackets rolled as a pillow. At their feet, their boots, practically standing in a "V" at attention. Even their helmets and backpacks were in a specified place.

The virtue of this arrangement was that they could wake up in the pitch dark for a night problem, guard duty, or any emergency, and they would always know exactly where everything was. Everything ready and waiting.

For them, and for us, as it turned out.

On occasion, without warning, the CO or First Soldier would spot check the guards at night, but after watching for a period, we noticed that those checks inevitably became less frequent the longer a given group was in the field.

Colte insisted that the plan he and Connelly had worked up required four guys. If his plan worked, it would be Barnum and Bailey night at the encampment. If he was wrong, he was frank to say, it would be throw another log on the fire, boys, but take his boots off first.

At the team meeting, Rozzelli sounded all of us out. I knelt there in the dark, listening to the rest of the team laughing and crowing as the details of the plan were firmed up. Naturally, when it came my turn to express my views, I told them exactly what I thought of this colossal piece of lunacy. "Well, Captain," I said, "It sure sounds great to me!"

Oh, well, what the hell. Of one thing I was very confident. This was clearly a game for the heavy weights. I mean this was for the guys on our team who *liked* this stuff! Dah-dee-dah-dit! Ditty-dum-dum-ditty! That was *my* game!

"OK, Colte," Rozzelli said at last. "It's a go, and it's your baby! You pick the night and the men."

Colte nodded. "Tomorrow night should be fine."

He pointed out that we would have to radio base to get them to send out an umpire in the morning to go along as an observer. His leer was satanic in the light from the fire. "You know. Just to keep the body count."

The choice of men was also simple. "Connelly, of course," Colte said. "It's his idea as

360

much as mine. And how about Denbeaux for muscle--I mean, if we're going to have a circus, we might as well have an elephant along."

That went over pretty well. Denbeaux waiting for the laughter to let up a little. Actually, I knew he was delighted that Colte had picked him, but he kept a straight face. "That's good thinking, Sarge. Now, let's see," he said. "That gives us an elephant, a hyena and a jackass. Now all we need is a monkey!"

Everybody joined in the laughter at Colte's expense, but all of a sudden he held his hand up and had that crazy look in his eye again. "You know something, Denbox, old buddy! You got something there. We *could* use a monkey. To sneak along and empty them tents. Someone really small, and nice and light on his tippytoes. Who do we have who fits that bill?"

Every head on the team swung to me, like they were all on the same string. Every face looking at me expectantly. What else could I do? I spread my hands, shrugged, and said, "Well, I'll be a ring-tailed baboon!"

Shit, Almighty. That took care of the attack team. I wondered if they could hear me throwing up.

****

For the rest of the night, almost until dawn, Colte drilled us on various aspects of the planned operation. Denbeaux and I were happy to get a couple of hours break while we went up to the radio station to encode and get off that night's message, which included our request for an umpire.

After that, it was back to the drill again, and Colte was relentless, since he wanted us to get in as much preparation as possible before it began to get light. All night long, over and over, we carried out our mock attack on the enemy encampment, and by morning light, when at last we quit to get some sleep, we knew exactly what we were supposed to do.

CHAPTER FORTY-FOUR

We took off in the late afternoon with about three hours of daylight left. We set a brisk pace through the heavy woods, even breaking into a light trot on the downhill slopes. We wanted to get close to the 82nd encampment before nightfall. We knew we'd need to take our time moving through that last stretch of pitch-black woods to get up next to the camp itself.

A few clouds were drifting along above us, but the sky was clear and blue. Connelly and Colte up front, took turns taking the lead. Denbeaux was behind them. Then me. Then the umpire.

Colte rarely had to stop to check our position because all four of us had been back and forth across this terrain any number of times. Still, we had to be careful. This was no time to get lost, even temporarily.

On balance, we were flying along. Colte was carrying the only rucksack and it was practically empty, only a can of burnt cork, five cans of C-rations, and a few supplies that we would need.

We were stripped for action. T-shirts, fatigue pants and sneakers. Each of us had a dark turtleneck sweater tied around our waists and stocking caps stuck in our belts. Cartridge belts hung with four grenades, canteens and our .45 sidearms loaded with blanks. Extra clips on the belts. The holster tips were tied to our thighs in true Wyatt Earp fashion.

That was it! No other weapons or equipment of any kind. Not a goddamn thing. But according to Colte, the four of us were going to take out the whole detachment.

The umpire, following in my wake, began regretting this assignment about an hour after we took off. A tall, young captain in his early thirties, on loan from Army Intelligence, he had been looking forward to this work for the experience. And he was certainly getting that.

Clearly, he was not used to running up and down these mountains the way we were, although he seemed athletic enough. He had planned for a day or so in the field, and was carrying his regular field pack, jammed to the hilt. A sleeping bag, poncho, extra blanket, a full change of fatigues, underwear -- the works. At Rozzelli's urging, he had lightened his pack at our team area, but not enough, as he soon found out.

He had kept a change of clothes and enough cigarettes, canned food, crackers candy and other goodies to keep a platoon happy for days. He also kept his heavy blanket because he knew it could get damned cold sitting out in those mountains for any length of time observing. With the pace we were setting, he must have felt like he was carrying a keg of beer between his shoulder blades.

I could tell, glancing back at him, that he desperately wanted a break, but the five of us were well spread out, and he would have had to yell to get Colte's attention. His pride kept him quiet. Or somewhat quiet. Occasional oaths from behind me marked a barked shin or a sudden slip during the first hour. Shortly, they became louder, longer and considerably more colorful.

At one point, a branch that I ducked easily, struck him rather forcefully in his chest and face. Still, I didn't feel that gave him the right to mutter those things about my parentage. Finally, Colte did stop, coming back past me to peer down the hill for the umpire.

We had, in fact, reached our stopping point, about a mile from the 82nd camp. We planned to stay there for a couple of hours.

The umpire finally staggered up to us, teeth clenched, head forward as he continued to force one foot in front of the other, almost colliding with Colte before he realized we had stopped. Colte grinned, "Cheer up, Captain, we're half -way there!"

We were in for a long evening. The woods were already turning pitch black and it would be well after midnight before we'd be ready to move. Sitting there, just inside the tree line, we could look out across the valley below us to where the encampment was set up, brightly lit, full of activity.

For the first few hours their lights blazed like a huge bonfire in an otherwise black night. By about nine, the blaze had been reduced to a few patches of light here and there. By ten there was only one small pocket remaining, its dim glow the only light left to be seen across the whole black valley. It came from one large, battery-pack spotlight strung between a couple of trees near the command tent. We knew it was generally left on all night, like a lonely streetlight, illuminating the open area at the right of the CO's tent where the half-track and the three other trucks were parked.

The woods at night are never silent. They are full of the scrabbling noises of small animals. The occasional screech of an owl. Sometimes, more unnerving, the terrified cry of some small animal caught by a larger one. Once in awhile, a bigger animal, like a deer will come plunging through the bushes.

Watching, sitting, listening, it began to get damn cold. The wind picked up. We could hear it sweeping and gusting through the trees. Still we waited, my teeth chattering slightly from both cold and nervousness.

We had each cut a number of long pine branches, which we laid over our chests and shoulders as some protection from the biting wind. That helped. Off to my right, the umpire sat huddled, warm and toasty in his fatigue jacket, with his GI blanket wrapped around his shoulders like a shawl.

For a while he had sat apart, still miffed by Colte's teasing, but after a couple of hours his good nature returned. After we had each consumed our dinner, consisting of one cold can of C-rations, the good captain moved over and broke out some of his goodies, which were gratefully accepted. For a while we sat munching crackers and sucking lemon sour balls in relative comfort.

To smoke we took turns going in pairs back over the rise and about fifty yards down into the woods on the other side, completely out of sight of anyone at the enemy camp. Even then, we kept our backs to the hill and the match flame and cigarette tips well covered in cupped hands.

By midnight we were pretty positive our enemy was not going out on any night searches tonight. We had kept track, and they had never started a search after eleven. We were confident that they were all tucked up for the night, except for their guards.

For the first time, our umpire guest was filled in on exactly what the plans were for the upcoming festivities. I can still see his eyes getting wider as Colte talked him once right through it.

We took turns applying burnt cork to our hands and faces, including the umpire. Colte gave us a last check, and we started off, Indian file, walking slowly. Trying to stay a few feet behind the man in front. Above all trying not to make a single unnecessary sound. The umpire, having left his gear by a tree, brought up the rear.

Each foot was set down cautiously. The weight shifting carefully forward. No branches were to snap like firecrackers. No stones were to go crashing off like minor avalanches. We had two hours, if necessary, to move less than a mile, and half of that was downhill.

We had time. We took our time.

Even after hours of adjustment to the dark, on that starless night, my eyes strained to keep the man in front constantly in view. Each time the lead man's hand went up, the man behind stooped cold, and so on down the line. Not a muscle was to move. Not a sound. Then, we'd start again. Step by step. Foot by foot. Yard by yard.

Rest in place. Deep breaths. Ease the tension. Wipe away the perspiration. Use your peripheral vision. Remember to blink. Don't stare straight ahead. Heart pumping. The adrenalin magnifying every sense.

Ready? Move again. Plant that foot. Shift your weight. Slowly. Move ahead. Again.

We circled around so that our last approach would be at the end where the half-track was positioned with the CO's tent just beyond it. The CO's tent between us and the two rows of pup tents. Here, we could stay well inside the darkened woods. The camp's single light was some thirty-yards beyond the CO's tent, on the opposite side from our line of approach.

Colte stopped. One finger raised for silence. Motioning the rest of us to continue until we were all within a foot of each other. It seemed like we had been moving for hours, but a time check showed it had taken us just over one hour to reach that point. We still had more than fifty minutes before the change of guard at two.

Colte moved past us to the umpire, silently showed him the time, and pointed off to our left. He put his mouth right to the umpire's ear to remind him to take his time moving to an observation point about fifty yards away, just inside the tree line. The captain nodded, and disappeared through the trees, moving very slowly in the direction indicated.

Colte divided up the gear, and it was our turn to move again.

Thirty minutes later we eased into place, settling down in the high grass right at the edge of the woods, about fifteen yards from the half-track. I could just make out the guard sitting up there behind the heavy machine gun mount, facing the CO's tent, his chin resting on his forearms, dozing and snapping awake now and then as his head rolled to one side or the other. Now we wait.

CHAPTER FORTY-FIVE

Lie still. Ignore the infuriating buzz of insects. The itches. The conviction that a hundred crawling things are moving under my shirt, on my legs. Feeling the cold again. The perspiration was icy in the small of my back.

Almost 0200 hours. The guard in the half-track stood up. Stretching. He climbed up on top of the machine gun mount, balancing himself. He was silhouetted faintly against the lighter darkness of the sky for a minute, looking out across the top of the CO's tent for the other guards. For his relief.

We could hear them coming on the other side of the big tent.

The half-track guard jumped down, almost lost from sight in inky blackness as soon as he hit the ground. We could barely see him as he crossed and started around the CO's tent.

A couple of minutes later, a new guard appeared. When he got to the half-track he flicked on his flashlight. Various parts of his body passed in and out of the beam as he climbed up.

He looked big. Goddamn big. Standing on the open-topped cab of the vehicle, then on the front seat. Leaning on the metal pipes that supported the canvas top when it was rolled closed. We could hear men walking around on the other side of the CO's tent, the footsteps dying out as they headed off toward the other end of the camp.

For about five minutes, the guard on the half-track stood in the cab, occasionally reaching up to stretch. His head and shoulders looked like part of the outline of the truck.

I knew we planned to go after him in another twenty minutes and my temples were throbbing along with my thumping heart. Starting to get nervous. All of a sudden the silhouetted head and shoulders disappeared.

Trying to see what was going on. Forgetting to use my peripheral vision. Was he climbing down, or what?

When light clicked on inside the open cab, it startled me. My head snapping like I'd been slapped in the face.

The guard had dropped into the driver's seat and flicked on his flashlight. In the beam of the light I could see three comic books. Those nice, thick jobs some kind relative used to buy you for a birthday present when you were about ten. I saw him shove two of them back inside his shirt, leaving his choice on the steering wheel in front of him. He began to read. I swear I could almost see the guy's lips moving.

Colte was five yards into the clearing, directly in front of me, before I realized he was moving. His eyes like two white silver dollars in the middle of all that burnt cork. He pointed to me, nodded and was gone into the darkness before I could even push up off the ground. Apparently, he had taken one look at our comic book reader and realized we didn't have to give this guy any more time to settle in. That would give us more time for later, when we'd need it. Basic Special Forces rule--stay flexible!

I pulled on my stocking hat, and moved out across the clearing, bent low, my eyes on the half-track. Ready to drop and freeze at the slightest movement from the guard. Once I moved out of the guard's line of vision, I picked up speed and headed for the rear of the half-track. Almost running over Colte who was stopped, crouched down, waiting for me.

Colte pointed to the front of my belt where we each had a number of lengths of rope and cloth gags hanging down, giving us the bizarre appearance in the dark of wearing moth-eaten hula skirts. I pulled out a cloth gag, two short and one long lengths of rope, and fell in behind him as we moved down the half-track, hugging the side.

As instructed earlier, I went around him and continued to the cab, stopping and crouching there on one knee, trying to breathe very quietly. Colte disappeared silently up and over the side of the vehicle, out of my sight. I got ready, but as hard as I strained to listen, I could hear nothing from Colte. I could hear the guard breathing just a few feet from me, and I could even hear the pages of his comic book when he turned them.

Colte's whisper, when it came, sounded to my straining ears like a coarse bellow. *"One move, one sound! And I'm gonna blow this sonafabitch off right in your ear!"*

I rocketed forward at the words, pulling myself around and up into the cab next to the guard. My hands were shaking, but the guard wasn't about to notice that.

Colte was lying on top of the half-track. One of his huge paws had the guard by the throat, his thumb and middle finger clamped on each side of the guy's Adam's apple. His .45 was sticking out of his other fist, the muzzle jammed right into the guy's ear. Hard into the ear so it hurt.

I'd heard about people's eyes bulging in fright, but I had never seen anything like this. The black pupils looked like tiny olives on two huge white saucers. The guy's mouth was wide open as though he were screaming, but not a sound was coming out.

His flashlight had dropped unheeded onto the floor between his legs, the beam pointing up at his crotch as it rolled slowly back and forth. The comic book was lying in his lap, the top against the steering wheel.

"*They're only blanks!*"

It was Colte again, the same hoarse whisper. "Just blanks, Sonny." He made every word count. "But if you make one friggin' sound I'll pull this trigger and the noise will blow your eardrums right out through your nose! *Got that!*"

Colte's eyes flicked to me as he mouthed, "Gag!"

I jumped up and jammed the big knot of the gag into the guy's mouth, shoving hard with my thumbs to get it all in. The guard making a strangling noise as Colte pulled off the guy's helmet, let go of his throat, and shoved his head forward hard, holding a fistful of hair while I pulled the ends of the gag up quickly and tied them behind the guard's head. Tight. I think the guy really thought we were going to strangle him.

Colte slid down then into the cab, shoving his .45 back into his holster, and went to work like a surgeon as I passed him the lengths of rope. Shoving the guard's face down on the seat, he tied his wrists behind his back, one tight knot, then another. Then, the ankles, the same. Then he pulled the guard up again, took the longest piece of line from me and began looping it expertly around the guy's torso, stopping first to open the top few buttons of the guy's shirt so you could see the comic books inside. Then jamming the third one inside the rope as he pulled it tight. Colte making sure the guy's sergeant knew what he had been doing when he was taken out.

Lastly, he looped the end of the rope around the steering post and wheel, braced one foot against the dashboard and leaned back to pull the line tight, the guard groaning as his chest was jammed up against the steering wheel. Colte laid in the last couple of knots and the guard was trussed up like a Thanksgiving turkey.

Colte standing on the seat, reaching a long arm straight up and waving it in a circle for Connelly and Denbeaux. In a matter of seconds they appeared out of the darkness just below us. Colte pulled a cloth blindfold out of his belt and leaned over the guard.

The guard's eyes swiveled up to Colte, fear rushing back into them as he wondered what this lunatic was going to do next.

Colte placed his face right in front of the guard's, nose to nose, as he whispered again. "There's only twenty of us, but we're going to be here the rest of the night. Got that? I'm leaving him right up here." Colte jerked a thumb at me and patted the top of the truck above the driver.

"He'll be able to see and hear you every minute." Colte gave the guy a short, sharp jab in the kidneys, hard enough to make him wince. "You make a sound, he'll jump off, land right here. You'll piss blood for a week! Your choice, Sucker!"

With that he pulled the blindfold over the guard's eyes, knotted it, and tied the tails to the top of the steering wheel. He motioned me to slip down quietly to the ground. I could barely hear his last words to the guard. "Be smart, Baby."

In a second he was beside us on the ground and the four of us headed off single file, plenty of space between us as we circled the CO's tent, aiming for the edge of the woods beside one row of pup tents.

Colte tapped his wrist and we all made a time check. 0220. Colte grinned. One guard down and we were fifteen minutes ahead of schedule.

We went most of the way down to the other end of the camp staying out in the open but just skirting the edge of the woods, being careful and quiet, but making good time. That area, in the 82nd way, had been carefully policed. Daily! Not a stick to snap. No stones to break our bones. No scrubby little bushes to fall over. How nice for us.

Near the far end, we stopped. Kneeling. Listening. I could hear nothing to indicate where the other guards might be. Motioning to us to stay put, Colte disappeared into the gloom.

Last in line again, I kept looking nervously behind me. If that guard on the half-track got loose, he could bring the whole camp alive like

Vesuvius erupting. I studied the woods to my right, planning my escape route.

Colte was back. I hadn't heard a thing, but there he was, motioning for us to follow. He led us out, across the camp to the other side, each man pointing out to the man behind him the tent ropes and pegs as we passed them. Inside the tents as we passed we could hear the snorts and snuffles of men in deep sleep.

Christ! Let them stay that way.

Entering the woods on the other side. Moving forward then, I heard it. Low voices. Men talking. We got closer. Glancing back, I could no longer see the camp. Deep brush and trees hid it completely. The voices were more audible, but still quiet. I saw their light on the ground.

Colte stopped and motioned Pat up to him. He pointed at his watch and held up three fingers. Colte gave us a hold sign as Connelly disappeared into the brush, heading to the right of the light. Denbeaux was motioned forward. The same routine, but he held up two fingers and sent him off to the left.

I was next, but when I got to him, Colte signed that I should follow him. Starting forward, one-step at a time. When we got closer, I could see what was happening.

The two guards were playing cards! Friggin' *cards!*

The light was a flashlight on the ground between them. A fistful of coins lay on the ground also. I could just make out the words, "Hit me."

Colte pulled two cloth gags from his belt. He raised a finger, looking at his watch. All of a sudden, Colte's finger dropped and there was a whoosh and a crash up ahead. Colte was up and on top of our card-playing friends in three huge bounds, but the game had already been called.

As Colte's finger dropped, Denbeaux and Connelly had struck.

At exactly 0250, they had both jumped forward, reached around the tree and grabbed a guard just as Colte had done earlier. The Adam's apple pinched between thumb and middle finger. The .45 slapped up against the ear and jammed in hard. Both guards writhing, their necks pinned up against the trees! Gurgling and frightened out of their wits.

And then there was Colte, towering over them like a giant oak come to life as I rushed up. "Not a *friggin'* sound, you bastards!" The words were whispered, but they got the message. Colte dropped to his knees. One hand shot out to pull off a guy's helmet, the other to jam a gag into that guard's mouth. He spun away and did the same to the other. Colte's huge fingers pawed and shoved at their faces, pushing their heads back against the trees as he did so. I decided right on the spot that he would have a bleak career as a dentist.

Connelly and Denbeaux tied off the gags.

Each guard neatly up against "his" tree. Each lifted in turn into a standing position with one ham-handed grab of a shirtfront. Denbeaux and Connelly quickly tied their wrists to their ankles. In each case a last loop was added, down between their legs and up to a branch. Those guys would have to saw off their nuts to sit down.

Colte shook out two blindfolds. While the wide-eyed guards watched helplessly, he whispered his instructions. "You two. Stay there in the woods between these guys and the camp, while I get the other men. They make one sound, one move to get free, kick their balls right up into their rib cages before you take off. Got that?"

To make his point, he turned and let go with a vicious kick at the nearest guard's groin, stopping it only at the last second, inches from the target. Even in the darkness, we could see the guard squeaking into his gag, almost fainting. And who could blame him?

In another minute, both guards were blindfolded.

Connelly spread the cards out in a nice fan and placed the still lit flashlight so that it made a pretty picture. Scooping up the loose change, about three bucks in all, Pat tossed it into the bushes with a grin at Colte. "They kept saying, 'Hit me,'" he whispered, "So we did."

CHAPTER FORTY-SIX

The four of us were again skirting the edge of the encampment but able to move more swiftly now. There were no longer any guards up and about. The two rows of tents stretched into the darkness before us. A time check showed that we still had well over an hour for the work at hand before the next guard shift would be likely to start stirring, and maybe getting suspicious that no one had woken them yet. There was always the danger of someone getting up to take a piss, of course, but we were all on alert to watch for that as we set about our work.

We got right to it. Just the way we had drilled it for so long the night before.

Colte and I took one row, Denbeaux and Connelly the other.

I tiptoed up beside the first tent on one side and dropped softly on to my belly. In went one hand to roll back the edge of a poncho. Out came a rifle. Don't slide it. Lift it. Hold the tent side up just enough and bring it out.

Up on my toes and hands, scooting two or three feet to the end. In went a hand, out came one boot. In again and out with the other. Pass the rifle and boots to Colte.

Reach out. Loosen the tent pegs as I pass. Just loosen them, but leave them in the holes.

Up on my feet, taking four or five careful steps. Stretching as I did this. Back down again on the other side. The same drill, emptying that tent of all rifles and boots.

Colte and I moved down the row. Inside the tents, snores. Heavy breathing. Snorts. Outside, total concentration. Not a sound. Be careful. The icy nervousness in my belly. *Hurry!* But concentrate and don't get careless.

Colte disappearing off toward the woods, a quiet step at a time, his arms loaded with rifles and boots.

Keep working. Alone. Careful. Down. Move. Up. Carry a rifle and boots with me and leave them on the ground for Colte. Down again and reaching in.

Colte is back. He picks up the boots and rifles and waits while I pass him more. *Oh, Jesus.* We've only done four tents. We must be running close to time. I start to look at my watch but Colte touches me lightly with a toe, shaking his head, motioning me to keep at it, to keep working.

Up. Down. Bring out the gear. Oh, *shit*, I forgot those last tent pegs. *Concentrate*, goddamn it. Concentrate! Moving to the next tent, and then the next.

Got to rest a minute. Get my breath, shake it out. Here comes Colte again. He winks at me. His face looks really excited. I look around as I stand up. *Jesus!* We're halfway down the row. *Halfway!* I look over and in the dark I can see the murky outlines of Denbeaux and Connelly only one tent behind us in their row. Christ, this is working! My tiredness seems to evaporate. Feeling much better.

Keep working. Concentrate. Back on my belly. Scooting along beside a tent.

CRASH! Oh my good Christ! I freeze. I can see Colte's feet just ahead of me, standing stock-still. I inch my head around to look.

The noise was off on the other side. Connelly or Denbeaux. Someone had dropped something. Colte was standing in a crouch, ready to race for the woods, three or four rifles dangling, his arms full of boots. I was in a sprinter's crouch, ready to bolt right behind him.

Silence. No sounds except our own breathing and the snores and snuffling noises from the tents. Colte motions me to continue. A little shaky as I reach under the next tent. I almost forget to roll back the poncho and I start to pull on the rifle and poncho together. Shit! *Concentrate, goddamn it!*

Continuing up the row, working quickly.

As I stand up beside another tent, all of my muscle are feeling the strain from this long stretch of tense, careful movements, Colte points at several rifles and boots beside him on the ground in front of me, motioning to me to pick them up.

Christ Almighty! Is he tired? Does he want me to do *his* work, too? But then I look around. *That's it!* That was the last tent in our row.

Giddy with relief, I gather up the last of our booty and follow Colte off to the edge of the woods. About ten yards in he tucks the boots under and into bushes, mixing up the pairs as he does this. I do the same. He takes the rifles a little further away and one by one he jams the muzzles down into the soft earth, twisting them hard, then shoves them under other bushes, as far in as he can. I do the same. Colte cups his hand around my ear, and his whisper is paper-thin. "Monkey see, monkey do. C'mon, monkey."

I grin, and fall in behind him as he heads for the CO's tent. Elation is building by the second. I glance at my watch. Just 0345. We still have the time we need.

At the CO's tent, Colte goes one way while I go the other, loosening the tent pegs. In few minutes, Connelly is beside us helping. Several guy wires to give added support lead off on each side, except from the front. They are tied to large stakes and small trees. Colte cuts these one by one, but he hangs on to them, leaning back to keep up the tension as he walks slowly in toward the tent, allowing the canvas to fold down gently against the poles and equipment inside. The big tent looks like a badly squashed toadstool when he finally lets go of the guy wires.

At the front of the tent, Colte slips a long line through a ringed opening at the top, on the ridge above the door, just as I hear soft footsteps coming along the side of the tent. I move past Colte and to that corner, crouched, ready to spring, but it is Denbeaux who rounds into view. He has a 'C-3' block in his hand. He gets Colte's attention and points to the trucks that are just barely visible to us. The umpire is sitting on the hood of the first one, identifiable only because of the white armbands and the white ring around his cap that he has now put in place. He gives us a wave.

Denbeaux continued on past us and over to put the last wooden block of mock explosives in place on the half-track. I can just make out part of the driver still immobile over the wheel.

Colte motioned Connelly, Denbeaux and me to take our positions. I crossed to the outside edge of the line of tents on our right, Connelly moving to the inside edge of my row. Denbeaux went to the far edge of the other row, and we knew Colte would take the inside edge of that line of tents. I could feel the adrenaline pumping like crazy as I looked down the long line of tents stretching out in front of me. What a beautiful feeling to know that every goddamn rifle and pair of boots had been pulled out of them.

Colte had the rope he had attached above the door of the CO's tent draped across one shoulder, and he had a grease gun in his left hand that he had slipped out of the CO's tent. Connelly, Denbeaux and I each pulled two grenades off our belts, jerked out the pins, but kept a tight grip on the hand releases. Only a firing charge in each one but they would still make a nice loud bang. Colte had four smoke grenades to toss behind him as we got down toward the other end.

Three of us crouched, looking at Colte, ready to go.

Jesus! It was Connelly! Both hands up signaling for attention, giving us a referee's "time out" sign with his hands full of grenades. He ran off around the CO's tent, heading for the half-track. *Shit!* This wasn't part of the plan.

He was out of sight for only a minute and then he came running back. Clutched under his arm, holding it awkwardly because of the grenades in his fists, he had the large field radio from the half-track. The radio had a five-foot antenna sticking out in front of Connelly and it bounced as he ran like a fishing rod. As he hurried back to us, rounding the last corner of the almost deflated tent, he tripped. He caught himself, but not without landing rather heavily for a step or two.

"WHAT THE HELL WAS THAT?"

It was a deep baritone voice, and it exploded out of the CO's tent just as Connelly righted himself and broke into a full run to get to his position. Colte gave us the "go" with Connelly five yards away but closing fast.

We all took off down the two lines of pup tents. I was swinging my left leg at the tent peg lines on my side, and swinging my left arm to knock over the tent pole at my end of each tent. Connelly was doing the same on the other end.

Behind us I heard the crash of the big CO tent and the startled outcries from inside it as it toppled all the way down. For the next several seconds, we heard a few voices calling out half-asleep in the tents around us, but all I could really hear was the pounding of our running feet as the four of us galloped, kicking and whacking our way, down the rows of tents.

We fell into a rhythm quickly. Step, kick, swing at the pole, step, kick. Step, kick, swing at the pole, step, kick.

Down went the tents, one after another, tent pegs flying.

Behind us all was confusion. Tents crashing down over guys still zipped in sleeping bags. Curses, squawks of surprise and fright.

Ahead, men still sleeping, startling awake as the uproar reached them.

"WHAT THE CHRIST IS THAT? WHAT THE HELL IS HAPPENING?"

Crash! Steps, kick, swing at the pole, step, kick. Crash!

We were three quarters of the way down the line when Connelly let loose a blood curdling war whoop that would turn the hair in your nose white. At the same time one of the grenades he had flipped over his shoulder went off like a giant firecracker and I heard the screaming whistle of one of Colte's smoke grenades sailing off behind us.

I let go a grenade, too, the loud "POW" following after a few seconds as I also heard Colte and Denbeaux yelping right along with Connelly, an unnerving screeching, the three of them sounding like a bunch of Comanches with hot coals in their breech-clouts. At the same time, I heard other grenades going off and Colte cutting loose with the grease gun, working the bolt like crazy with his left hand and firing blank after blank. That was when I heard someone else hollering and bellowing. After a surprised second, I realized it was me!

All hell had broken loose behind us, and as I bore down on the last two or three tents in the line, I could hear yelps and cries of alarm from in front of us as well. Guys trying desperately to get out of sleeping bags, reaching for boots and weapons that weren't there, and then buried in canvas as we raced by and their tents crashed down on top of them.

Suddenly, coming right up out of a swirl of canvas in the next to last tent in front of me, a huge, rangy guy stood up, shaking his pup tent loose from his shoulders and jumping right out into my path barefoot. His eyes were blinking wildly as he tried to come fully awake and I know he never saw me.

It was damn sure not the time to be polite. Tucking my chin on to my chest and with my forearms leading, I ran headlong right into him, one elbow hammering into his stomach just below the rib cage and sending him over backwards and down on to the end of the last tent in line. I could hear the air whooshing out of him as he fell.

Catching myself with my hands before I fell myself, I ran straight across his chest, veered half-right and was off for the woods like Jesse Owens practicing sprints.

Jee-sus, did I run!

I hit the woods doing sixty miles an hour and still accelerating. The next thing I knew, I hit something and found myself going head first through the air, my legs pumping even as my feet and shoulders leveled off. I bounced off at least one huge bush and then off a couple of small trees like a three cushion billiard shot. When I finally slid to a stop I had about six pounds of gravel down the front of my pants.

I had started to throw my left hand out in front of me for protection as I fell, but realized with surprise that I was still holding one of the goddamn grenades. It was clamped in my palm like a huge wart, with my fingers still locked around it.

I scrambled to my feet, just as two barefoot, bullshit guys in T-shirts and under shorts came bursting out of the bushes only eight or ten yards behind me.

"Grenade!" I yelled, swinging my left hand up in an imitation softball pitch. Even in the dark they saw the metal blob in my hand, and without a pause, both of them dove headfirst and automatically into the thick bushes to either side of them. I was off again, running a zigzag course to throw off my pursuers, the grenade still snug against my sweaty palm.

Three or four more minutes of hard running and I slowed long enough to heave the grenade as hard as I could behind me, up into the trees. I was already pounding off again when its loud 'POW' sounded through the woods, swears and yelps from my pursuers accompanying the loud bang.

My hat gone, my face slapped into hamburger by unseen branches and pine needles, I ran on, zigging in and out between the trees and bushes, occasionally bouncing off of one I didn't see in time. I was already a mass of bruises and welts, and I knew I was making only slightly less noise than a hippo in heat, but for a while the clamor of a lot of angry men right behind me drove me even faster.

A hollering, swearing uproar was following me, all right, but after awhile they did seem to be falling back, and dropping off. The troopers who had actually caught sight of us at the edge of their camp had taken up the chase bootless and weaponless but in full hue and cry. Calling for their fellows, they had raced heedless into the woods behind us. They knew by then, no doubt about it, that it was those goddamn Special Forces turds who had done them in, and catching sight of one or two of us, of our real live bodies fleeing, they had taken off after us with a laudable and venomous determination.

Even as I ran, the fear like a lump in my throat that I couldn't swallow, I was treated to a series of sounds that gave me an horrific delight. Even today, I can recall the most memorable of those sounds vividly. They resulted whenever one of my pursuing vigilantes, their bare feet churning hard in the darkened forest, came hard down upon a nicely bent twig, or slam-bang, toes-on into a good sized rock, or excruciatingly down with a bare instep upon a rough and ragged stone. One by one, as these howls attested, they literally fell by the wayside. Not even a trained marksman with a night vision scope could have dropped those poor barefooted bastards in their tracks with more efficiency.

Sad I am to relate, even at this late date, the shameful, uncouth pleasure with which I greeted each and every one of their screams of anguish, and the gleeful smile with which I acknowledged every one of their howls and screeches as I pounded off into the forest blackness.

CHAPTER FORTY-SEVEN

The umpire's report, when we finally got a copy, gave the essentials, but the most satisfying details came from Captain Rozzelli after he found and had a heart-to-heart talk with the umpire who accompanied us on the night of the "wipe out."

The aggressor camp had been left in total confusion. No boots, no rifles, their tents collapsed all over them, everyone shouting, gunfire and grenades popping. Even when they did climb out of the debris they didn't have a clue as to what had happened.

All around them, their fellow troopers were clad only in boxer shorts and T-shirts. A few were hopping around trying to pull on pants, or standing wide-eyed with a shirt half on staring at the chaos around them.

One young guy about eighteen had pulled on socks and clapped his steel pot on his head, and he kept running back and forth yelling at the top of his lungs, "It's an attack. Don't panic! It's an attack. Don't panic!"

He kept this up until he almost collided with one hardened and furious sergeant who was coming down the line surveying the wreckage. That worthy reached out and jammed one hand hard on top of the kid's helmet, stopping him in his tracks, then he dropped him to a sitting position. Whipping off the kid's helmet, the sergeant brought up one hand in a short, stinging slap. The erstwhile Paul Revere came out of it, blinking in surprise.

Grabbing the young man's arm, the sergeant pulled him to his feet and gave him an encouraging pat on the back. "OK, Audie Murphy," he had grunted. "You're doing fine. Just take a break on that running back and forth before you kill someone!"

The sergeant continued down the line pulling guys out from under their tents, and up onto their feet. He winced whenever he heard one of our pursuers out in the woods bellowing in pain as he left the best part of a foot on some rock or broken branch.

Each time that happened, the sergeant would spit viciously and turn furious eyes to heaven while he called on God, the devil or anyone within hearing to do the right thing! To fry those Special Forces mother-humpers in hot oil until their jump wings melted into their blackened hearts.

It was this sergeant, about ten minutes later, who rallied a couple of dozen troops at the end of the camp. "Alright, you bastards," he ordered, "grab some boots! *Any* boots, you dumb shits! Just shove your goddamn feet in, grab a rifle and follow me!"

A minute or so later, as those guys began to run after him into the woods, carrying rifles in the usual port arms position, he spun furiously on them in a rage. "Dandy!" he bellowed. "What the hell ya gonna do with those? Yell, 'bang, bang you're dead, you meanies!'"

With that, he pulled a rifle from under a bush, growled once when he saw all the mud and crap jammed into the barrel, but then he demonstrated. Gripping it at the end like a baseball bat, he advanced into the woods furiously beating the bushes on all sides with the stock as he went.

Branches snapped off, flying in every direction. Whole bushes were uprooted and sent flying off the stock of his rifle like divots on a golf course. "This is how to use this useless piece of shit, you assholes!"

The whole group then fell upon the woods as they followed along in the direction in which we had fled, all following the sergeant's enthusiastic example.

"Oh, Christ," the umpire heard the sergeant cry out as he disappeared into the woods, continuing his furious attack on the hapless greenery, "Why, oh why don't' they give us *live* ammo! Jesus, I'd give my sixteen years in this good-for-shit army for just one clip of live ammo, a clear field of fire, and just one of those mother-humping bastards in my sights!"

At the other end of the camp, the Lieutenant and the First Soldier had crawled out from under the flattened CO's tent. The sergeant had a large flashlight in one hand and he looked around him with an expression like a housewife who has just found dogshit in the middle of the marital bed.

The lieutenant was in shorts and T-shirt, but he did have his boots on, and he had his .45 in one fist. For several seconds, he crouched, ready for action, but then he slowly straightened up, surveying the total chaos around him.

From his left, the tall lanky figure of the umpire made his way toward him, stopping to waive his arms every few steps and yell "Umpire, umpire!" when troopers, catching sight of the unknown in full uniform, charged at him, determined to wreak a terrible vengeance. Stopped by that announcement, their disappointment was evident. Clearly, more than one considered giving the skinny sonofabitching bastard a shot anyway, one that would make his white armbands spin for a week.

"Sorry about this, Lieutenant," the umpire said, coughing slightly, and then having to raise his voice considerably to be heard above the din. "I'm going to have to call this a total. A wipe-out!"

He reached into his back pocket to pull out his notebook, and he shook his head, looking around. Even he had trouble taking it all in, and he knew the plan. He opened the notebook, and whistled softly as he began to write. "Jesus! This was Little Big Horn all over again. No offense, Lieutenant, but your name isn't Custer, is it?"

Now, a slow fury had started to build up inside the lieutenant, but at these words, he got really hot. "Oh sure! Oh, great! That's easy for you to say. You come waltzing in here in the middle of the night, after my men have been hit by a..." He paused, his hands waving, "...by a whole goddamn company of those Special Forces bastards!"

Warming to his topic, his rage poured out. "What kind of shit is this, anyway? We're told they'll only be a *handful* of those bastards on this problem, and then they send in a whole company to hit us in the middle of the night! What the Christ do they expect? Of course it's a friggin' wipe-out!"

The captain stopped writing long enough to hold four fingers up in the air. "Four men, Lieutenant!" He let that sink in for a moment, still holding up the four digits, then he went back to writing, and he said it again. "Four men, Lieutenant. Your guys were deep-sixed by four men!"

The lieutenant stared at the captain, his mouth open to speak, but the umpire held up his hand. "I came in with them, Lieutenant. I was with them all night. I had the plan. I saw them set it up. I saw them do it."

The lieutenant began spluttering. His arms straight out, his gesture taking in the whole camp, and his voice had a break in it, almost a whine. "Now wait a goddamn minute! Just hold on here! Look...just look at this! You *have* to be wrong! Four men! My Jesus, that *can't* be right! I had guards out! We...we..."

The umpire sighed and started to write again. "It will all be in my report, Lieutenant." And then, to himself, the captain had added, that poor bastard. He'll be wearing this stink around his neck like a bag of garlic, and no one will ever understand.

The lieutenant, subsiding, his arms dropping to his sides, looked around dazed. His beautifully organized, beautifully laid out encampment in total ruin. He started to protest once again, but the words died silently on his lips as the awful truth sank in.

A total wipeout. By *four* goddamn men! He didn't want to face it, but in his heart he knew. Oh, yes. He *knew!*

CHAPTER FORTY-EIGHT

Out in the woods, I continued my serpentine ascent toward the tall tree line at the top of the grade, listening for sounds behind me and never moving in a straight line. I was able to move quietly again, still going as fast as I could in the circumstances, but picking my way now, and trying not to trip or run directly into anything. Listening both for my own teammates and for pursuers.

Occasionally, one weird sound kept reaching me that I could not identify. It came from some distance behind me. It was sort of a *SCAAREEEEEEeeeeee-BAAWAAAAAAaaaaaaaaaang* that seemed to linger and echo in the treetops.

I kept on, working hard, climbing up and over one rise, then trotting down the other side and climbing up again toward an even higher rise beyond. Determined not to stop for anything, I kept on until I was hacking and gasping for breath. I must have sounded like a jackass with pneumonia.

Finally, though, I had to stop. I stood, bent over at the waist, hands on my knees, taking deep breaths. I had one last steep stretch to the top where we were supposed to rally.

A crash that practically drove my heart through my Adam's apple!

Leaping away from the tree as the bushes in front of me erupted like they had been blown apart with C-3. A huge, dark blob hurtling right at me.

The figure slamming into me, sending me flying backwards. I went over like the mountain had been jerked out from under me, my upper back hitting the ground and knocking the little breath I had recovered out of me.

Denbeaux! Recognition of the charging figure came to me just as I bounced up into a sitting position. Just before he ran right over me. A size twelve sneaker landing right on my breastbone and hammering me backwards into the same depression in the soft earth that I had made just a second earlier. That depression, however, became considerably deeper as he landed and then vaulted off of me.

Following Denbeaux's rather short progress after that second collision was no problem. There was a loud, surprised squawk as he stomped on me. I heard his short, but I thought rather pithy expletive, *"Balls!"* as he sailed over me. I actually enjoyed the earth-jarring crunch with which he landed.

Lying on my back, embedded in Mother Earth up to my ear holes, this conclusion to Denbeaux's journey did not upset me. He piled in with a lovely "OOOOOMMPH!"

It was a second or so later, while I was still lying there trying to breathe through my eyes, that I heard another noise. That damned broken guitar again, but now much closer and louder.

SCAAREEEEEEeeeeee-BAAWAAAAAaaaaaaaang!

Very strange indeed.

Again, the bushes exploded to life just beyond where I lay and another figure came hurtling out. Whether it was my anguished howl, or just good night vision on his part, I'll never know, but this time the huge figure skidded to a halt inches before my spread-eagled nether parts were trampled into pulp.

Connelly! Leaning over me, blacker than the night except for his gleaming eyes and teeth.

That goddamned noise again. BWAAANG! BWAAANG! SCRRREEeeeeee! Something swishing in the air right above my nose. Something whip-like. Then I knew. That goddamn antenna on the 82nd's radio.

Pat still had it pointed out in front of him like a bizarre divining rod. That crazy bastard had run all the way from the camp like that, with the foolish antenna slashing the air in front of him and getting caught up in every bush and branch he hit along the way. When I asked him much later why he had never turned the radio around, he gave me that demented smile and said, "I liked it that way. I knew that sound was driving our pursuers crazy!"

Now he leaned over me in the dark. "That you, Fitz? For, chrissakes, you lazy Irish bastard! This is no time for a nap. Up and at 'em!"

I rolled painfully up onto my knees, ducking the slashing path of the rapier antenna whipping by my ear. Behind me, Denbeaux groaned and sat up.

"Who's *that*?" Connelly aimed a hoarse croak at our fallen elephant. "Denbox? Was that you in front of me, you crazy bastard! Call this a covert operation, with you throwing yourself around like a great sack of cowbells? Up, Man! Up!"

Connelly galloped around me and slapped Denbeaux on the rump as Bill hoisted himself off the ground. "Jesus, what a crew I got for sleeping! Colte must be half way back to the team area by now, and here are you two going beddy-bye on me!"

Denbeaux and I were both up, slapping the worst of the dirt off and discovering which parts were still moveable.

"Listen! Hear that?" It was Connelly again. We did stop and listen. The sounds were still well down the slope below us, but unmistakable. The scrabbling and swearing, the yelling, the noisy babble of a lot of men crashing about in the woods and making their way toward us.

Connelly's croaking whisper was almost a chortle. "In about ten friggin' minutes, maybe even five, that whole company will be on top of this here mountain looking for balls to bust and asses to kick. One glimpse of any of us and they will never stop if they have to chase us a week. Now me, my plan is to deny them that pleasure and haul our asses out of here."

With that, he was off again ahead of us now, his long legs swinging as he climbed, effortlessly.

Denbeaux and I scrambled after him in the dark, working hard to keep up. I had all I could do at times to keep the two of them in hearing. At the top of this last rise, Connelly and Denbeaux stopped to let me catch up.

Just as I came out of the tree line on to the barren, scraggly top to join them, there was a long, low whistle, and Colte stood up from behind a bush where the woods started again down below. "Hey, GI's!" he stage whispered. "You got chocolate for my sister?"

For the next hour and a half we moved on automatic pilot. Trotting downhill single file, then climbing steadily up the next rise, staying under cover almost all the time. Working hard. Using the dirt roads and winding paths whenever we could. Getting plenty of distance, between the angry eighty-two and us. By the time the first grey light of dawn began to open up the woods, we were long gone and we knew it was too late for daylight to give them any help.

Trees and bushes gradually came into three-dimensional focus. For quite awhile, the steady, clop-clop of our feet had been the only sound we heard. Then the birds woke up and their chatter kept track of our passage. Then the colors brightened into muted greens. Then the sunlight turning certain patches to an orange fire. Reds and oranges and greens all around us as we slowed at last to a walk.

We left the path then, cutting down through the woods to a brook we knew was below us. Falling into it face first when we got there. Rolling in it, laughing, splashing ourselves and each other. Miles and miles from the 82nd. Far away in those deep and beautiful woods. Safe.

I don't remember who started it, but I remember Connelly, practically foaming at the mouth as he kicked his legs up and down in the brook, sending spray all over us. "Oh, my Jesus. Did you hear that goddamn CO when I tripped? '*What the hay-ell was that?*' Well, he sure as shit knows now, don't he?"

All of us laughing at the memory.

Denbeaux spluttering. "Oh my sainted aunt. That poor CO! He'll never, ever live this down! Never!"

Colte, picking it up. "He'll have to get out, go home. He'll end up wearing suspenders and selling shoes!"

Finally, we got up to move on again. Not tired at all anymore. Connelly looking around. "We'd better stick to the woods, Gunnar, stay away from the roads, even the small dirt ones. They've still got the trucks we supposedly blew up. Now you know they'll damn sure pile into those as soon as that umpire leaves, try to speed ahead, cut us off somewhere."

Denbeaux interrupted. "I really don't think so, Sarge. Maybe tomorrow. But not today. Those trucks aren't going anywhere today."

Bill's hand came out of his pants pocket with the rotor from one truck. Pulling up his turtleneck sweater on one side, he cupped his hand and two more rotors dropped into it. Denbeaux turned sideways then to show us a huge red welt, speckled with blood, where the metal had driven into his side.

"When that goddamn Fitzpatrick tripped me, I thought for awhile I was going to wear these stupid baubles permanently next to my heart. Me, who's always hated junk jewelry!"

Connelly held out the rucksack. "Drop 'em in here, Denbox, my man! Right here in the old goody bag. By Jesus, you amaze me. I always knew you were a con man, but I never dreamed you were an accomplished thief."

Denbeaux dropped the three rotors into the rucksack, trying to look pained. "Just be careful what you say about me, Slats. Remember. An elephant never forgets."

CHAPTER FORTY-NINE

Dusk. The sun was just below the horizon. The sky was turning darker by the minute. Aside from Connolly and me, about a dozen men and boys were gathering in the woods beyond Turner's barn. Most of them were between fourteen and twenty, not counting Mr. Turner. Two more figures coming out of the woods, past the meadows, past the outhouse, coming up to where we waited. Harvey Samuels and his nephew Calvin. Our "army" for this night's work almost complete.

Nelson Tolliver Turner called each of them by name for us as soon as they came in to view. No binoculars needed. One squint into the distance enough for Turner. Squatting on his heels now, part of the inevitable north Georgia male ritual, poking a sandy spot in front of him with a stick. No sign of fatigue although he had been in that position for over half an hour. At eighty-two, Mr. Turner loved war games.

"Ah knowed Harvey and Calvin would be a little late," he told us. "Not their fault. They has their chores to do. Harvey's pappy, now, Festerin' Lester we call him, he ain't done him a lick of real work since that boy was old enough to reach up and squeeze a cow's udder. Unless it was to pick up a stick and hit Harvey. Ol' Lester he ain' worth an open box of feathers in a high wind, but them two boys, they is as good as you kin get. In these parts, or anywheres else. Fine boys."

Turner introducing the last two arrivals as they came into the clearing. Harvey, at 16, towered over me. His long farmer's fingers almost snapping my hand off at the wrist as he enveloped it and shook it vigorously. But what the hell. I had a whole half-inch over Calvin, the fourteen year old.

Inspection of arms. Everyone had brought a weapon. Not a big problem in this area where every boy learns to hunt before starting school. Damnedest collection of rifles and shotguns I'd ever seen. But what did I know? I'd never touched a firearm before I came into the army. Beautiful pieces. Passed down within families, most of them. Lovingly oiled and polished. Spotless. The mechanical parts sliding easily, smoothly.

A Winchester pump-action rifle. Geez! Red Ryder lives! A long-barreled single-shot rifle on which you have to thumb back the hammer each time. Must be fifty years old. A .22 here and there. A double-barreled shotgun that could cut a small tree in half if you gave it a chance.

One of the younger boys shyly held out a treasured weapon. A long thin barrel, a lot of shiny wood and brass studs, the butt of the piece ending in a concave half-circle that fit neatly around the shoulder. Mr. Turner beaming. "Now that," he told us, "that there is what you call your fowling piece."

The troops followed us into the woods for a two-hour hike up the mountain to our team headquarters. To a clearing where some optimist had once built a house, probably felling every tree, pulling every stump, and moving every boulder by hand. The remnant empty now, as it clearly had been for many years. Parts of the collapsed and rotting house still black from the fire that had brought it down. Most of what was left lay tumbled into and on top of the basement. The stone foundation, with its empty holes where windows used to be, still standing. And the long, high porch across the back stood there, still in place, almost intact. One set of steps led to the ground.

Rozzelli and Colte were sitting on that porch, legs dangling, as we trailed in. An oil lamp at one end lit the deck and the immediate area, but it was not visible through the heavy woods until we were almost on top of it. Equipment, rucksacks and rolled sleeping bags were spaced out like markers on the deck as though measuring its length, and its tall, lumbered legs looked naked and embarrassed as we gathered in front of them.

Gomez and Hadley arrived at almost the same time from a different direction with another fifteen friendlies in tow. A few of these guys were older. All looked eager and shy at the same time, looking a little cowed as they came right to the headquarters of "them there parashooter fellas." Hey, look at this! Two of them were proudly wearing their old army fatigue shirts. Veterans, for chrissakes! Another guy wearing a grey military shirt, blue dungarees and a sailor hat. The navy was here, too! By God, we'll build us an army yet!

Gomez putting an arm around the sailor's shoulder and leading him proudly up to Rozzelli. "Look what we got here, Captain. Able Bodied Seaman Clyde Bellows, only home for a couple weeks liberty. Says he'll be glad to help us out much as he can for as long as he can stay."

Rozzelli vaulted lightly to the ground, Colte a half-second behind him. Rozzelli moved among our recruits, getting introductions. Taking his time and getting the names. Our locals obviously liking that. *Why he's a regular fella, ain't he?*

Our volunteers were used to doing a man's work and it showed. Lean, hard-muscled frames. Calm, steady eyes.

Rozzelli talking to each one in turn.

"Sixteen? Hell, I'd of said eighteen, easy. You can serve in my outfit any time, son. Proud to have you with us."

Stopping to examine a weapon, expertly. Colte holding a flashlight for him at the breech while Rozzelli peered down the barrel, whistling softly. "Take a look at this one, Gunnar! Now here's a man knows how to clean a rifle. Knows how to shoot one, too, I'd bet my bars on that." The fifteen-year-old swelling with pride. The others nodding.

Special attention to the two young army vets and the seaman. Getting their histories. The first had a year in Korea as a cook. A little embarrassed at the attention.

"I didn't never see much action, Cap'n. Leastways, not much. Mostly worked in the rehab kitchen, Sir."

"Very glad to have you with us, Soldier." Soldier! Wow!

The second guy, Leroy, a different story. Infantry basic and sent direct to Korea. He was almost on top of the landmine when it went off. On his way back home in less than three weeks and then out of the army with a pieced-together leg that would never hang straight again. He was clearly afraid that Rozzelli would turn him away. "Ah cain't run like I used to, Cap'n, but I kin hop so good on this sumbee that I kin fly right by a lot of the fellas. Jest ast them!"

Everyone nodding. Everyone watching Rozzelli intently. "Very proud to have you with us, Son. It's an honor to have a veteran wounded in the service of his country come up here to help us out. An honor." Leroy stepping back with relief flooding his features, his teeth gritted so he wouldn't break right down and cry.

Rozzelli stopped in front of Mr. Turner. Another worried candidate afraid his age would send him packing. Rozzelli's face the one wreathed in pleasure this time. Getting Mr. Turner's service history. "Ah had me two years in the Yew-nited States Army, Cap'n. In a war I betcha you never heard tell of. Down thataway," he said pointing over his shoulder toward the South. "They called it the Mexican Border In-cee-dent at the time. But it was a shootin' war alright. A rastlin' war, too, when we got in close enough. Got my jaw busted once by one of them fellas. Got his big ol' sombrero in my face, blinded me, then busted me one with his rifle butt. Never did get to shoot me any of them slant-eyed Mex's myself, but plenty of 'em tasted our lead, an that's the truth."

Rozzelli crooked a finger and called someone to him. Flicking his flashlight on to Hector's shirtfront, he said, "By the way, Mr. Turner, have you met our medic yet? Say hello to Doctor Pancho Villa Gomez."

Turner was aghast as he read the name tag. Everyone dissolving in laughter. Even Turner finally, as Rozzelli suggested to Hector that he would be wise to leave his sombrero in his rucksack while Mr. Turner was with us.

One of our new troops spoke up. "Tell the Cap'n about the medal, Mr. Turner. The medal!"

Mr. Turner's embarrassment deepened. Finally, his voice soft, he told us, "Ol' Blackjack Pershing hisself give it to us. To my whole regiment. We all got one. I don't think I kin rightly say the words, but it's on the paper what come with the medal and some of these here fellas has seen it. Says it was for like conshipictures gallontrees, or somethin' like that. Meaning we fought real hard and good, as I got it anyways."

Rozzelli nodded. Everybody now looking at him. They'd all heard about the medal, but no one knew what it was for. "You know, I heard about that. They told us about that when I was studying to be an officer. About your regiment. It's in the books. The 1916 Mexican War. General Pershing singled out your entire regiment and cited all of you for conspicuous gallantry in the field."

"That's it!" Turner gurgled, almost unable to speak. "Them's the very words, the very words!"

"General Pershing considered it a great moment in history when he awarded that medal."

The collective awe that spread through the watching group was palpable.

Everyone was staring at Turner. Turner's jaw hung open as he stared at Rozzelli. Squaring his shoulders, he looked around at our army. His words were unspoken but we could all hear them anyway. *Now did I or did I not tell you true? It's in the book!*

Turner then turned to Gomez. "Sergeant, ah surely hope I gave you no offense with what ah said. Ah swear, they is times ah has got the biggest and dumbest mouth in the whole county. Will you 'cept my apology, Sir? Ah offer it sincerely."

A big smile split Hector's face, and he took Mr. Turner's hand and shook it firmly. Then, drawing it out, singing it, he said. "Si, Siiiiii Seenyor!"

Everyone loving that.

The troops were called to order by Colte. Fall in. Two straight lines. Everyone hurrying into place. *Ten shun!*

Colte swore them all in. Honorary, temporary members of 10th Special Forces Group Airborne. Everyone repeated the words. Everyone trying to stand taller than everyone else. Not a smile among them as they took the oath. Rozzelli called me forward. "Got your radio pad there, Fitz. Some things we're gonna need to get these men operational."

Everyone was glued to his words. *Back packs. Pup tents. Ponchos. M-1's.* The sucking in of breath at those words was like a twister passing by. *Rations. Cartridge belts. Fatigue caps.* His voice ticked off the list, then stopped.

"And I'm also going to need the following insignia of rank. For my troop leaders." He pointed to our sailor and to the former army cook. "Two sets of sergeant's stripes for these two men."

Wow! The two guys actually blushed. Everyone else looked on delighted. Except Leroy, the gimpy-legged vet. I could read his mind. *Sheeesh, I get my laig half blowed off an he makes a goldurn swabby a sergeant!*

"And for this man," Rozzelli continued, pointing right at Leroy, "a set of Lieutenant's bars. First Lieutenant's bars, Fitzpatrick. He's earned them."

A rebel yell from somewhere in the second rank, and everyone joined in for a minute. *Leroy, an officer! Don't that beat all?* Then everyone quiet, watching Rozzelli.

"And one set of gold major's leaves. For Major Tolliver Nelson Turner."

Bedlam. Everyone broke ranks and crowded around the old gentleman. They were looking at an eighty-two year old man who had just been re-born, spanked on the ass, and baptized all in one fell swoop. Major Turner he had become, and Major Turner he would remain, to his dying day.

Our army was ready for the field. And that was for danged sure.

CHAPTER FIFTY

Heavy-duty training on the weekend. Most of our army arranged to get Friday off to be with us, with their families and bosses cooperating. Everyone enjoyed the game.

Basic training. A minimum of marching. Just enough so they could fall in and out without knocking each other's brains out every time they turned with their new rifles. We weren't training them for parades. We got right down to the important matters. The team astonished and pleased at how quickly our locals learned, at how eagerly they ate up our instructions. These country boys, hunters all, were right in their element.

We put them through three long days and nights of fieldwork, letting them catnap between exercises. Showing them how to attack as a group across an open field without killing each other, and us, if they'd actually been firing live ammo. Moving fast and quietly through the woods and staying low and invisible in the fields came naturally to this crew. We taught them hand signals so we could give them silent directions from a distance, and flashlight signals for essential communications at night.

We showed them how to set up booby traps, modified to startle and scare, but not to maim or kill, and designed to identify the location of pursuers or to secure an area from surprise attack. They worked tirelessly, hanging on our every word.

At one point, I did come close to having a small coronary when I discovered that, from long habit, the two squads I was leading in an attack across an open field all had live ammo locked and loaded in their widely assorted weapons. *Dear Mr. and Mrs. Fitzpatrick, we're not sure how the buckshot got in your son's ass because he swallowed his tongue at the time and he is not talking.*

We set up a night drop on the first Saturday, delighting our army. The plane swooped in right on time, filling the starry sky with silken chutes drifting down. Our troops had the bundles unloaded in minutes and the DZ cleared and empty. We ran them for two hours to clear the area before we finally let them stop to inspect their loot.

The look on their faces was priceless as they hefted the new M-1's and carbines, opened the boxes of neatly packed grenades, and salivated over the olive drab cans of C-rations. *Hal-le lu-iah, brothers! We have died and gone to heaven!*

All day Sunday, in a small clearing well up in our mountain safe area, we put them to work, stripping and reassembling the weapons, memorizing the order of pieces. Cleaning them, and cleaning them again. *Mr. Fitzpatrick, I'm all done cleaning your .45. Kin I do your mess gear now, kin I? I'll make it shine like glass.* Well, if you *insist.*

Some of them ran several miles home to do chores, then ran all the way back. Not wanting to miss a single minute. *C'mon, Clyde! Let me carry the radio gear this time. You carried it last time.*

Mr. Fitzpatrick! Make him give me that gear this time.

Sunday night late, the troops were standing in formation in front of our lonely deck, still bright-eyed and bushy-tailed despite three full days and two nights of hard work. Not one of them would admit he was tired. Our team stood on the porch watching Major Turner tally up the results of their training. Compliments here and there, but also special attention to the inevitable foul-ups.

"Comin' through them woods after that drop last night, why I could hear some of you more'n two miles away. What if them there aggressors had been around then, huh? Why you'd all be rounded up and jailed and all our new gear'd be back in Fort Bragg! Is that what you iggerant crackers want? Fight them airborne sojers with huntin' rifles?"

Then he gave them good news, that another air drop was set for Monday night, for those who could get free to join us. Rebel yells rolled off into the night. "No AWOL's, now, boys. Only those what kin come without no angry parents coming up here after our hides. You younger fellows, you be dang sure you have permission if you jine us that night. It's going to be a late one. Might not get home until two, three in the morning."

Major Turner's unexpected last words to the troops got the attention of our whole team. "For those as kin make it, we'll all meet right chere at Rattlesnake Gulch."

At *where?* What did he just say? Standing up there on the porch, our eyes shifted covertly, first to each other, and then over our shoulders to where the caved-in, rock-filled, debris-strewn basement of this former house vegetated silently in inky blackness.

Our army dispersed then, disappearing quietly into the woods. Only our team and Major Turner remained. Rozzelli, returning his salute, stopped his departure with an upraised finger, and called him closer. I believe all of us noticed his reluctance to come much closer than he already stood, which was about twenty yards from the long porch on which we stood, nor could we casually ignore the obvious care with which he swept the ground in front of him as he did manage one or two grudging steps in our direction.

I think that was when the full recognition dawned on me. Of the fact that, until that very moment, I had never seen Major Turner, or any other of our local troops, come as close as he was now to the deck we routinely used for our sleeping quarters and as our equipment storage platform. Indeed, in the more than one week in which we had been assembling them up here, not one member of our army had ever stepped as close to our make-shift home as had Major Turner at that moment.

Rozzelli, with what I considered to be a rather thin and forced smile, pointed his index finger to the deck below his feet. "*This* place. It's called, 'Rattlesnake Gulch'?"

"Why, shorely," Turner answered, clearly surprised by this question. "Ever since the Jasper family, what lived here back in the twenties, was all kilt that freezing night when the rattlers come right up into the house to huddle near their stove and covered the floor like a blanket whilst they was all in bed. No one knows why they jumped up and tried to run through them snakes, but they was all bit to death afore they could get out. Man, woman and children. All four of them."

It is an understatement to say that the silence on the deck at that moment was memorable. None of us moved so much as a hair, while Turner continued. "Course the townspeople, we come out and shot us a passel and burnt this place to the ground the day after the funeral, but that didn't get rid of the snakes, of course. We knowed that. But it made us all feel some better. Hit's been called Rattlesnake Gulch ever since, and nobody around here ever comes up here. Haven't none of us come near this snake pit in years."

Turner spread his hands, registering anew the astonishment that they had all felt at out arrival. "And then here come you parashooter fellas, and you camp right *here!* You throw your stuff right up there on the porch. Why, hay-ell, y'all boys sleep right there on them old planks! When ever one around these parts heard that, why we just knowed you was the bravest fellas what ever..."

He stared up at us in the light of the one oil lamp. "Why, Cap'n, you ain't saying, you didn't *know?*"

"About the Jaspers?" Our leader's short, explosive laugh made my tensed bones jump. "Of *course*, we knew all about *that,*" Rozzelli lied.

Rozzelli looked to us for support, our heads nodding on rigid necks. "*Everyone* has heard about the Jaspers," he continued. "That's exactly

413

why we came here, made this our headquarters. We just didn't know the *name* of the place, that's all."

"Oh, *right!*" Turner acknowledged, reassured. "Of course. That there name, it ain't on no map that way. *We* named her that. Of *course* y'all wouldn't know the name."

After a few more minutes, with a last salute and wave, Turner headed home. The rest of us stood there as though our feet were glued to the planks. Except Coy, who was laughing delightedly. "Rattlesnake Gulch. Now who woulda thought?"

Gomez finally moved, turning to the back of the deck and shining his flashlight downward, the beam a bit unsteady as I followed its passage. Everything quiet, still. *Whoops!* What was that? The beam returning, moving back. *Oh, my god!* That space down deep between those boulders was alive. An ocean of snakes slipping and sliding away from the searching light. Up, over and around the rocks, under and over the charred beams. Past bottles, cans and other flotsam. The whole caved-in basement seemed alive with slithering movement!

"*Santa Maria!*" Gomez.

"*Jumping Jee-sus!*" Colte.

"*Oh, my God I am heartily sorry ...*" Fitzpatrick!

An outburst of furious activity. Our gear disappearing into our rucksacks so fast you couldn't see our hands moving. At high noon, you wouldn't have been able to see our hands moving. No one wanting to be last this time.

Two hours later, we had all found places and settled down in Turner's barn "The aggressors," we told him. "All over us up there."

"A surprise raid," Rozzelli had added. "They were almost on top of us when they tripped a few flares we had rigged, and we bugged out just before they could encircle us."

"Dang and tarnation," Turner sympathized. "They must of heard our bunch crashing around in the woods when they headed home last night. Coulda heard them rebel yells of theirs in Augusta when I announced the drop for Monday. Dang it all anyways. I've gotta teach them boys to move soft. It's my fault, it purely is."

The major tried to make it up to us. Fried chicken, hot coffee and a couple of jugs of white lightning. Turner trying to cushion our vast disappointment at the forced move, at having to abandon our cozy quarters at Rattlesnake Gulch. The first jug made a slow but continuous round. Two hours later, with Turner home in his own bed, I studied my teammates through the Venetian blinds that used to be my eyelids.

Colte, the second jug now cradled in his arms like a baby, enunciated each word with exaggerated clarity. "Do not mind snakes. One snake. Two snakes. Three snakes. Do not like them by the dozen. Do not like them in piles."

Connelly. "Me neither. Partic-a-lar, don't like piles of rashel shnakes."

Denbeaux took the jug from Colte, took a long drink, and made a face as it burned its way down. Turner's stuff was definitely not the smoothest we'd had.

Denbeaux held the jug up and stared at it with his one open eye. "Could have poured this in that basement," he slurred, "used their rigid l'il bodies, make a fence."

Rozzelli rolled up to a sitting position from where he had been dozing and snoring. "What we need," he announced, holding up one finger for emphasis, "is a raw hide rope! A nice, big fat one."

That took a supreme effort, it was clear, because his speech degenerated rapidly after that. "What cha do, see, is you put it all around us." He demonstrated, waving both arms to indicate a big circle on the barn floor. "Then we shleep in here, inside it. Scc, the secret is," taking us into his confidence with a hoarse whisper, "shnakes won't never, ever cross it."

Rozzelli waved a finger back and forth like an upside down pendulum. "Never."

"Why is that, Captain?" I asked, unable to follow that logic. Or any logic.

"Shnakes," he told us, "they won't crawl over warhide mopes on account of they ish their bellies."

Hector Gomez sat up. "I'll bet old Major Turner has got string in his house. Bet he's got a whole big ball of it." He burped loudly. "Will that do?"

Rozzelli thought that over and then nodded firmly. "Perfect."

From that point on, the whole evening seemed to go downhill.

CHAPTER FIFTY-ONE

For some reason, snakes and I have never been close. It's not that I can't deal with them, because I certainly can. It's just, well, changing my underwear afterward that's a pain.

Why none of us suspected the truth about Rattlesnake Gulch earlier remains an unanswered mystery. Well, maybe Coy knew. In fact, as I think back, I am goddamn sure Coy knew. That sucker had three belts done, and two more underway the day Turner gave us that unsettling news about our home away from home.

Coy knew when to keep his mouth shut. Oh, yeah. Another week or so and he could have opened a store.

Gomez should have suspected *something*. Solid, built low to the ground, he was not exactly high-jumper material.

"Who needs water?" That simple question came from Gomez as about five of us had been sitting on the edge of the porch, legs dangling.

Most of us passed over our canteens. Hector, two or three in each hand, had swung himself off onto the ground to head for the creek a couple of hundred yards down the mountain. He landed solidly enough. I can still see his shoulders stopping right about level with the porch deck, right beside my knees.

"Y I I - I I I - I I I - P E! ! !

My teeth still hurt when I think of how they slammed together as that blood-curdling yelp left his lips.

C A A A - - R A A A S H H! ! !

Gomez rose like a rocket, landing on the porch in one mighty bound, his boots slamming down inches from my naked hand. Canteens bounced away on all sides.

What in Christ?

Everyone leaned forward, looking down. Watching what seemed like an endless row of black and white diamonds riding a piece of fire hose across the clearing and disappearing into the high grass.

Oh, Gomez should have known alright. And why didn't I know? Maybe three mornings later, after first hanging over the edge and studying the ground under the deck *very carefully*, I jumped down myself, towel in hand, shaving gear in my fist, and headed down the trail to our dammed up stream for my morning ablutions. Almost down to the creek, singing a happy song and stopping to set down my gear. That's when I saw the eyes.

Snake eyes! And I don't mean dice.

No more than five feet from where my hand had stopped, still holding my shaving kit, everything in it rattling now like I was using it for a castanet.

Staring eyes! Staring, it seemed, right at my crotch. At where the proud symbol of my manhood used to hang out. Until a second or so earlier, when the cowardly worm took off to find refuge somewhere up in my rib cage.

Snake eyes on a damn big head. On top of several disgustingly fat coils.

What in hell do you do? Say, *nice snaky?* *Snaky want a cracker?*

What the hell is that? *"Seeeee the peer-ay-mids along the nyyy-allll!"*

Oh, suffering Jesus! It was Coy! Coming down the path behind me.

SSSSSS—SSSNNNNNAAAAAAKE!

What in the hell was that?

Balls! That was *me!* Trying to sound a warning. Trying to warn Coy before he walked past me and stepped right on the sonofabitch.

Second try, lips still not moving, but getting it out between clenched teeth! "Coy! Snake! Snnnaaaaaake!"

Coy, in a voice that rattled the trees. "WHAT'S THAT, FITZ?"

Oh, shit. We who are about to die salute you. "SNAKE!"

Oh, he heard that. Footsteps stopping behind me. A fuzzy white apparition at the corner of my peripheral vision, leaning around me. Coy in a T-shirt. "Hot day-em! Ain' he a beauty, Fitz! That ol' boys asleep! Sleepin' like a baby. Keep a eye on him, will ya, while I get me a stick."

Great jumping Jesus! A stick! He's going to *tease* the bastard!

Jump, I told myself. Jump back. Jump anywhere but forward! But it was as if all the connections between my brain and the rest of my body had been severed.

Bent double, a human question mark, I was frozen in place.

HEEEEE—YAAAAAA!

Coy, that incredible madman! Appearing out of nowhere at the edge of the creek to my left. In his bare feet! Splashing through the water as he jabbed at the snake like a knight at a dragon.

The snake's head shot up, and a terrible rattling noise thundered from the rock where he lay coiled. A throbbing ripple ran down the whole body. ZWAP! He flashed out, striking directly at Coy! Landing on the gravelly edge of the stream at his full length, but with his head a good twelve inches from Coy's extended bare foot.

I parted the bushes to get a better look. *Bushes?* How the hell did I get over here in the bushes? I found myself bouncing up and down on a large mass of leaves and branches, weighing the bush I was sitting on almost to the ground. My feet, chest and face were still pointed at the stream—but I realized, shocked, that I was now a good eight feet away from where my shaving kit lay dropped and forgotten on the ground.

PDDDDDrrrrrrrrrrrrrrrrr—chicka...chicka chicka!

Another warning as the snake curled, rose and struck again at Coy's stick. Again, the snake landed flat out on the ground. WHAP, WHAP, WHAP! Coy moving in, hammering again with the thick stubby end of his short stick. I pushed myself up on to shaky legs. The snake was trying to pull into a coil yet again, but its head was now almost flattened, a gooey mess of flesh and bone. Coy's blows were now unerring. He struck again and again until the snake was still.

Coy trotted back to the path. "Keep a eye on him, will ya, Fitz, while I run up and get my knife."

Coy going past me, gleeful. Near the top, I heard his yell. "Hey, you guys! Colte! Gomez! Come see the big ol' snake Fitz and me just killed!"

Dorchester city boy sitting on a stump. Watching the last, occasional and slow ripples of the biggest snake I'd ever seen. Looking at the almost headless body, the rest of the snake as untouched as if civilization were a thousand miles away.

The body, in truth, was absolutely beautiful with the light playing now along its length, and I felt really low looking at it. Wondering if it was really asleep there in the sun when I first got there. While I stood frozen in fear. Oh, yeah. It *was*. Sleeping like a baby in the morning warmth. If I had only known, only realized. I'm really sorry, old timer. Really sorry.

Coy came down with his knife and took the head off in one quick slice. He held it up by the tail for the others coming down to see. Everyone admiring the kill. Coy telling his tale and including me in it all the way. "So then, ol' Fitz, he kep' a eye on it while I got me a stick...and ol' Fitz, he moved over there to head him off, 'n case he tried to go for the bushes..."

Didn't he *know*? Didn't he see me at all?

After the others went back up, and with Coy's prize lying over on the shore, Coy began to shave, chuckling as he slid the blade along his jaw line. Confidential now, for my ears only. "Fitz, old pal, I've seed grasshoppers jump, I've seed big old country hares could jump a mile, but I've never seen nothing go up in the air like you did when that snake made that first strike. You could have used oxygen up there, Fitz, and that's no shit!"

Oh, he knew alright. He saw. Coy saw *everything.*

"It ain't fair, you know?' he added. "Me tryin' to kill me a big ol' snake, and you getting me to laughing so hard I coulda got myself bit. Fitz, if you could only do that backward leap regular, you could make a fortune in the circus."

Oh, yeah, we should have known, all right, and long before Major Turner made his little announcement. But we were Special Forces troopers. We never missed a trick.

CHAPTER FIFTY-TWO

From the back seat, next to the window, I had to lean left to see the speedometer between Bill and our driver. It was edging up over ninety as we hit the curve, tires screeching. All of us were thrown to the right. Harvey Samuels, one of our locals was on my left. He let out a whoop as we broke out of the wrenching turn, then sagged back against Dubois who was jammed up against the other window. Our souped-up, long-nosed Packard raced on, never slowing.

We went downhill, picking up even more speed and hitting a patch of gravel that sent us skidding and fishtailing for several heart-stopping seconds. Our driver immediately returned to his casual, one-handed grip on the wheel as soon as we straightened out. "Jest a little sand, boys," he told us, his voice calm, the words slow and easy. "We get lots of that round here."

Another curve was coming up fast ahead, the speedometer over a hundred. Our driver turned halfway in his seat to look at those of us in the back. "How you fellas doin' back there? Y'all okay? Y'all didn't let that patch of sand skeer you none, did you?"

We had no chance to answer as we hit the curve. All of us were thrown to the left this time as we squealed into it, and both of the driver's hands returned to the wheel. We rocketed around the turn like we were in a roller-coaster bucket-car.

A lone car going past on the other side of the road from us, and one millisecond glimpse of the farmer at the wheel tooting his angry old horn at us. Taking in a deep breath, I saw that at least we had a clear road ahead for a bit. Our driver, smiling happily, used this opportunity to skid the back of the car out and across the road, twisting the wheel to send the front with it, skidding us all the way across until we bumped up on the shoulder on the left hand side. Then he did the same in the other direction to send us skidding and skating back across until we bounced up on to the shoulder on the right. Only then did he skid us back out on to the road. "See how nice this baby handles?" he asked no one in particular. "Hell, you kin take this here honey *anywheres*."

Conroy MacAllister, our driver and entertainment secretary of the moment, was the middle son of the legendary, in those parts, Moonshine MacAllisters. The three sons and their father before them, had been running white lightning out of those mountains for years, first, in fast wagons, and later in souped up cars like the one I was turning parchment-white in. They had been doing this under the noses of the local law, who, frankly, didn't give a damn, but they had also managed to keep one step ahead of the Federals, and that was no minor accomplishment. The Feds had been hell-bent for years on putting the whole MacAllister family behind bars.

Everyone in those mountains knew that the revenuers had only come close once. That was when the oldest boy, Hardy, seventeen at the time and still a bit careless, tried to get the Buick he was driving to have sex with an eighteen-wheeler which had suddenly slowed in front of him as he came around a turn with the Feds right on his heels. No one, seeing the wreckage, could believe that Hardy had actually walked away, and he hadn't exactly. He had come out running, and was already deep in the woods before the pursuit car, which had just missed crashing into the wreck itself, could get stopped, turned around and back to the scene. We were told that you could still smell the shine along that stretch of road every time it rained.

Hardy had been quoted in the papers while we were down there as saying that racing at Indianapolis didn't hold a candle to running shine over the mountains in a driving thunderstorm with the Feds sucking on your exhaust all the way.

Another chuckle from Conroy at the top of the next rise. "Y'all will like this one," he lied. "We'uns around here call it Bobsled Run."

Harvey was beside himself with excitement in the back seat, jumping around and inadvertently passing bruises out equally between Dubois and me. "Oh, boy! Bobsled Run! Let 'er rip, Conroy, let 'er *riiiip!*"

We went over the rise at the top with all four wheels in the air, and plunged down the other side with the accelerator flat to the floor.

We knew, of course, that McAllister was hell-bent on scaring the living shit out of us, out of Harvey's parashooter pals. Personally, I found it hard to defecate with my colon wrapped around my esophagus.

Initially, Conroy McAllister had disdained Harvey's suggestion that he join us in our war games against the eighty-deuce. Twenty-six, married, with a good income running shine, he was what you'd call mature and settled for those parts. He didn't cotton to the idea of running through the woods playing "sojer boy." On the other hand, most of these guys who had joined up with us were his pals and relatives and, of course, he did hate the Feds with a mighty passion. He managed to ignore the fact that most of us were both Yankees and federals, enticed by the stories of what wild men we were supposed to be. I think he suspected we might be as crazy as he was. And, the idea of giving a whole company of regular 82nd troopers the screaming fits, well, that was a real enticement, no question.

This run over the mountains, we understood, was Conroy's way of finding out what we were made of, what we had inside.

I was pretty sure that Bobsled Run was about to show him exactly what I had inside. My only concern at that moment was whether I'd be able to reach his lap.

Screeching down the other side and leveling out at the bottom of the impossibly steep incline. The trees going by were nothing but a solid blur of green and I felt the car swerve out and around a horse and wagon as we were almost at the bottom. The speedometer was resting at the top right of the dial when I heard Conroy's, "Hang on, boys!" That's when he slammed down the brakes again and held them there as the needle dropped to seventy, to sixty, and finally to forty. That was when Conroy swung the wheel first left, then hard right and sent us spinning around backwards in a one hundred eighty degree turn.

I had been hammered back against the seat so hard as we had raced down that hill that I thought I might end up in the trunk, but then I was thrown forward as Conroy spun the car around to send us sliding backwards into a long, road-blistering stop, so that I actually had to push myself off of the back of the front seat as we finally ground to a stop.

Conroy calmly dropped the car into first gear and began rolling forward again, with nothing but our heavy breathing to be heard in the car. Even Harvey was gasping and breathless. Then I could hear Conroy up front, laughing softly.

Cruising. Coming back to pass the horse and wagon which was now plodding toward us. Conroy leaned out the window and tipped his hat. "Sorry about that, Mr. Carlyle. Hope we didn't skeer you none, Sir. Just showin' the boys here what this ol' heap of mine kin do."

The farmer, hunched over the reins, registered no change of expression as we slowly passed. "Nope. Your father skeered me once, Sonny, but that was years ago."

Conroy pulled off the road and turned off the motor to look us all over. Taking his time about it. "Well, leastways didn't none of you faint on me. I'll give you that."

He looked at me just as I was re-swallowing the last of my breakfast, for maybe the third time. A wide grin. "Didn't skeer you none, did I, Mr. Fitz?"

"Well," I said, "I have to admit, you almost had me when my dick fell off."

Conroy guffawing and slapping Denbeaux on the thigh with a crack like an M-1 firing. "Wait'll I tell Paw that one, William. Oh, he'll love that one, Paw will."

Harvey brightened considerably. "Does that mean you'll jine up with us, Conroy? Kin we tell Cap'n Rozzelli that you are agoin' to hep us out?"

Conroy let his eyes pass once more over each of us. Then the calloused hand came out, first to Denbeaux, and then to each of us in turn. "Hell, yes, Harvey," he said. "These yere boys are alright. They got the stuff. Hell, yes, you can count me in."

People down in Alabama must have turned to look, the way Harvey's rebel yell rolled off through that countryside.

****

The gravel crunched under the tires as we rolled slowly to a stop. The woods were completely black all around us as we sat there listening. Denbeaux tapped his watch, the glow from the crystal the only light in the front seat. "We're a few minutes early. They'll be here shortly."

Dim figures moved toward us. Coming out from under the trees. Rozzelli, his grease gun across his middle, stocking cap on his head, his face and the backs of his hands blackened, reached through the driver's window. "Mr. McAllister? A pleasure."

Other members of the team and of our "army" surrounding the car. The locals with their issue of shiny new M-1's, and with grenades all over their upper bodies like hives. Conroy leaned out to look them over, giving a low whistle.

428

"Shoot! You men ready foah a war, alright, and no mistake. Thet there umpire fella show up?"

Rozzelli grinned, his crooked teeth showing. "Better than that. They sent us three umpires for this wind-up. That means one of them gets to ride with you!"

He leaned down to the window and dropped his voice to a whisper, and I saw the crooked smile. "I didn't mention anything about who the driver would be. I just told them that one of the umpires could ride along. They drew straws for the honor!"

All of us in the car laughing, but my mind raced ahead. Does this mean that one of us will have to walk? *Don't wait, Asshole. Volunteer!*

I opened the door on my side and stuck a foot out. "Damn it! I guess that means one of us has to walk, Captain. Shit! I knew my luck was too good to last!"

"Hole on there, Fitz. Hole on jest a second there."

It was Conroy.

"Hey, Cap'n! Whyn't we let Ol' Fitz jump right up here in front with Denbox and me. Then that there umpire can still get in back. No sweat."

"Aww, that's okay, Conroy. I really appreciate it, but I don't want to crowd you. I mean not with the kind of driving you may have to do tonight an' all."

"Shoot, Fitz! Get on up here with us, Boy! Ain't no sweat. Sometimes I drive with a case of corn sittin' in my lap. Hop up here, Ole Buddy. Right up here with us!"

Oh, terrific! Denbeaux got out and stood to one side to let me in. Whispering as I went by. "Nice try, Hotshot. Nice try!"

Out in front of the car, three men came toward us. The white on their arm-bands and helmets made a fuzzy blur as Rozzelli's flashlight picked them out. Two captains and a major. One captain was smiling, the other two officers looked sour. The smile came over to us, grinning at Rozzelli. "Aha! I see my chariot has arrived!"

He went by Harvey who was holding the door open for him, heading for the middle of the back seat, but he straightened just for a moment first and wiggled his fingers at the other two umpires. "Well! Ta-ta for now. You fellas be sure to keep up now, when these guys start trotting up and down these mountains. Don't want to disgrace Army Intelligence now, do we?"

With an explosive chuckle he climbed in. Harvey followed, slamming the door.

Conroy stuck a hand out the window and waved everyone off the road. Then he glanced back at the umpire who grinned back at him. A happy grin. "Well, now men," the umpire said, "you guys fill me in. What have we got on for tonight, anyway?"

Conroy McAllister was still looking back over his shoulder when he put the accelerator to the floor.

A long second of delayed reaction, about like you get when a missile fires off. A terrible, whining roar of tires spinning on dirt and gravel. Then the car shot straight ahead, going from zero to sixty in eight or nine seconds. The umpire found himself plastered against the back seat between Dubois and Harvey, his pupils contracting in fright. The car tore ahead into the pitch darkness, without lights, still picking up speed.

Conroy, one quick glance ahead and then he looked into the back again at the umpire as he tramped down even harder on the accelerator. A cloud of dirt and stones plumed up behind us. "Now, y'all jest set back there and relax, Cap'n, and enjoy your ride. Ah knows this here road *real* good!"

CHAPTER FIFTY-THREE

Rolling down the Toccoa Road. Conroy swept out and around the slower traffic. Squeezing between the lines of passing cars at breakneck speed, he gave his horn several loud blasts just as we sailed past a truck doing seventy. "That's it, Big Guy," Conroy said. "You stay over there on the right, 'n you cain't keep up with us little fellas."

An angry return blast from the truck's horn. *Eeeee-Awww! Eeeeh-Awwww!*

A mile further and Conroy took a sharp right, going up on two wheels for most of the turn, bouncing back again onto the four tires. We turned off the main road and headed back into the foothills of the mountains.

A narrower road. When the oncoming traffic saw Conroy coming at them at 80 plus, they veered over to the shoulder to let us pass. Conroy kept the heel of his hand on the horn, jamming it down every five seconds and staying right out in the middle of the road as he roared past the slower traffic. "Move it or lose it, Gents, move it or lose it!"

Not daring to shut my eyes, which I wanted to, I braced a hand against the dash, trying to stay in my seat as we rolled into the curves. Denbeaux, I noted, was doing the same. Passing one truck as another one came right at us in a thundering blur. Both trucks veered as we shot right between them. Conroy was clearly not bothered by the deafening roar, but my ears were popping. We careened out the other end like a cork out of a bottle. Conroy gave me an elbow.

"Traffic sure is light tonight, ain't it, Fitz? Ever body must be to home listening to their radios, I guess."

From the back seat, a hoarse croak, but the words when they came were clearly distinguishable. "STOP! Stop this car. This instant! That's...that's an ORDER!"

Barreling on down the asphalt and closing fast on the taillights in front of us. McAllister turned to look past me into the back seat. He turned back just in time to see more headlights coming at us in the other lane. Swerving right up on to the shoulder, he roared past an ancient old Ford plodding along in front of us in our lane. All of us except Conroy were bounced around in our seats, almost crashing into the roof as we jolted along on the rough shoulder. Conroy held on to the wheel, barely moving at all as he steered us back out on to the road. We left the slower car in the dust, the faces of the elderly couple inside peering out at us in shock, but visible to us for only a split second as we flashed past.

Conroy chuckled as we fishtailed and skidded, gaining speed, and his thumb jerked toward the back seat. "Did you hear the ol' Cap'n back there, Fitz? That umpire fella? This here is a ORDER he says. Ah think that ol' boy thinks I'm in his aah-mee!"

Conroy chortling noisily at the idea. Yep, that's a real laugher, Conroy. Hee hee.

The road flattened out, and there were now more houses on either side, but not many. Lights appeared up ahead. Conroy braking down to 60, then 50, then all the way to 40 as we cruised toward the lights.

Conroy nodded. "Ah do believe that must be them, jest like your Cap'n Rozzelli told us. That there's Elroy's Truck Stop, sure enough, and he sure do seem to have drawed a crowd for this time of night. Them army fellas must of got that there alert, alright. Girdin' they loins for battle now, I spect. Whyn't we roll in there, boys, give them their wake-up call?"

Four two and a half ton trucks were lined up facing the road just beyond the gas pumps, their noses even with the front of Elroy's store. Troops were out and milling about them. On this side of the pumps, nose-to-nose, there were two jeeps with several men standing around in full battle gear. A knot of men was gathered around the jeeps comparing maps, holding them up so that the lights above the pumps shone down on them. "Officers," Bill said. "And heavy-stripers. In a nice tight group. Get ready, guys!"

Bill, Harvey and Dubois were at the windows with grenades in both hands, the pins already pulled. Not much bang to them without the explosive, but lots of flash and noise at least. We rolled across the gravel, driving right up to the group of officers.

Conroy slowed to a stop, putting the gears in neutral and racing the motor loudly. Helmeted heads above annoyed faces swung in our direction. Harvey, our delighted local, yelling it out good and loud. "Special *dee*-livery, y'all! From the Special Forces!"

Three grenades dropped down out of the darkness into the light, hitting the ground and rolling in among the officers and the two jeeps. No one moved. They all watched them, surprised, the way you'd watch a kid's soccer ball that dropped over a fence into the middle of your barbecue party.

Conroy was already back in gear, flooring it, and behind us as we roared past the pumps, we heard the "POW! POW! POW!" as the first three went off. The officers and NCOs jumping back then, high-stepping and yelping in anger as they saw another three already bouncing across the gravel toward them.

Conroy swung the wheel sharply, doing a breath-taking U-turn and then racing back again past the pumps on the other side. The men were still clustered near the jeeps, but they were jumping for cover now as we roared back grenades already sailing at them through the air. Stones and gravel flew out from behind our wheels. A dust cloud! Conroy fishtailing the back of the car to send the gravel spewing over the officers and NCO's, who ran bent over, covering their faces. Maps were loose and flying everywhere as we shot past.

Dubois, his head and shoulders hanging out the window, gave them the word this time. "Deeeeaaad!" he hollered. "All of you fuck-aaaiiirs are deeeead!"

Across the road, out of the lights, and we were racing back down the road into the darkness.

Denbeaux reached back to slap the umpire on the leg. "Write it down, Captain. A major, two captains, a lieutenant, two SFC's, and both of those fucking jeeps. You saw it, Captain. Those last grenades rolled right under them. A wipe-out!"

Conroy already over sixty and still accelerating when the Captain answered. "I...I'm...I'm going to be SICK!"

SCCCCCCCCRRRRRREEEEEEEEEEEEEeee eeeeeeeeeeeeeeeeeeeeee!

Conroy standing on the brake. I was on the dashboard, my forehead kissing the windshield. A loud "OOOF!" from Denbeaux, beside me as he rammed into the glove compartment and his head did bop once off the windshield. The car bouncing up on to the shoulder even though it was over twenty, and still braking hard. "Not in *my* car, you ain't, Pal," Conroy exploded. "OUT! Harvey, don't sit there, boy! *Push!*"

The captain outside on the ground, on his hands and knees. Retching. Then flooding the ground in front of him with the effluvia of that last good meal he'd eaten before he joined up with us. Buckets of the stuff. Wearing a lot of it on his chin and shirtfront as though he was reluctant to see it all go. "Oh, boys," he wailed pathetically, "just leave me right here, oh, pleeeeaaase. I'll...I'll square it with you later. You can come back and get me and..." Another retch and heave. And I'll...I'll put anything you want in the report, boys. Just, leave me here. I can't...can't take any more of that car."

Bill tapped him on the shoulder and pointed. The captain's head came up slowly to look. "Look at that, Captain. Doesn't that pink piece right there look just like a rat's kidney? Look at it!"

The captain, gulped, cried out, gurgled and let fly again. Another great whoooosh, but this time producing only a small, greenish puddle.

436

Harvey giggled, slapping his thigh. "I think he's empty now, Conroy, I truly do. I think ol' Bill here just turned the captain inside out like an old sock."

McAllister was satisfied. "Alright, then. Drag him back in, men, and let's haul ass. But Harvey, you put that old boy next to the window this time, and you be sure his head goes out, 'n he decides to fertilize this here county any more tonight, y'hear?"

Conroy U-turned again and headed back now for the same lighted clearing. This time the trucks all in a line, troops on board, and motors roaring. The jeeps had moved but the officers were *still* in a group settling the last details.

Conroy was doing at least fifty as we tore across the gravel. Another six, seven, eight grenades sailed out, rolling under the trucks, a couple bouncing off the sides and rolling over spinning to the gas pumps. The yelling of the guys on the trucks as they saw us flashing by mingled with the loud "POWS" of the grenades going off as Conroy braked and veered out on to the road again, braking so hard that our front bumper touched down on the asphalt sending a shower of sparks off on both sides. The hood lifted then as Conroy accelerated, and we peeled out of there with the nose of the car pointed up like a combustion-engined surfboard.

"Got that count, Captain?" Denbeaux hollered above the noise. "At least two of those four trucks gone bye-bye! Nothing but nuts and bolts left. And they were loaded with troops, too. Put that in your book, Captain. Write it down!"

A long, low moan came from the umpire, with his eyes squeezed shut as Harvey held his head out the window, the road flying by beneath him. Dubois responded. "I don't think he 'ear zat, Denbeaux. You keep zee count. I 'ave zis feeling he weel take your word, yes?"

Five minutes down the road, Conroy pulling over to the side, shifting in to neutral, and idling there, watching the rear-view mirror. Two or three more minutes. I had a cigarette out, just ready to light it. "Here they come. Hear 'em?"

The unmistakable whine of the jeep leading the trucks as they came around the bend about fifty yards behind us. Harvey chortled. "They got one of them sy-reens, boys! Why they is as loud as our fire truck, I swear. Just listen to that!"

Conroy rolled back out onto the road, but not too fast at first. Making sure they were close enough to see us. Coming very fast for them, especially after they crested the rise and moved onto the flat behind us. Pushing us up to sixty now with their siren screaming.

We followed the winding road through the valley for another few miles. "Better pull that umpire fella in now, men," Conroy said. "This next road's gonna be a might more narrow with lots of trees. Don't want him hurt none. He ain't even filled out that there report yet."

We turned off and branches began whacking the car as we drove past. Conroy, slowed and opened his door to make our interior light came on, to make us more visible. He listened to be sure they were following. Elated, we saw the headlights turn in behind us, the siren still roaring full blast.

The road curved in front of us toward a tributary of the Chattahoochee River. With the river to our left, we drove along an old winding path that slashed its way between the canyoned walls now rising on both sides of us. The water, about fifty feet below, was strewn with boulders and smaller rocks.

"There she is, boys! Ain't she purty?"

Conroy pointed over the wheel at the bridge that had just become visible in front of us. The pursuing trucks and the siren sounded much closer now. The road in front of us took a sharp left across the steel-framed, narrow bridge, and then turned right on the far side to continue along beside the river. The water, white and foamy, rushing by under the bridge, splashed up as it collided with the rocks and boulders.

We made the turn, thundering across the metal bridge. "Knowed a fella," Conroy advised us, "a suicide, jumped off this here bridge. Despondent over some little ol' gal. Banged hisself up good, too. They put him away for being stupid."

The siren was really screaming now. "They can see us!" Harvey yelped in the back seat. "They can see our taillights, Conroy. They speedin' up now, alright! They are comin' fast as they kin!"

Conroy was still driving slowly on the bridge. He kept that same pace until we saw the jeep swing into its turn and speed up as it neared the other end of the bridge. Then Conroy flooring it, taking the turn at the end on two wheels and racing off down beside the river. We were doing close to fifty on that dirt road when Conroy yipped, "Get ready!"

439

Swinging the wheel left and then right, he did another of his hundred and eighty degree turns. A dizzying spin! Skidding backwards down the dirt road and stopping with our nose facing back at the bridge.

The jeep was halfway across and going flat out. Just as it cleared the bridge, braking hard to make the swing down to face us, it saw that we were stopped and waiting and it hit its brakes, gravel flying everywhere, screeching to a stop. Its siren wheezed to a halt, gave a last "oink" and quit.

In the few seconds of quiet that followed, we could hear the trucks rumbling across the bridge. Then we heard that other sound. An older motor, much louder. A battered old truck came driving out of the woods behind the jeep. It lumbered to a dead stop across the roadway, right at the end of the steel girders, sealing off this end of the bridge entirely. It was an old, cumbersome cement truck, its round carrier no longer turning. It sat across the end of the bridge like an abandoned dinosaur.

The cab door flew open and we saw the driver jump out and race back for the woods, the guys in the jeep all standing and looking back. *Now what the hay-ell is this?*

An officer leaped from the jeep and began running. Back toward the bridge. Yelling at the top of his lungs at the first of the trucks slowing to a stop as it neared the cement truck. "Go back!" the officer bellowed. "Go back! It's a trap!"

Bill counting trucks out loud. *Four. Five.* The sixth turned onto the bridge, too far away to hear the officer on our side shouting. Rolling on across and braking to a stop behind the others. Guys at this end jumping out of the trucks. A lot of shouting and confusion. Other guys yelling "Get back in! Get back in the trucks! It's a trap! Back up, back up!"

At the far end of the bridge, we spotted another set of headlights coming fast. Coming up to the far end of the bridge just as the sixth truck began to back. To my right, Harvey whooping when he saw it. "Whooo-eeee, boys! That'll be old Sylvester, right on time! Bottle 'em up, Sylvester, bottle 'em up!"

A big, old farm truck with high wooden sides, loaded with lumber. Its lights continued past, not turning on to the bridge. Stopping with the mass of its big wooden body blocking off the other end like a sliding door. Again, the driver jumped out on the passenger side and ran for the woods. We could hear Sylvester's triumphant rebel yell all the way across the river as he disappeared among the trees.

On the side of the farm truck a white sheet dangled down. Denbeaux read the big red letters with his binoculars, calling out the words for us.

"HOWDY, Y'ALL! IT'S BOOM TIME!"

Our men coming out of the woods and all around us now. Others coming out from under the bridge. They pointed their weapons at the three men standing by the jeep, as they trotted by, firing off a few blanks at them.

Our local army.

Already on the scene, their work nearly done. Colte came up from under the bridge with wires in his hand, trailing them out behind him.

Coming over to where Calvin waited with the detonator. Green emerged from the woods with another half a dozen men. Then we heard Major Tolliver Nelson Turner, his voice carrying well in the night air. "Fall back, men! Everyone over here! We a-goin' to blow that bridge! Where's that umpire fella? Get him over here!"

Another pair of our locals appeared, the umpire captain dangling between them, his eyes still glassy when a flashlight lit up his face. Colte showing him the detonator, pointing at the wires leading to the bridge. The umpire nodding, trying to sit down, but being held up by his keepers. Another bellow from Turner.

"LET 'ER RIP! BLOW THAT SUCKER!"

Colte, his teeth glowing white in the middle of his cork-covered face, plunged the handle down. Two or three others firing flares into the air at the same time, the sky lighting up over the bridge as a series of sharp "POWS" began going off under the girders, the detonator caps firing. Turner exhorting the troops. "Don't just stand there, men! Yell 'BOOM'! Fire them weapons!"

Everyone yelping and shouting, firing off grease guns and M-1's. Others throwing grenades at the jeep where the officer, his NCO aide and a driver now sat glumly, looking helplessly back at the trapped trucks and the confused soldiers milling about on the bridge. One of our locals grabbed their radio from the front seat as he ran by. The three men in the jeep did not even react, just watched it go.

"Let's go, men," Colte yelled. "Everyone this way, double-time. That bridge is GONE! It's a wipeout! That bridge is halfway to Gainesville

442

right now. Double-time, men! We still got work to do. Follow the major and me!"

Running ourselves then, back to the car. Harvey and one of his pals hanging on to the umpire's belt and running him along with us. "You see the way them charges was set, Cap'n? Both ends of that bridge a-goin off in what we call a sequence? Would been sliced away like you'd cut you a hunk of butter, that bridge, if the damn C-3 was there. That French fella, he taught us good, didn' he, Cap'n? He taught us *good*!"

Piling in to the car again. The umpire coming to life and bracing himself against the outside of the car door like a crazed cat trying to stay out of a carrier. "Oh, no, boys! Not *again*! Oh, Jesus, leave me here this time. Lemmee go with the others! Oh, pleeeaaaase!"

In he went, the rest of us piling in behind him. Conroy already on the accelerator as the doors were still shutting behind us.

VVVVRRRRRRRR—ROOOOOOOOOMMMM!

Another plume of dirt and gravel swirled off to our rear.

Conroy, a nasty laugh as we hit fifty, already flying down the bumpy road without headlights. "Well, boys, leastways, this time the Cap'n is empty!"

CHAPTER FIFTY-FOUR

I woke up with a decided cramp in my neck and it was several minutes more before I opened my eyes.

I was curled up in a corner in the back of the truck heading back to North Carolina. Sitting up, I worked my head around on my neck to get the juices flowing again. The field jacket I had pulled over myself as I had fallen asleep was lying on the floor by my feet.

I picked it up, gave it a shake, and stuck it through the straps on my rucksack, being careful because Gomez had his head propped against it as he slept.

The whole team was stretched out or curled up in assorted positions all over the back of the truck, along with rucksacks, weapons, radio equipment, the bazooka and all kinds of other gear which was stashed here and there. Some of the items were standard Government Issue, others were relics of the Georgia problem. Sleeping with his back propped against the truck cab, Coy still wore several dried snake skins tied across his chest, from shoulder to waist, like a frontiersman's version of a Sam Brown belt.

Most of the team was asleep, or trying to sleep. Except Denbeaux. He was sitting at the end with one foot up on the tailgate, looking out. Watching the road roll by.

Stretched out in the middle of the aisle, right at my feet, his head on his rolled-up sleeping bag, his mouth open and emitting a series of impressive snores, was Captain Rozzelli.

Instead of taking the seat next to the driver, an officer's prerogative, he had elected to climb in back with the rest of us for this return trip back to Bragg. Once we were underway, out on the highway, he had brought out a parting gift from our Georgia locals. One last jug of corn. It was sitting over by Connelly now, almost empty.

It had been almost 2300 hours before the convoy finally got rolling, one full day after the problem had wound up. After our big finish.

For the first couple of hours, we had done almost nothing but laugh, passing the jug. All of us were feeling both elated and down at the same time. Elated by the way things had gone on the wind-up, but down because we were sorry to see it all end. We drove into the night leaving behind not just the Georgia mountains that had been our home for the last ten weeks, but also new friends, delighted followers, our local army.

The last two days of Operation Cleo had more than exceeded our expectations, and our expectations had been high. For the wind-up in particular, it had seemed as if half the male population of North Georgia had joined our rag-tag army. Running through the woods beside us. Giving the Feds "what fer"! And having a ball while they were at it.

What we did in ten weeks in Georgia should have provided an unforgettable lesson for the Pentagon, but one is never sure how much sticks over the long haul to the brass-bound brain matter of the regular military. There were those who had made it clear that they simply did not believe in the wisdom or value of developing special elite troops and forces within our army, who didn't think they were appropriate in the regular army of a democratic government. Others were simply convinced that no group of soldiers in our own army could ever be trained to go into the field and, on their own, effectively raise a guerilla army and conduct devastating behind-the-lines warfare—to act as "force-multipliers."

What happened in those Georgia mountains was in striking ways a mirror reflection of what had happened behind the lines in France to the German army in the pre- and post-invasion days of world war two. To those who had strongly objected to the idea of such a force, for any of the reasons mentioned, Operation Cleo must have been a hard swallow indeed.

Our handful of nine-man teams, dropped like dragon-seeds all over the Chattahoochee National Forest, had blossomed in a two-month period into an army of hundreds. More, as we had amply demonstrated, it was an army capable of swooping down out of nowhere to confuse, misdirect, hogtie, trap and even wipe out whole segments of some of the best-trained troops the U.S. Army could put in the field. What happened in Georgia was more than you could blame on luck, or blunders, although we certainly knew that those had been involved as well.

The way tents were lined up for us in nice neat rows, in an encampment which, in retrospect, should have been named "easy pickin's." The way senior officers and non-coms gathered in a group to study maps and discuss their plans right out in the open in what was supposed to be enemy territory. The way troops were mustered at a gas station because it happened to be a well-lit area, a decision that totally ignored the incendiary implications of such a location if an attack were to take place. The way truckloads of troopers, armed to the teeth, were allowed to end up trapped in their vehicles because they pointlessly chased fleeing guerillas out onto a bridge in the middle of nowhere.

We understood now, of course, that those were the kinds of things that will happen when no sensible or effective anti-guerilla plans or strategies have been developed for an army in the field. It was sobering to me to see companies of crack troops rushing around in circles, spoiling for a fight, but unable to find or come to grips with their enemy. To see the weak points of a force superior in numbers and equipment located and exploited, and to see this done in ways that gave that superior force no real warning or opportunity to react effectively. To see how their superior weaponry could simply be avoided, bypassed or deflected. It was, in fact, an incredible thing to see from our perspective as guerrilla operatives in the field.

That, in sum, was Operation Cleo.

In the assembly area, before we loaded up for the trip home, Colonel Bank himself came through for a visit, bringing his elated senior staff along to congratulate the men. They moved from team to team collecting stories, with only a few preliminary umpires' reports in hand, but even those were illuminating. The colonel on hand himself, though, to get the nuts and bolts direct from his team leaders. The Aaron Bank way.

Our turn came in due course. Standing proudly in our sweat-soaked, muddy fatigues and listening as Bank was told about our ambush at the gas station, about the six truckloads of troopers trapped on a bridge. One of Bank's assistants confirming the highlights from his own notes of an umpire interview. Rozzelli, Colte, Connolly getting the full treatment.

Rozzelli stepped back, I noticed, to widen the circle. To make sure we all got a handshake from the man, a moment in the sun. Then, just as he was about to move on, he stopped Colonel Bank "With all respect, Colonel, if I could just dump these screw-ups here and get me a real team next time, there's no telling what I could accomplish."

All of us hooting. The colonel and his staff laughing as they moved on. Connelly jabbed Colte and grabbed Rozzelli by an elbow. "What do you say, Gunnar? We still got time to find us one more irrigation ditch before the trucks take off."

The first two hours in the truck remain a pleasant blur, all of us laughing, passing the corn, needling each other. Feeling the liquor burn on the way down, and then the warmth spreading out, and then sitting back suffused in the wonderful glow. The world never looked better. Falling asleep listening to the stories, the laughter of my teammates.

Piss Call

Everyone was pretty drunk by the time we piled out by the side of a long, deserted stretch of road, about thirty miles West of Spartanburg, South Carolina. Standing in a wavy line to spray the foliage. Stretching afterwards and doing knee bends. Then back into the trucks.

Everyone gradually quieting down, dropping off to sleep, exhaustion taking over as we continued to roll along the otherwise deserted country roads.

It was about 0300 hours when I woke up and found Denbeaux the only other one awake in the back of the truck. Where the hell were we now, anyway?

I got up and made my way carefully to the tailgate, stepping over and around bodies and equipment. I moved Connelly's feet from the end of the seat and placed them on top of a rucksack, and then I dropped down across from Denbeaux. I shook out a cigarette and lit up as I sat back to stare out at the passing countryside.

It was a bright, starry, cloudless night, ironic after the teeming rains of three nights earlier, the first night of the wind-up. So wet, I'd thought I'd never be dry again.

Rounding a bend I could see another six or seven trucks behind us, lights on as always in convoy, but unneeded on this moonlit stretch of road.

Denbeaux pointed off to the horizon behind us. "Just went through Monroe about ten minutes ago. We've been in North Carolina for almost an hour. We're about halfway home, I'd guess. Maybe two, three hours to go."

Shit, I thought. *Home?* He's kidding, right? 0600 reveille. Hit the deck. Morning runs. How's about some PT, guys? Shine those friggin' boots. Fall in, fall out. *Looky here, Fitz, you on KP again!*

Home my sweet Irish ass.

Geez! It just hit me. This is September. I've only been in the army one year. At times it seems to me like I was *born* in this goddamn army. And, golly gee, another whole year yet to go! *Ain't that grand?*

Denbeaux reached over and tapped me on the knee, jerking a thumb at our snoring team leader. "Hear what Rozzelli told me last night, Short Stuff? You, me, Dubois, Green, we're all getting our corporal stripes in about two months. As soon as we hit the minimum required time in grade. Not bad, huh?"

I shrugged. "Big deal," I said. "With all the stripes already running around in Special Forces, corporal stripes don't mean dick. In a regular outfit a corporal may be a little god, but what's two stripes good for in this outfit?"

Denbeaux dropped his voice to a whisper and his eyebrows went up and down. Groucho Marx in fatigues. "Well, for one thing, we'll need a whole bunch of new patch jobs, we have to get all those stripes sewn on!"

That's *right!* I had forgotten that. I wondered if our honey was still at the old stand. Hadn't had a chance to check, really, since just before Free Legion.

"*And* more pay," Bill added. "Don't forget that. And then in your case, think of the hit you'll make with all those knobby-kneed lovelies that hang around the Fayetteville bus station. Hell, when they see your new stripes, you'll get freebies, Fitz. Freebies!"

I used the appropriate digit to let Bill know he was still number one as he sat back laughing. Friggin' Denbeaux. Always a step ahead.

We sat in silence for a while, the countryside rolling steadily by. Endings were always a little sad, even good ones. Like the wind-up yesterday. Mustering our local army for the last time to say our goodbyes. *Shit.* All of us having to step back in to reality. Collecting our equipment from our troops. Taking back the newly shined M-1's and packing them up for shipment back. Cartridge belts, bed rolls, pup tents. Counting everything twice, like a goddamn bunch of CPAs.

Wait, Mr. Fitzpatrick, sir! You forgot this here army knife. 'Member? You give it to me two weeks ago so's I could cut them fuses right. I shined it all up, and I sharpened it real good, too. Is it okay, Mr. Fitzpatrick? Is it?

Hell, if I were permanently assigned to the field, work with guys like that, I could almost stand this goddamn army. It's the barracks I hate.

We're havin' a full field inspection tomorrow, men. 0900 sharp. Get all your gear scrubbed up and shiny. Don't plan on no sleep tonight, guys. Gotta get that floor scraped down good. Gotta scrub them windows.

Pisser. Sometimes I feel like I'll go nuts if I have to spend one more week in this damned army. Shine one more piece of brass. Pull one more night of KP.

"What're you looking so glum about, Fitz?

"Denbeaux," I replied, quietly, because as far as I could tell everyone else was still asleep. "There are times when I feel twice as old as Tolliver Nelson Turner, and that's no shit. There are times when I feel like I just can't wait to get out of this army."

I leaned forward to see whether he was following me. "Do you know what I mean, Bill? Shit. Just to think about being, you know, a free man again, makes my mouth water. Get up when you want. Got to bed when you want. Not have to take any shit from anyone. Be able to tell them all to go suck eggs. Know what I mean, Bill? Can you understand how I feel?"

Denbeaux snorted. "You know what your problem is, Little Brother? You don't know when you're well off. Seriously. All over this country there are millions of guys going at it every day, nine to five. Working their asses off in jobs that are about as exciting as a pair of tits in a girls' locker room. And here you are, with the Korean War over, getting to jump out of planes, run around all night playing cops and robbers, the government picking up the tab! And, shit, feeding you to boot. Jesus, Fitz, count your damn blessings, Buddy. This life we're leading ain't half bad. Take my word for it."

I stared at him and then down at the asphalt road flashing by beneath us. "I know, I know. You have a point. It's just that the whole thing seems so goddamn endless. One whole year behind us, but another whole year of this crap to go. I mean, sometimes it just seems like it will never end."

Denbeaux pushed back and put both feet up on the tailgate. "Oh, it'll end all right, Fitz. Soon enough. And some day, twenty or thirty years from now, if you ever become a lawyer like you say you wanna be, you'll be cooped up in an office somewhere, trying to keep your weight down, and keep your clients happy, and worrying about ulcers. And you'll be making sure your tie is straight so you don't offend some judge."

He shook his head. "And you know what, Pal? When that day does come, the only thing you'll remember then is the good times. You'll forget all the bullshit, all the day-to-day crap. You'll look back then and the only thing you'll remember is the laughs. The good times."

"Oh, *yeah*?" I said, taking the heat then. "Oh, *yeah*? In a pig's ass, I will!"

****

On 11 November 1953, Colonel Aaron Bank commanding, the 10th Special Forces Group (Airborne) sailed for Europe from Wilmington, North Carolina, aboard the U.S. Army Transport Ship General A. W. Greely, deploying 800 enlisted men and 150 officers to the port of Bremerhaven, and then by train to Flint Kaserne in Bad Tolz, Germany--the first time a United States Army Special Forces Group was ever deployed overseas.

James Fitzpatrick, William Denbeaux, and their whole team, under the command of then Captain Roger Rozzelli, were aboard. While they were there...

Ah!...but that's another story.

"The author and Sgt. McInerney on Aaron
DZ, Bad Tolz, Germany, December, 1953."

BIOGRAPHICAL NOTE

A native of Boston, Edward F. Fitzgerald is one of the original Green Berets. He joined the 10th Special Forces Group (Airborne) right after Jump School when it was being organized at Fort Bragg, North Carolina, and he became a member of one of the first A-teams made field-operational in North Carolina and Georgia. He later deployed with the 10th to Bad Tolz, Germany in November of 1953.

After leaving the service, he became a Massachusetts trial lawyer, the author of numerous law review articles, and the author of a textbook on intoxication test evidence that is annually supplemented and widely used in this country by trial attorneys and experts. For a number of years he has restricted his legal practice to consulting with attorneys on alcohol test cases, and he still lectures regularly on that subject for the bar and bench.

Thanks to an inspired burst of sanity in 2000, he and Ginny, his wife of more than thirty years, moved across the country to Arizona's beautiful Valley of the Sun where they now reside with five annoyingly literate cats who, after napping on all the earlier drafts, grudgingly approved this final manuscript. Ginny is an excellent ballroom dancer who keeps Ed in condition chasing after her over every dance floor from Apache Junction to Sun City, whenever he is not otherwise engaged at his computer or emptying litter boxes.

Give The Gift Of **BANK'S BANDITS** To Your Family, Friends And Military Colleagues

☐ YES, send me ___copies of **Bank's Bandits** for $20.95 each.

Include $4.50 shipping and handling for one book, and $1.00 for each additional book. For quantity orders and bookseller discounts please contact the publisher.

Payment must accompany orders. Publisher usually ships within 48 hours.

My check or money order for $_____ is enclosed.

Please charge my:

☐ Visa   ☐ MasterCard   ☐ American Express.

Name: _____

Organization: _____

Address: _____

City/State/Zip: _____

Phone: _____E-mail_____

Card # _____Exp. Date: _____

Signature: _____

Or Call Toll Free: 1-877-BUY BOOK (289-2665)

☐ YES, I am interested in having Ed Fitzgerald appear to speak and sign books at my veterans association or other organization. Contact the author by e-mail at: ed@edwardffitzgerald.com or through the publisher (see below).

Infinity Publishing.com
519 West Lancaster Avenue
Haverford, PA 19041

Printed in the United States
19292LVS00003B/10